To

From

Date

Teach me your ways, Lord

366 DAILY READINGS

NINA SMIT

SCB
STRUIK CHRISTIAN BOOKS

TEACH ME YOUR WAYS, LORD

Published by Struik Christian Books
An imprint of Struik Christian Media
A division of New Holland Publishing (South Africa) (Pty) Ltd
(New Holland Publishing is a member of Avusa Ltd)
Cornelis Struik House
80 McKenzie Street
Cape Town 8001

Reg. No. 1971/009721/07

First edition 2007
Second impression 2010

Unless otherwise indicated, Scripture quotations are from *The Holy Bible*,
New International Version (NIV) © 1984, International Bible Society.

Project management by Reinata Thirion
Translated by Lizel Grobbelaar
Edited by Nick Collins
DTP design by Tessa Fortuin
Cover design by Joleen Coetzee
Cover image by Gallo Images/Getty Images
Printed and bound by China Translation & Printing Services Ltd, Hong Kong

ISBN 978-1-4153-0154-8

www.struikchristianmedia.co.za

We pray for you all the time – pray that our God
will make you fit for what He's called you to be,
pray that He'll fill your good ideas and acts of faith
with his own energy so that it all amounts to something.

– 2 Thessalonians 1:11, *The Message*

A Christian is someone who is still on the way,
someone who has not necessarily made much progress,
but who at least has some idea of Whom to thank for it.

– Frederich Büchner

Contents

Live for God!

When people are asked what they want most of all, they usually answer that they should like to be happy. Happiness is something everyone strives for. However, few people realise that only one factor guarantees true happiness: loving God above all and obeying Him implicitly. If you are prepared to love God, to live for Him and to obey whatever He asks in his Word, you will find that you will receive joy as a gift. True happiness is impossible without God in your life.

This month we will discover together Who this God is Who makes us happy, exactly what He requires of his children and how you will be required to live to please God.

January

One wish

READ: 2 CORINTHIANS 5:1–10

So we make it our goal to please him, whether
we are at home in the body or away from it.
– 2 CORINTHIANS 5:9

Paul had one all-important wish. He cherished a dream – not a dream which concerned himself or the things he wanted, but a dream to please God in everything. Although he was looking forward to heaven, he wanted to obey God while he was still on earth. He was willing to remain courageous on this imperfect earth because heaven was awaiting him.

'A turn of the year is a time for reflection,' writes Dirkie Smit, 'a time to see that things could be different. Could be renewed. That it's never too late. We easily forget that we are not prisoners of yesterday, but children of tomorrow, and that this year, life could be different for and through us; that everything does not merely have to be more-of-what-has-already-been.'[1]

Because Jesus died for you, you should be willing to live fully for Him; to trust in the Lord, cling to Him and obey Him regardless of the negative circumstances which might await you this year. Today is the first day of a brand-new year – and you could learn to be really happy by making Paul's dream your own. You could become a new creation this year, tackle things differently and live in a new, exciting way by living according to God's will.

❧ Heavenly Father, I want to make Paul's dream my own. Please help me to live in a new and different way this year and to obey your will. Amen.

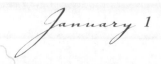

January 1

A new you for the new year

READ: 2 CORINTHIANS 5:14–19

Therefore, if anyone is in Christ, he is a new creation;
the old has gone, the new has come! All this is from God,
who reconciled us to himself through Christ and
gave us the ministry of reconciliation.
– 2 CORINTHIANS 5:17–18

In John 12:24–25 Jesus says: 'I tell you the truth, unless a grain of wheat falls to the ground and dies, it remains only a single seed. But if it dies, it produces many seeds. The man who loves his life will lose it, while the man who hates his life in this world will keep it for eternal life.'

Two days ago you stood at the 'grave' of the old year. Before you can live fully for Jesus this year, you have to be prepared to die to yourself and become new – like the new year which lies ahead. You have to surrender to Him all those things which are now so important to you that they sometimes usurp God's rightful position in your life. This year you will have to be willing to do God's will and, like Paul, exchange your own dreams and ideals for those which God has for you. The renewal which will take place in you will be God's work. You cannot do this yourself. He sent his Son to the world to pay the price for your sin. Jesus came to make peace between you and God and between you and those around you. Because He did this, you can – if you believe in Him – be a new person with a new lifestyle this year, someone who will follow in the footsteps of Jesus Himself!

❧ Lord Jesus, make me new and holy. Thank you for reconciling us to God and for giving us the ministry of reconciliation. Help me to follow in your footsteps this year by living in peace with other people. Amen.

January 2

Time, opportunity and commitment are important

READ: ECCLESIASTES 9:7–12

Whatever your hand finds to do, do it with all your might ...
time and chance happen to them all.
– *ECCLESIASTES 9:10–11*

One of the very best resolutions at the beginning of a new year is to make the most of your time by seizing the opportunities which come your way. We do not know how long we will still be healthy, or how long we will live. We should therefore welcome every opportunity which comes our way with enthusiasm. Every day brings new opportunities. It is your responsibility to notice them and do something with them.

The Preacher agrees wholeheartedly with this: Live with a joyful heart, he recommends his readers (v 7). Enjoy life with those you love (v 9a). Do everything your hand finds to do with all your might.

However, not everything will run smoothly this year. In verses 11–12 the Preacher warns, 'Food [does not] come to the wise or wealth to the brilliant or favour to the learned; but time and chance happen to them all. As fish are caught in a cruel net ... so men are trapped by evil times that fall unexpectedly upon them.' Whether you will be successful or happy in the year which lies ahead, or whether you will make a positive difference in the world where you live will largely depend on yourself. And with God's help you will be able to do it; He will teach you to choose your time and opportunity wisely.

 Lord, I should like to be happy and successful this year. Please help me to use my time wisely, to seize the opportunities and do everything with all my might. Amen.

January 3

In God's strength

READ: ISAIAH 40:27–31

Those who hope in the LORD will renew their strength.
They will soar on wings like eagles; they will run and
not grow weary, they will walk and not be faint.
– ISAIAH 40:31

At the beginning of a new year you are usually filled with energy and game for everything. However, as the year drags on, you start running out of steam – until, towards the end of the year, you eventually feel ready to drop.

The secret of how to flourish this year, how to make your positive energy last all year, is to place your whole life in the hand of God and tackle every challenge which confronts you through Him. Paul was very familiar with this secret. Regardless of his circumstances he was able to testify that he was able to do everything expected of him because God helped him. 'I can do everything through him who gives me strength,' he wrote to the church in Philippi (Phil 4:13).

While they were in exile, God's people thought He no longer even noticed them, and they reached the end of their reserves. But the prophet Isaiah gave the discouraged people a beautiful promise: God cannot grow tired. He gives the weary new strength. If only they would turn to their God again, He Himself would give them new strength.

If you remain close to God this year and rely on his strength, you will discover that He is able to do much more for you than you can ask or even think (Eph 3:20).

❧ Heavenly Father, I should like to claim your power right at the beginning of the year. Please give me enough strength every day to meet my obligations. Amen.

January 4

A recipe for success

READ: 1 SAMUEL 18

In everything he [David] did he had great success,
because the LORD was with him.
– 1 SAMUEL 18:14

Everybody wants to be successful. Perhaps you have already wondered whether your ideals will be fulfilled this year, whether the things you should like to achieve will ever be realised. If you want to be successful, your success has to be built on the right foundation. True success starts with yourself. You have to be prepared to give your all to be able to achieve the right kind of success. However, it always ends with God. Only He can crown your efforts with success. You may be the most successful person on the face of the earth, but if you refuse to acknowledge God's sovereignty in your life, your success will be meaningless because it will not really make you happy.

'Commit to the LORD whatever you do, and your plans will succeed' (Prov 16:3). Follow King David's example in the year which lies ahead – live close to the Lord and build your success on a relationship with Him by remaining close to Him. Pray before you act. Study your Bible so that you can submit to God's will for your life. If you seek the will of the Lord in your effort to be successful, He Himself will help you to achieve success. And once you achieve success, always remember to give God the glory for it!

❧ Heavenly Father, I want to commit to You everything I do this year. Please help me to achieve success because You are with me. Amen.

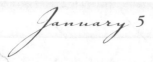

January 5

When success seems to elude you

READ: GENESIS 39:1–21

The LORD was with Joseph and he prospered.
– GENESIS 39:2

We already know that God's children are not exempt from problems. However, they have a promise that no-one can take away from them: Regardless of how awful their problems are, God is with them, in the midst of the problems. Joseph's life reads like a thriller: His brothers sold him as a slave and his owner's wife accused him falsely so that he, an innocent man, eventually landed in jail – despite God's presence. But we read that God was with him, even in jail. Genesis 39:20–21 reads, 'But while Joseph was there in the prison, the LORD was with him; he showed him kindness.' When Joseph was released from jail, he became Pharaoh's confidant and eventually saved his whole nation by bringing them to Egypt during the famine.

Although Joseph suffered considerably during his life and success apparently eluded him time and again, Joseph's life was an exciting success story in the end. The presence of God in your life makes the difference between success and failure. With Him on your side, nothing will overpower you this year; problems will not break you; you know you can rely on the infinite power of God when your own strength fails. Even when success apparently eludes you, you can hold on to God knowing that He will make all things work together for your good.

❧ Heavenly Father, I praise You for the promise that You will be with me this year, that You will help me in times of trouble. Amen.

January 6

Work on your marriage

READ: ECCLESIASTES 9:7–10

Enjoy life with your wife, whom you love,
all the days of this meaningless life that God
has given you under the sun – all your meaningless days.
– ECCLESIASTES 9:9

The Preacher is a great pessimist – he believes that there are few good things left in the world, but one of them is a happy marriage! Those who know say that satanists meet throughout our country regularly to pray for the failure of Christian marriages. Perhaps this explains why so many Christians are unhappily married and also why divorce is increasing at such an alarming rate. You cannot really be happy if your marriage is unhappy. If you as a married person therefore desire happiness in life, you will have to work hard on your marriage this year.

Marriage was instituted by God Himself – and it is his will that a married couple who loves Him and each other should be happy together for ever. However, a happy marriage requires unselfish marriage partners who are prepared to serve and forgive each other. 'Do nothing out of selfish ambition or vain conceit, but in humility consider others better than yourselves,' Paul wrote to the church in Philippi (Phil 2:3–4). If you obey this instruction in your own marriage and you as well as your husband undertake to serve and obey God, you will discover how wonderful it is to enjoy life with the marriage partner you love.

❧ Lord, today I want to pray for Christian marriages throughout the country. Grant that married couples who know You will be considerate towards each other and love and obey You. Amen.

January 7

Your children as living witnesses

READ: ISAIAH 8:13–18

Here am I, and the children the LORD has given me.
We are signs and symbols in Israel from the LORD
Almighty, who dwells on Mount Zion.
– ISAIAH 8:18

The prophet Isaiah and his followers declared here that they were living witnesses of God in Israel. Although the majority of the nation had turned away from the Lord, they were still prepared to follow and obey Him wholeheartedly.

Perhaps you and your children are among the few people who are still faithful to God in your town or city at present. Society is becoming increasingly backslidden, rejecting the Lord and his commandments. Very few people are still prepared to obey Biblical instructions and to live the way God expects from his children in their homes and families. Nevertheless some believers still rear their children for the Lord – and these families are still living witnesses for God where they live.

The world in which our children are growing up differs widely from the world we knew as children, and parents sometimes do not know what is expected of them. Adults therefore tend to be increasingly tolerant regarding their children and virtually ignore discipline. Your children definitely need your unconditional love, but they also desperately need parental discipline. Children may protest against rules, but ultimately flourish as a result, provided the rules are fair. Your primary responsibility towards your children is to fulfil your baptismal vow towards them and share your faith with them. Then you will be happy together as a family this year.

❧ Father, help me to keep my baptismal vow and to rear my children in such a way that they will one day be living witnesses for You where we live. Amen.

January 8

Your family will have to choose

READ: JOSHUA 24:14–24

[But] if serving the LORD seems undesirable to you,
then choose for yourselves this day whom you will serve …
But as for me and my household, we will serve the LORD.
– JOSHUA 24:15

Joshua told Israel to choose: They had to choose once and for all whom they wanted to serve: the God of Israel or the heathen idols. He made his own choice and the choice of his family very clear: 'As for me and my household, we will serve the Lord!'

Christian parents should serve and love God within their family circle in such a way that the members of their family will have no doubt regarding their choice of whom théy will serve. Your husband and you should furthermore involve your children in this choice. You should tell them from a tender age that the Lord loves them and that they should submit themselves to Him – that is after all what you promised when they were christened. Calvin often said that the family of a believer should, as it were, be a miniature church. Is this true about your family? If not, why not pay special attention to persuading your family to choose the Lord this year?

The way you live in your home is a much clearer testimony of your faith than verbal instructions to your children. Decide right now to help your family to choose the Lord once and for all, and persuade them by your prayers, words and deeds to remain faithful to this choice for the rest of their lives.

❧ Heavenly Father, I should like to persuade my family this year to choose You as their Redeemer and to serve You for the rest of their lives. Show me how to do this by my way of life. Amen.

January 9

Remain calm!

READ: JOHN 14:27–31

Peace I leave with you; my peace I give you. I do not give to you as the world gives. Do not let your hearts be troubled and do not be afraid.
– JOHN 14:27

Crisis situations are very common these days. While I was writing the daily readings for this month, a security guard was shot and killed in front of the shopping centre where I do my shopping, and in a neighbouring town an elderly lady was bludgeoned to death with a hammer. Violence and bloodshed have become so much part of our lives that most people suffer from some degree of fear. We no longer feel safe anywhere. And it is not very easy to remain calm in a world of violence and danger.

However, Jesus promises you his peace this year ... If you are troubled at the moment as a result of all the negative things which are happening around you, ask God to give you his peace in your life. Jesus promises that He will give his children a different kind of peace, not the peace the world gives – a peace which will remove all frear from our hearts. This peace will reign in your life despite problems and dangerous situations, despite hijackings and assaults and murder and bloodshed, because the peace of God passes all understanding. If you remain close to God, this peace will guard your heart and your mind all year (Phil 4:7); your behaviour will be characterised by this peace and it will be passed on to your family and everybody with whom you come into contact.

❧ Lord Jesus, I want to receive your peace. Give me your peace in abundance this year, and reassure me that I do not have to fear anything because You are always with me. Amen.

January 10

Caring for others

READ: GALATIANS 6:1–9

*Carry each other's burdens, and in this way you will fulfil
the law of Christ. Let us not become weary in doing good …*
— *GALATIANS 6:2, 9*

Happy people are people who are always helping others, people who notice the need of others, who always reach out to others to help them and whose wallets are open to give. This is what Jesus asks of you this year: pass on the love which his Spirit pours into your heart to those whom He brings your way. The translation of the core verse in The Message reads as follows: 'Stoop down and reach out to those who are oppressed. Share their burdens, and so complete Christ's law.'

In the place where you live there must be societies which desperately need your help. Get involved in the charitable work of your church, visit the sick in hospital, support the soup kitchen of your congregation, visit the lonely in a home for the aged in your neighbourhood. 'We all look forward to heaven where God is, without realising that we can be with God in heaven this very moment. But rejoicing in the Lord here and now means loving like Him, helping like Him and saving like Him,' Mother Theresa of Calcutta once said. If you will follow her example this year, happiness will always be close to you.

✤ Lord Jesus, please help me this year to become intensely involved with those who need me so that I can help to bear their burdens the way You did. Amen.

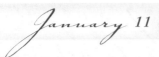

January 11

Let us praise Him!

READ: PSALM 95

Come, let us sing for joy to the Lord;
let us shout aloud to the Rock of our salvation. Let us come
before him with thanksgiving and extol him with music and song.
— Psalm 95:1–2

According to a beautiful legend, God called his angels at the end of the fifth day of creation to show them all the wonderful things He had made. They were amazed and impressed. 'This is incredible ...' an angel said with respect, 'your creation is perfect, nothing is lacking.' 'No, something is lacking,' a small angel said hesitantly. The Creator stooped down to the little angel. 'And what, I pray, is lacking?' He asked, highly amused. 'Voices to praise the magnificence of your creation,' the little angel said shyly. According to the legend, God thereupon made man.

Man is the only being who can really appreciate God's natural wonders, who can notice them and 'extol Him with music and song', who can praise God's omnipotence and greatness, his knowledge and the work of his hands. 'Great are the works of the Lord; they are pondered by all who delight in them. Glorious and majestic are his deeds' (Ps 111:2–3). Make this your intention this year to notice the beauty around you every day and to praise God for it. Concentrate especially on adding your voice to those who extol God's creation and praise Him.

❧ Heavenly Father, the world You created is incredibly beautiful. Thank you for my ability to notice this beauty and to extol and praise You for the beauty of your creation. Amen.

January 12

The being of God

READ: ACTS 17:21–34

The God who made the world and everything in it is the Lord
of heaven and earth … [He] himself gives all men life and breath
and everything else … in him we live and move and have our being.
– ACTS 17:24–25, 28

When Paul visited Athens, he found altars dedicated to the different idols worshipped by the Athenians. One of these altars was dedicated to 'The Unknown God'. Paul immediately saw a way of introducing the God he worshipped to the Athenians. He told them that God created everything, that He gives everything life and that we live and move and have our being in Him only.

Your life can be meaningful only if this God forms part of your daily existence, if you have an intimate relationship with Him. We cannot see God. He is great because He is unfathomable and mysterious. 'By faith we are in contact with a Mystery which we cannot hold, but Who holds us,' writes Willem Nicol. 'We understand very little about God. He gives us reflections of Himself by which we can experience his closeness and by which we live, but we never see a photograph of Him.'[2] If you want to draw closer to this glorious God this year, make time for Him: Set aside a special time to talk to Him in prayer, to study your Bible in depth and spend time with other Christians. In this way you will get to know Him better every day.

✿ Heavenly Father, I worship You as the Creator God Who holds me in his hand. Thank you for the assurance that You, the great and holy One, love me and care for me. Amen.

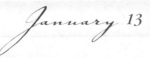

Who is God really?

READ: ECCLESIASTES 11:1–6

As you do not know the path of the wind,
or how the body is formed in a mother's womb, so you
cannot understand the work of God, the Maker of all things.
– ECCLESIASTES 11:5

We do not have to try to understand God – and his miracles – with our limited human minds because we will never be able to understand Him. He is, after all, infinitely greater than we are. However, the central message of the Bible explains who God wants to be for us. In his book, *Godsdiens wat werk*, Willem Nicol gives us a beautiful description of who God is: 'God is the Infinite One, the Foundation of our existence. He has a burning desire for us. He paid the highest price to enable us to be part of Him forever … We see Him in Jesus. Basically life for us should consist of being different from others, of no longer living for ourselves. Because we follow Jesus. Eternity makes this possible for us because He gives his Spirit to live in us and to lead us.'[3]

This is exactly what God wants to be for you this year: He wants to be the reason for your existence. He wants you to be part of Him forever. He sends his Son so that you can be his child, and He gives his Spirit to show you how to live. You no longer have to try to understand Him – you merely have to be still and cherish his love for you.

❧ Lord my God, how great You are! Thank you for loving me first; for sending your Son to pay the penalty for my sin and for sending your Spirit to be with me for ever. Amen.

January 14

Meditate on the Word of God

READ: PSALM 19:8–12

The law of the LORD is perfect, reviving the soul.
The statutes of the LORD are trustworthy, making wise the simple.
The precepts of the LORD are right, giving joy to the heart …
– PSALM 19:7–8

God reveals Himself by his Word. Few things are therefore as intensely satisfying as studying your Bible in depth and hearing the voice of God speaking to you personally. The more you study your Bible, the better you get to know God, and the more you become aware of his majesty and greatness and of his unfathomable love for you – a love you can never earn or understand, but which you can accept by faith.

By means of his Word, God communicates with his children personally. Your Bible gives you ways in which you can experience God consciously. If you memorise verses, you will have those words with you wherever you go. 'The words of your Bible open the curtains to the secret world around you,' writes Willem Nicol. 'You can meditate on them quietly until they form a precious deposit in your heart. You will notice that God is behind them and that He is revealing Himself through them so that you experience Him and are open to continue experiencing Him when you close the oldest book and enter life.'[4]

Don't wait any longer to start a new, more intimate relationship with God by discovering your Bible in a brand-new way this year!

✿ Heavenly Father, I praise You for the wonder of your Word by which You speak to me personally. Thank you that I may study your Word in peace and get to know You better and better. Amen.

January 15

Servants and stewards

READ: 1 CORINTHIANS 4:1–7

So then, men ought to regard us as servants of Christ
and as those entrusted with the secret things of God.
– 1 CORINTHIANS 4:1

The image Paul uses here is that of servants or employees who, in the absence of the owner, have to manage his possessions on his behalf and then report back to him on his return.

God's children are his representatives in the world. We are the ambassadors of the greatest King ever, and it is our responsibility to show others who do not know God what He really looks like. We can never get away from this fact. The only way unbelievers can come to know more about God first-hand is by looking at God's children. Others see our faith by the way we live; for example, by the way we handle crises, or by our love for others – and this is the only picture they have of what our Father is like.

In the year which lies ahead you should therefore once again realise that God has placed you in this world to serve Him and others the way Jesus did when He was on earth. We are the servants to whom God has entrusted the management of his property. The possessions God has given you do not belong to you either – they belong to God … and you are merely a steward. Remember this year that you are God's servant and the manager of his property, and that you will have to give account to Him some day.

❧ Lord, thank you for trusting me to be your servant and steward on earth. Help me to live in such a way that people will see You when they look at me. Amen.

January 16

God requires faithfulness

READ: 1 CORINTHIANS 4:1–7

Now it is required that those who have been given
a trust must prove faithful ... My conscience is clear, but
that does not make me innocent. It is the Lord who judges me.
– 1 CORINTHIANS 4:2, 4

In his letter to the Corinthians, Paul admits that he is in the world to serve God, but that he is not at all concerned about what others say about his work. That God should be satisfied is good enough for him. Like Paul, you are also God's servant and manager on earth – we discussed this fact yesterday. Today we will look at the kind of manager you should be. God is looking for faithful managers to do his work on earth, people with a clear conscience. This means that others as well as God must be able to rely on you; that you have to be a woman of her word. However, reliability seems to be scarce these days. Promising something but not keeping the promise seems to have become a way of life today.

It is very easy to deceive others, but you cannot deceive God. Nothing can be hidden from God, He knows all about you. He even knows what you are thinking. Therefore, try your best to be absolutely reliable this year. Try to keep every promise you make. And remember that God is the One Who will eventually judge you (see verse 4).

🌸 Heavenly Father, I want to be an absolutely reliable steward for You this year. Please help me to succeed. Amen.

January 17

What God asks

READ: DEUTERONOMY 10:10–17

And now, O Israel, what does the LORD your God ask of you but
to fear the LORD your God, to walk in all his ways, to love him,
to serve the LORD your God with all your heart and all your soul?
– DEUTERONOMY 10:12

It is God's will that his children should be reliable. However, this is not all God expects of you this year. In Deuteronomy 10 Moses preaches his farewell sermon. The desert lies behind them and he cannot accompany them to the promised land, but he once again shares the Lord's instructions. God demands five things of his people: They have to honour God, do his will, love, serve and obey Him.

If you will really absorb this list of instructions, the year which lies ahead will be happy and prosperous. Decide right now to honour God's Name in everything you do this year; to give Him the glory for all your success. Study your Bible so that you will know God's will for you very well – and then do it! Undertake once again to love God with your whole heart and soul – and ask Him to enable you to love your neighbour like this as well. Be prepared to commit yourself totally to God and to obey the commandments which He sets out in his Word. If you do what God asks, you may claim the last part of verse 13 for yourself: 'For your own good'.

❧ Heavenly Father, please help me this year to do what You ask: to honour You, to obey your will, to love You sincerely and to serve You with all my heart and soul. Amen.

January 18

The desires of your heart ...

READ: MATTHEW 7:7–12

If you, then, though you are evil, know how to give
good gifts to your children, how much more will your
Father in heaven give good gifts to those who ask him!
– MATTHEW 7:11

Long ago I read the story of a young man who went with his dad to select a car for his birthday. On his birthday he received a squarish parcel from his father. On opening it, the lad found a Bible. He was so disappointed because he had expected the promised car, that he threw down the Bible and left without even saying goodbye to his parents. Shortly afterwards his dad died. The son went home for the funeral and on taking up the Bible which he had received on his birthday, he found a cheque inside – for the exact amount the new car would have cost.

Sometimes you also ask God for things you desire – and when God does not give you what you ask, you are also disappointed like the young man in our story. Although God does not always give his children what they ask, He promises to give you good things when you pray. However, remember that He will do so in his own time and in his own way.

Should you feel God does not hear your prayers this year, read Psalm 81:10 again: 'Open wide your mouth and I will fill it.' However, remember that what we think we need, and what God knows we really need, are two different things.

❧ Heavenly Father, thank you for all the good things I receive from You every day. Fill me with gratitude and help me to be willing to wait on You. Amen.

January 19

Follow the right footsteps

READ: PSALM 23

The Lord is my shepherd, I shall not be in want … he restores my soul.
He guides me in paths of righteousness for his name's sake.
— PSALM 23:1, 3

The New King James Version of Psalm 23:3 reads: 'He leads me in the paths of righteousness for his name's sake'. This verse always reminds me of the well-known television advertisement of a little boy, fishing-rod resting on his shoulder, stepping carefully into the footprints of his dad in the wet sand on the beach.

Be sure to step accurately into God's footprints while you follow Him on your path of life this year. If you follow the Good Shepherd in the year which lies ahead, He Himself will guide you to follow the right footsteps. He will show you exactly where to step to avoid being snared and to reach the right destination eventually. God not only guides you in the paths of righteousness, but He also promises to lead you by going ahead. In John 10:27 Jesus says: 'My sheep listen to my voice; I know them, and they follow Me.' Led by such a Shepherd you do not have to fear anything which lies ahead this year; not even 'the valley of the shadow of death' to which David refers in Psalm 23:4. Even then He will go ahead and lead you through the darkness until you reach the house of God safely, where you will be received as a guest of honour and be home forever.

❧ Lord Jesus, Thank you that I can know You will lead me this coming year - that I only have to follow your footsteps to reach my destination safely. Amen.

January 20

God's plan

READ: PROVERBS 3:1–8

Trust in the LORD with all your heart and lean not on your
own understanding; in all your ways acknowledge him,
and he will make your paths straight.
– PROVERBS 3:5–6

It is good to realise early in the year that everything that comes your way this year – the good things as well as those which are not so good – forms part of God's plan for your life. God is omniscient and He therefore already knows what is going to happen to you. He is also omnipotent and He can therefore use everything in your life in a positive way. For that reason you can rely on God totally instead of making your own little plans. Share your dreams and plans with God and you will experience his help and support personally.

God has a plan with our lives. According to Norman Wright's devotional, *Together for good,*[5] we have to consider three words in this plan this year: initiative, timing and surrender. Let these three words work for you this year so that God's plan for your life can be fulfilled. Swop your own plan for God's initiative which He sets out in his Word; work out your time carefully; see to it that you do the right thing at the right time – and be prepared to accept God's timing if you are uncertain. Finally: Surrender your whole life and all your dreams to the Holy Spirit – if He is the Helmsman of your life, all things will work together for your good.

Father, I trust You for the year which lies ahead. Show me your will for my life and make me willing to surrender the control of my life to You. Amen.

Disappointments

READ: ROMANS 10:5–13

*As the Scripture says, 'Anyone who trusts
in him will never be put to shame.'*
— ROMANS 10:11

As in the case of suffering, all of us experience disappointments. No-
one escapes disappointments – you can also expect several disappointments this year. And nobody enjoys shattered dreams. 'Hope
deferred makes the heart sick, but a longing fulfilled is a tree of life,'
says the writer of Proverbs (Prov 13:12). God nevertheless uses these
disappointments to teach precious lessons.

All of us have at times been disappointed by others. Most of us
have already discovered the fact that we cannot really rely on people.
However, God is different. He never disappoints his children. He is
absolutely faithful and He keeps all his promises down to the smallest
detail. What Paul wrote to the church in Rome in our core verse is
true: 'Anyone who trusts in him will never be put to shame.' God is the
same yesterday, today and for ever. He promises to care for you in the
future the way He cared for his people throughout history.

Expect disappointments during the coming year, but see them as
opportunities to learn something. Know this: You can rely on God –
He will never disappoint you. He will also be with you and support
you in difficult times so that you will be radiant with joy even in times
of trouble (see Ps 34:5).

ॐ Heavenly Father, I know You use disappointments in my life to teach me
precious lessons. Thank you that no-one who trusts in You will ever be put to
shame. Amen.

January 22

God never changes

READ: PSALM 102:18–28

In the beginning you laid the foundations of the earth,
and the heavens are the work of your hands. They will perish,
but you remain … But you remain the same, and your years will never end.
– PSALM 102:25–27

As we grow older we realise all the more that the world around us is changing – and that these changes are occurring at a tremendous and ever-increasing rate. New scientific breakthroughs occur daily, technology progresses daily and man is now able to do things which seemed totally impossible only a few years ago. These days I sometimes feel as if I simply cannot keep up with all the progress and changes!

The beginning of a new year is one of those times when we are reminded even more of these changes – and not all of them are as favourable as the progress in technology and science. Food, accommodation and products are becoming more expensive practically daily; inflation is increasing steadily; violence is increasing at an alarming rate; moral codes change practically from day to day. Yet, if you are a Christian, it is very comforting to realise that something in our changing world always remains the same: God. He is still the omnipotent God who created the world and sustains it day and night by his powerful word. He is also the God who holds your life and your future in the hollow of his hand and who promises you that He will help and support you. If the changes upset you again this year, do underline Hebrews 13:8 in your Bible: 'Jesus Christ is the same yesterday and today and for ever.'

❧ Lord Jesus, thank you that, in the midst of everything which is changing around me so rapidly, You remain exactly the same yesterday and today and for ever. Amen.

January 23

Trust and hope.

READ: ISAIAH 8:11–17

I will wait for the LORD, who is hiding his face
from the house of Jacob. I will put my trust in him.
— ISAIAH 8:17

Two things will be absolutely indispensable in the new year: trust and hope. Trusting God will mean that you will trade in your fear of the unknown, and your fear for things which might go wrong this year for the assurance that God is there for you, that He will help you – that He will carry you and save you regardless of when or where you might need Him. You can rely on the fact that God will hold you in the hollow of his hand; you can rely on the fact that He will make all things work together for your good. He will never disappoint you. This assurance is found in Psalm 32:10: 'The Lord's unfailing love surrounds the man who trusts in him.'

Trusting in God requires that you look past all the negative things in the world which will rob you of your hope; you will have to look to God, the God in Whom you place your hope. Hope always indicates future – you cannot hope on things which are already past. 'Christ in you, the hope of glory,' Paul writes in Colossians 1:27. If you love Jesus, you not only have positive hope for the year which lies ahead, but you already know that you will one day have eternal life.

Nothing will overwhelm you this year because you know you can trust God and hope in Him.

❧ Heavenly Father, I praise You for the privilege of trusting in You and of building my hope on You for the year that lies ahead. Thank you that I may know that You will be there for me. Amen.

January 24

With God on your side

READ: ISAIAH 12

Sing to the LORD, *for he has done glorious things;*
let this be known to all the world. Shout aloud and sing for joy,
people of Zion, for great is the Holy One of Israel among you!
– ISAIAH *12:5–6*

The Israelites could always claim God's presence with them. He enabled them to win their wars, to pass through the sea without getting
their feet wet, to survive the trek through the desert which lasted forty
years. All the other nations were aware of this presence of the God of
Israel, the way they were blessed – they could not but notice the 'great
things' God did for his people.

If you love the Lord, the core verse for today is specially for you.
God is still the same as in Old Testament times. He is still able to do
great things for his children – and they can still be assured of his presence. With this God on your side you can tackle the new year with
confidence. No problem will be too complicated for you, no burden
too heavy, no temptation too great if God is with you. In Psalm 18
David tells us what God's presence meant to him personally: 'My God
turns my darkness into light. With your help I can advance against a
troop; with my God I can scale a wall,' he said (v 28–29).

Should you be in a tight spot this year, remember you are not
alone. You have God on your side. He wants to do great things for you
this year.

❧ Heavenly Father, I praise You for the assurance that You are with me
every moment of every day. Please do great things for me this year. Amen.

January 25

God wants to make your paths straight

READ: PROVERBS 3:1–10

Trust in the LORD with all your heart and lean not on your own understanding; in all your ways acknowledge him and he will make your paths straight.

– PROVERBS 3:5–6

When people receive the Word of God and are prepared to do what He asks of them; when they are prepared to give everything in their relationship with Him, He, in turn promises to 'keep them on track', according to the translation of the last part of the above verse in *The Message*.

Dr Charles Stanley compares a Christian who does the will of God to someone floating rapidly downstream in a boat. There are rocks to avoid; at times the oars have to be used to keep the boat away from the rocks; boats can be nudged ashore at certain spots along the bank. However, the person in the boat does not have to row to float downstream; all he has to do is to flow with the current, trusting God.'

Likewise, you should surrender your life to God and trust Him to keep your life on track this year and to guide you to the right destination. He promises to give you the necessary strength and wisdom this year to complete your journey successfully.

Entrust the oars of your boat of life to God. You no longer have to struggle against the current to the point of exhaustion. Although our core verse does not use the image of a boat but refers to our paths of life, the idea remains the same: we do not take the initiative, God does, and He keeps us on the right track.

❧ Heavenly Father, I want to acknowledge You in everything I do this year. Please make my paths straight and help me to reach the right destination. Amen.

Make the most of today!

READ: ECCLESIASTES 7:1–10

Do not say, 'Why were the old days better than these?'
For it is not wise to ask such questions.
– ECCLESIASTES 7:10

People who live in the past, achieve very little in the present. Those who cling obstinately to the way they used to do things will not achieve much either. One of the best new year's resolutions for this year is to be less narrow-minded and to stop yearning for the things of the past. Learn to make the most of today. Seize the opportunities which come your way today. Be prepared to broaden your horizons this year, to start doing things in a new way, to risk, to investigate new possibilities and make them part of your life.

'It is not because things are difficult that we do not take risks, but things are difficult because we do not take risks,' the philosopher Seneca said centuries ago. Decide to seize the unavoidable changes in your life this year instead of opposing them – and even to initiate change yourself. Risk doing things in a brand-new way: have a new hairstyle, read books by other authors and explore new music. Consider holidaying somewhere else, making new friends – the possibilities are endless. Try reaching towards the future this year, instead of wallowing in the past.

🦋 Lord, I am inclined to hark back to the past. Forgive me and help me to approach this year with expectations; to make the most of every day and to start doing things in new ways. Amen.

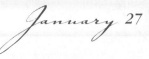

Choose the right thoughts

READ: PHILIPPIANS 4:6–9

*Finally, brothers, whatever is true, whatever is noble, whatever is right,
whatever is pure, whatever is lovely, whatever is admirable – if anything is excellent or praiseworthy – think about such things.*
— PHILIPPIANS 4:8

If you are serious about making the most of your opportunities this
year, you should be aware of the tremendous importance of your
thought patterns. What you think will also determine the way you
live. If your thoughts are always negative, your view of life will reflect
that negativity. Job himself complained that the things he had feared
had come upon him. Negative thoughts increase when one dwells on
them. Fortunately this is also true about positive thoughts. Positive
people draw positive things like a magnet. If you follow Paul's advice
to the Philippians and focus your thoughts on 'whatever is true, whatever is noble, whatever is right, whatever is pure, whatever is lovely,
whatever is admirable – if anything is excellent or praiseworthy', you
will definitely find that all will be well. The choice is yours. Decide
now what you prefer: pessimistic opinions about how bad everything
is, or optimistic faith in those things which are in agreement with
God's will. Ultimately your choice will determine the quality of your
life. The things on which you focus your thoughts will grow and mul-
tiply in your life.

Therefore, think cheerful, grateful thoughts, focus your thoughts
deliberately on things with positive values for life and eternity – and
the year which lies ahead will be a year of celebration for you!

❧ Father, please help me to focus my thoughts on the right things - because
I know my thoughts will lead me either in the right or the wrong direction.
Amen.

January 28

What you have is very good!

READ: ECCLESIASTES 6:1–9

Better what the eye sees than the roving of the appetite …
– ECCLESISATES 6:9

Once upon a time a man sold his house to travel throughout the world to find a treasure – which he never found. After his death, however, the man who bought his house found a treasure in the back garden.

Man is a very strange creature. Very few of us are satisfied with what we have. If we live in the country, we long for the city lights; and if we live in the city, we yearn for the wonderful silence of a farm in the Karoo. If we are tall we would rather be small, if we have curls, we would rather have straight hair. And so on and so forth. Very few people in the world are really content, but this year you could learn to be satisfied with what you have.

Focus on all the blessings God has given you; enjoy all the things you already have, instead of being unhappy about everything you desire but cannot afford. The desire to have more turns you into a discontented, disgruntled person. It's much better to be grateful and sincerely glad about every blessing the Lord gives you.

Make a decision of the will this year to be satisfied with the things you already have, to be truly grateful for them and to forget all those would-like-to-have's you cannot have.

❧ Lord, forgive me for still yearning for so many things I would like to have that I quite forget about all the things You have already given me. Make me satisfied with what I have. Amen.

On God's way

READ: DEUTERONOMY 5:31–33

*Walk in all the way that the LORD your God has commanded you,
so that you may live and prosper and prolong your
days in the land that you will possess.*
– DEUTERONOMY 5:33

God's people discovered time and again, to their own sorrow, that things soon went wrong when they strayed from God's way. They left God repeatedly for heathen idols only to turn to Him again for help when things went wrong. And God was always ready to help them. Even when they were carried away as exiles through their own fault, He showed them mercy again and allowed them to return to their country. There is only one way in which you will be prosperous all year, and that is to follow Moses' advice to Israel: Walk in the way the Lord has commanded you … The way outlined for you in his Word.

On your journey through life, you really don't always feel like following God's way. Sometimes the by-ways seem much more fun and interesting. But God helps you even when you stray. 'Whether you turn to the right or to the left, your ears will hear a voice behind you saying, "This is the way; walk in it,"'says God Himself through the prophet Isaiah (Isa 30:21). Ultimately you always realise that God's way is the only right way for you. He gives you his Word as a light for your feet, and his law as a route map. If you walk all the way according to the instructions of God's Word this year and obey his law, He Himself will make your way prosperous.

❧ Heavenly Father, this year I want to follow the way You have pointed out in your Word. Grant that I will obey your law so that I can be successful. Amen.

January 30

When God works

READ: JOHN 5:17–23

Jesus said to them, 'My Father is always at his work
to this very day, and I, too, am working.'
– JOHN 5:17

When Jesus dared to heal a paralysed man on the Sabbath, the Jews
were furious. However, Jesus told them plainly that his Father was
working ceaselessly, regardless of whether it was Sabbath or not – and
that He was also doing the work of his Father. On studying the life of
Jesus we notice that He did nothing without first consulting his Father.
'The Son can do nothing by Himself; He can do only what He sees the
Father doing,' He says in John 5:19. Even when Jesus was deeply troubled and was praying in Gethesemane that God should take the cup of
suffering from Him, He was nevertheless willing to conclude his prayer
with, 'Yet not my will, but yours be done' (Luke 22:42).

Sometimes our personal plans and schemes fail because we insist
on carrying out our own plans regardless of the cost. We try to do
God's work for Him, instead of waiting patiently for Him to work
through us. If you believe in Jesus, it means that you may relax, as it
were, and allow Him to take control of your life. Stop making your
own plans – you already know they always fail. Stop doing things on
your own without considering the will of God. Make this your new
year's resolution: Allow God to work in your life.

Heavenly Father, I apologise for being so wrapped up in my own plans
and schemes. Please work through me so that your will can be done in my
life this year. Amen.

Heavenly Father,

grant that this year will be a meaningful year in my life –
that I will be happy, learn to live in a new way, redeem the time,
seize my opportunities and be committed to my work.
Thank you for your power which You make available to me
and for the promise that You will be with me every day this year.
Bless my marriage and my children –
and grant that I will have your peace in my heart
despite the prevailing unrest.
Please give me compassion for others,
and grant that I will be absolutely reliable.
I want to get to know You better this year by studying your Word.
Thank you for trusting me enough to make me your servant
and steward in the world.
Please keep me on track –
make my way straight, Lord.
Help me to approach the year with faith and hope in You,
to make the most of every day,
and to focus my thoughts on the right things.
I praise You for always remaining the same,
and that no-one who believes in You will be put to shame.
Lord, I want to give the control of my life to You this year.
I want to surrender my own will and plans
and allow You to do your work through me.
Please make this possible, Lord.

Amen

Bear fruit!

After sharing the last supper with his disciples, Jesus spoke to his distressed disciples for the last time. He kept the most important things He wanted to convey to them to his last conversation. In his farewell teaching, Jesus told his disciples to bear fruit for Him in the world.

The image He used here to explain the process of fruit-bearing was well-known to the people of Israel in those days: that of the gardener and his vines. Jesus wants his followers to bear 'spiritual' fruit for Him. His farewell message is also directed at you.

This month we will follow Jesus' teaching on how to be fruitful in his kingdom. My prayer is that you will bear much more fruit for Him after working through these devotions than ever before.

February

Jesus, the true vine

READ: JOHN 15:1–8

I am the true vine, and my Father is the gardener ...
I am the vine; you are the branches. If a man remains in me and
I in him, he will bear much fruit; apart from me you can do nothing.
– JOHN 15:1, 5

In viticulture the type of vine planted is extremely important. Competent wine growers make sure that they use vines which grow strongly . The quality of the grapes depends on the quality of the vine which bears the branches. Jesus told his disciples that He was the true vine – the vine which enables the branches growing from it to bear much fruit.

We are the branches which grow from the Vine (Christ). In nature, branches which have been pruned away cannot bear fruit because the branches depend on the vine for energy and food. Branches which remain in the vine, and are attached firmly to the vine, branches which obtain their energy and food from the vine, can bear much fruit.

God is the gardener – He tends the vineyard and looks after the branches. The gardener sees to it that the vineyard is watered and pruned properly, so that it can bear as much fruit as possible.

If you belong to God, you are part of God's vineyard. You are one of the branches from which God expects fruit. To bear fruit, you have to remain close to Jesus, the Vine, because you will only be able to bear fruit if you have a relationship with Him.

❧ Lord Jesus, I want to bear fruit for You. Show me how to remain close to You day after day - I know I cannot do anything without You. Amen.

February 1

Created to bear fruit

READ: JOHN 15:9–17

You did not choose me, but I chose you and
appointed you to go and bear fruit – fruit that will last.
– JOHN 15:16

If a wine grower plants a new vineyard on his farm, the branches which have to bear fruit some day have no choice about where the vines will be planted. It is the farmer's responsibility to choose the best spot, the right vines and to graft the right branches onto the vines. In the light of this Jesus told his disciples that they had not chosen Him, but that He had chosen them to be his followers. And since He had chosen them specially, He had also appointed them to bear fruit for Him – to spread his good news throughout the world.

This instruction also applies to you: God chose you to be his child long before the creation of the world. Paul writes in his letter to the Ephesians: 'For He chose us in Him before the creation of the world to be holy and blameless in his sight' (Eph 1:4).

God therefore chose you specially to be a branch on his vine. He chose you to bear fruit for Him. And Jesus also specifies the type of fruit you have to bear: 'fruit that will last'. He wants you to bear lasting fruit. God's children 'must make a permanent difference in this world', is the direct translation of this verse in *Die Boodskap*. Live in such a way that the world around you will be a better place because *you* have had a positive impact on it.

❧ Lord Jesus, Thank you for choosing me to bear fruit for You. Grant that my fruit will be lasting - that it will make a permanent difference in the lives of those around me and the world where I live. Amen.

February 2

The fruit of the Spirit

READ: GALATIANS 5:16–26

[The] fruit of the Spirit is love, joy, peace, patience, kindness,
goodness, faithfulness, gentleness and self-control.
– GALATIANS 5:22–23

In Galatians 5 Paul sketches a picture of what the life of a Christian who bears fruit for God looks like. In the life of such a person the qualities which were so clearly visible in Jesus' life come to the fore. Note that the Greek word translated here as 'fruit', is in the singular. Paul is talking about one fruit, not nine different fruits. However, this fruit which Christians have to bear, has nine different qualities – if even one of these qualities is lacking, something is wrong with the fruit. All nine qualities should be visible in your life to bear the right kind of fruit for God.

To be able to bear this type of fruit you have to rely on the Holy Spirit to inspire these qualities in your life. You will be able to be loving, full of joy and peace, patient, kind, good, faithful, humble and self-controlled only if He is the helmsman. In your own strength you cannot achieve this, because your old sinful nature is much too strong. However, God will enable you to bear the fruit of the Spirit, but then you must also be willing to be changed by the Holy Spirit. Only then will this fruit be visible and only then will the good things which are indications of the fruit in your life increase and not decrease.

❧ Holy Spirit, I want your fruit in my life. I want You to determine my conduct from this moment so that I will reflect all nine qualities of this fruit in my life. Amen.

February 3

Pruning is essential

READ: JOHN 15:1–2

He cuts off every branch in me that bears no fruit,
while every branch which does bear fruit he
prunes so that it will be even more fruitful.
– JOHN 15:2

The gardener in Jesus' parable does two things with the branches of his vines: Some are pruned to correct their growth and others are cut off. The fruit-bearing branches are pruned to correct their growth so that they will bear even more fruit. This looks like a contradiction in terms, but anyone who has visited a wine-farm (or has grown up on one), knows that the vineyard has to be pruned in late autumn. The dead wood on the vine must be removed before the new branches which sprout in spring can yield the maximum crop. When the bunches of grapes are still young, the excess berries are also pruned away so that the remaining berries can be bigger and the bunches more attractive.

This pruning process is never pleasant or easy for the vine, but it is essential in order to yield a bumper crop. God prunes his children like the gardener prunes his vineyard. He removes from our lives those things which hamper our Christian lives, which prevent us from bearing fruit for Him. And, as in the case of the vine, we do not like this pruning process either. Things such as trouble and hurt are nevertheless essential in the life of every Christian because they stimulate us to remain close to God and bear more fruit. When you experience difficult times, know that God is pruning you to be able to bear even more fruit for Him.

❧ Heavenly Father, I now see that the difficult times in my life are merely your pruning process so that I will be able to bear more and better fruit for You. I am willing to be pruned by You until all the wrong things in my life have been removed. Amen.

February 4

Be glad about the pruning process

READ: 1 PETER 1:3–9

In this you greatly rejoice, though now for a little
while you may have had to suffer grief in all kinds of trials.
These have come so that your faith … may be proved genuine …
– 1 PETER 1:6–7

A newly pruned vineyard is not attractive at all. Instead of the lush green leaves and bunches of grapes seen in summer, all that remains after the pruning process is a vineyard pruned down to brown, dead-looking stumps. Sometimes the painful events in our own lives remind us of God's pruning process. No-one likes negative things to happen to them – yet, according to Peter, we should be glad about God's pruning process in our lives. God uses this pruning process to test the genuineness of our faith. Just as ore has to be crushed and melted before gold can be obtained from the rock, God sometimes 'crushes' his children in the mill of hardship to test whether their faith is genuine enough to pass the test of hardship.

Therefore, when you experience problems in your life again, rejoice! Just as the gardener trims the remaining branches on the vines, God wants to remove the impurities from your life by allowing you to struggle for a while. God does this to purify and strengthen your faith – after the pruning you will be a better, stronger Christian than before, because God's pruning process is always done in love and is always to your advantage.

❧ Heavenly Father, forgive me for complaining so much when You are pruning me to correct my growth so that I can bear more fruit for You. Enable me to rejoice because You are testing the genuineness of my faith. Amen.

February 5

God's discipline is good for you

READ: HEBREWS 12:4–11

No discipline seems pleasant at the time, but painful.
Later on, however, it produces a harvest of righteousness
and peace for those who have been trained by it.
– HEBREWS 12:11

We have already heard that the gardener has to prune his vines to encourage a bigger crop. Although this pruning process is never pleasant, it is essential if the branches are to yield their maximum crop.

Just as the gardener prunes the vines with a view to improving fruit-bearing, God disciplines his children to make them holy. Although this is difficult to understand while we are being disciplined, all of us who have children know that we cannot rear them without discipline. In fact, we discipline them because we love them. And during this process our children are not grateful at all, but eventually, once they are well-adjusted adults, they will most definitely see that the discipline had actually been a training process which had turned them into better adults.

'Endure the hardship as discipline; God is treating you as sons,' the author of Hebrews wrote (v 7). God disciplines you for your own good 'that [you] may share in his holiness', says verse 10. What the writer of Hebrews is saying here is that you should actually be worried if your llife is running too smoothly! See hardship as God's discipline and training in future, and know that this hardship which He permits in your life is always for your own good – that it actually proves that God is treating you as his child and that He cares for you.

❧ Heavenly Father, thank you for the new understanding that difficult times prove that I am your child and that You really love me. Amen.

February 6

The secret of fruit-bearing

READ: JOHN 15:4–8

Remain in me, and I will remain in you. No branch can bear fruit
by itself; it must remain in the vine. If a man remains in me and
I in him, he will bear much fruit; apart from me you can do nothing.
– JOHN 15:4–5

The secret of a branch which bears much fruit is that such a branch
should remain part of the vine. As soon as a branch is removed from
the vine, it withers and is thrown away. These branches are collected
and thrown into the fire, says Jesus. If you want to bear much fruit for
God, you have to remain close to Jesus to develop an intimate relationship with Him and see to it that nothing will come between you
and Him. However, to develop a relationship with God you have to
spend time with Him.

'We can produce more fruit for God by doing less for God and
being more with Him,' wrote Darlene Wilkinson.[1] The closer you are
to Jesus, the more time you will set aside for Him, and the more fruit
you will bear for Him. Don't think that you have earned the fruit which
you bear – this is God's work in your life. He is the One who saves you
and grafts you to the vine so that you can bear fruit. However, bearing
fruit is partly your responsibility. If you already belong to God you
have been grafted to the vine – and now you have to bear fruit. Good
vines bear good fruit and are recognised by their good fruit.

❧ Lord Jesus, I want to remain close to You, so close that I will bear much
good fruit for You. I know this fruit follows when I remain in You. Amen.

February 7

Remain in Jesus

READ: JOHN 15:4–8

Remain in me, and I will remain in you. No branch can bear fruit by itself;
it must remain in the vine. If a man remains in me and I in him,
he will bear much fruit; apart from me you can do nothing.
– JOHN 15:4–5

Jesus' command that we remain in Him comes after the pruning process has already been completed (cf John 15:3). To remain in Jesus means that you spend time with Him, wait on Him; that you make an effort to get to know Him better and better; that you thirst for Him like the deer thirsting for streams of water in Psalm 42:1–2. Remaining in Jesus means that we, as Christians, cannot survive without Him.

To me the very best bonus of retirement is that I now have much more time in the morning for devotions. I can read my Bible at my leisure and pray unhurriedly. And while you spend time with God, study his Word and listen to his voice, one fact becomes clearer: the incredible magnitude of his love for you. God loves you so much that He gave his only Son to die for you; Jesus loves you so much that He laid down his life for you and the Holy Spirit loves you so much that He will never forsake you. He remains in you, He teaches and guides and prays for you every day.

Enveloped in this Divine cloud of love, nothing can ever really go wrong in your life.

❧ Lord, thank you for your cloud of love which enfolds me, thank you for living in me through your Holy Spirit and that your Word reassures me of your love for me every day. Amen.

February 8

Remain in Jesus' love

READ: JOHN 15:9–17

*As the Father has loved me, so have I loved you. Now remain
in my love. If you obey my commands, you will remain in my love,
just as I have obeyed my Father's commands and remain in his love.*
– JOHN 15:9–10

Here Jesus gives us an example of exactly what it means to 'remain in
Him'. He says that He loves us the way the Father loves the Son. We
already know that Jesus demonstrated his incredible love for sinners
on the cross. Because He loves us so much, He was willing to die on
the Cross so that we could be reconciled to God. In gratitude for this
love we should remain in his love. We do this by obeying Him: by
obeying his commands.

However, this concerns a relationship with the Lord, not obeying
certain laws. You cannot bear fruit without God – fruit is borne only
when He accomplishes it in you through his Spirit. However, it is also
vital that you deliberately remain in Him in order to bear fruit for
Him. It is interesting to note here that we are not commanded to bear
fruit, but to remain in Jesus' love.

Encourage and cherish your relationship with God. And remember that obeying Him proves your love for God. Be willing to obey
God's commands in his Word if you want to remain in his love

❧ Heavenly Father, You know that I love You very much, that I want to
remain in your love. Please enable me to prove my love for You by obeying
your commands. Amen.

February 9

Spending time with the Father

READ: JOHN 15:7–8

If you remain in me and my words remain in you,
ask whatever you wish, and it will be given you.
– JOHN 15:7–8

Jesus' ministry on earth was characterised by regular communication with his heavenly Father. Whenever He had to make important decisions, He spent additional time with his Father. For example, before He chose his disciples, He spent a whole night in prayer. After He had been tempted by the devil in the desert, He also went to his Father to be strengthened. Before He was to be crucified, He went to Gethsemane where He pleaded with his Father to remove the cup of inhuman suffering from Him. Whenever Jesus set aside time for his Father, He received the necessary power for his earthly mission.

You also need time with God. The busier you are, the harder it will be to make time for God – but you will need that time even more! Never neglect the time spent with the Lord because you want to do so many things for God. There is a very real danger that Christians can be so busy working for the Lord that they lack time for the Lord Himself. Jesus promises that, if you remain in Him and his words remain in you, you can ask anything from Him and He will give it to you. Therefore, make time for God's Word every day – so that you can make this promise part of your life.

❧ Lord Jesus, forgive me for sometimes being so busy doing things for You that I am too busy to just be close to You. I want to remain in your love, and make your words part of my life so that I can bear much fruit for You. Amen.

February 10

If there is no fruit

READ: JOHN 15:1–6

He cuts off every branch in me that bears no fruit …
You are already clean because of the word I have spoken to you.
– JOHN 15:2–3

A farmer will not tolerate an unfruitful vine in his vineyard if, year after year, it yields no grapes. He will definitely remove it and replace it with a vine which will yield fruit. Likewise God removes the branches from his vine which do not yield fruit for Him. It is possible to be a child of God yet bear no fruit for Him, but such an unfruitful Christian is useless to Him. 'If anyone does not remain in Me, he is like a branch that is thrown away and withers; such branches are picked up, thrown into the fire and burned,' Jesus warns the disciples in John 15:6.

Some people are quite happy being nominal members of a church. They are seen only when they get married, have their children christened or when they are buried. Church members who do not have a living relationship with God will be cut off by God at some stage. Because He loves you, God will discipline you to bear fruit for Him. This discipline compels you to be more fruitful in future. However, if you refuse to bear fruit for Him, you might eventually be cut off from the vine completely. Do listen to the warning in today's verse and turn your life around – do your best to be an active branch from today onwards and to bear fruit for God.

❧ Father, I have to confess that I bear so little fruit that I am probably also running the risk of being cut off from You. I undertake to change my life from now on. Please enable me to do this in the power of your Spirit. Amen.

February 11

Sin prevents you from bearing fruit

READ: 1 JOHN 1:6–10

If we confess our sins, he is faithful and just and will forgive us our sins and purify us from all unrighteousness.
– 1 JOHN 1:9

Bruce Wilkinson gives an interesting interpretation of John 15:2. He writes that the Greek word *airo* translated here as 'to cut off', can also mean 'to lift up'. Jesus therefore says here that God will 'lift up' those branches which do not bear fruit so that they will be able to bear fruit again. Branches lying on the ground easily become heavy with mud so that they cannot bear grapes. Sin in our lives is like the wet soil which covers the vine leaves and prevents them from bearing fruit. The mud-covered branches on the ground which cannot bear fruit must therefore be washed and lifted up by the gardener so that they can receive light and air and be able to bear fruit again.[2]

If you therefore still have sin in your life, you have to be disciplined ('lifted up') by God so that you will give up your sin and be able to bear fruit for Him again, even more fruit. If you ignore God's warnings to stop sinning, He will allow suffering so that you can listen. When I was young, giving a naughty child a proper hiding was still acceptable! My granny used to call it an 'ear-opener' – the punishment given to a child so that he could hear the parent. Sometimes God gives us, his children, 'ear-openers' so that we can hear Him and give up the sin in our lives.

❧ Heavenly Father, I now understand that I sometimes have to struggle to hear your warning - help me to be willing to give up the sin in my life. Amen.

February 12

The unfruitful fig-tree

READ: MARK 11:12–14; 20–25

*Seeing in the distance a fig-tree in leaf, he went to find out if it
had any fruit. When he reached it, he found nothing but leaves,
because it was not the season for figs. Then he said to the tree,
'May no-one ever eat fruit from you again …'*
– MARK 11:13–14

Jesus and his disciples passed a fig-tree. Being hungry, Jesus pushed
aside the leaves to see whether the fig-tree had any figs. As the tree
had no fruit, He cursed it. When they passed the tree again the following day, the disciples noticed that the tree had withered from
the roots.

We probably feel that Jesus was rather unreasonable to expect figs
out of season. He furthermore cursed the tree so that it withered because He had not found any fruit merely because He was hungry.
However, Jesus was using the fig-tree symbolically: God expects fruit
from his children – and if He does not find fruit, punishment follows.
If, to date, you have been one of God's unfruitful children or one who
has borne very little fruit, it is time to change your life, and focus
particularly on bearing as much fruit as possible for Him. A Christian
who does not bear fruit is useless in the kingdom of God. Therefore,
do not wait until it is too late for you – as in the case of the fig-tree
– before you make a real effort to bear fruit for God.

❧ Lord Jesus, forgive me for not always finding fruit in my life. Please help
me to make a special effort to bear fruit for You in future. Amen.

February 13

Fruit in season

READ: PSALM 1

Blessed is the man ... his delight is in the law of the LORD,
and on his law he meditates day and night. He is like a tree
planted by streams of water, which yields its fruit in season
and whose leaf does not wither. Whatever he does prospers.
– PSALM 1:1–3

You now know that you have to remain close to Jesus if you want to bear fruit for Him. If the branch is not grafted onto the vine, it cannot bear fruit – likewise you cannot have a fruitful life if you live your own way, separated from Jesus. In Psalm 1 a believer who spends time in the Word of God, who meditates on it day and night, is compared to a tree planted by a stream of water. The roots of such a tree always have enough water therefore the leaves remain green throughout the year and the tree bears fruit in season.

God reveals his will to his children in his Word. If you therefore want to bear fruit for Him, you should spend enough time studying your Bible. People fed by the stream of God's Word are filled with God's power. And since God blesses them, they are successful in everything they do. John 15:7 contains a beautiful promise for Christians who make God's words part of their lives: 'If you remain in me and my words remain in you, ask whatever you wish, and it will be given you.'

❧ Lord Jesus, Thank you for your Word. I want to memorise your words and meditate on them and make them part of my life so that I can bear fruit for You in season. Amen.

February 14

The life of a fruit-bearer

READ: GENESIS 49:22–26

Because of your father's God, who helps you,
because of the Almighty, who blesses you …
– GENESIS 49:25

The life of Joseph is a striking picture of what someone who bears fruit for the Lord should look like. Although practically everything went wrong for Joseph, he remained faithful to the Lord. His brothers sold him as a slave and in Egypt he landed in jail although he was innocent. However, the Lord was with him. Joseph never became discouraged, he trusted the Lord implicitly and God had him released from jail and enabled him to explain Pharaoh's dream.

Ultimately Joseph saw the hand of God in everything that had happened to him. When his brothers came to him to buy food, he did not even try to take revenge on them for the terrible things they had done to him. He comforted them saying, 'And now do not be distressed and do not be angry with yourselves for selling me here, because it was to save lives that God sent me ahead of you' (Gen 45:5).

When Jacob later blessed his son Joseph, he called him 'a fruitful vine near a spring' and promised him God's blesssing.

If, like Joseph, you are willing to remain faithful to God, even when your own life is rocked by incomprehensible catastrophes, you will also be like a vine near a spring. Remember: You may always rely on God's presence and blessing in your life.

Heavenly Father, I want to remain close to You all my life. Please bless me and make me a vine near a spring like Joseph - a vine that will bear fruit for You. Amen.

February 15

The fruit of love

READ: 1 JOHN 3:11–18

Dear children, let us not love with words
or tongue but with actions and in truth.
– 1 JOHN 3:18

Love is the very first quality of the fruit of the Spirit listed in Galatians 5:22. The unconditional love which Jesus has for us is the essential quality which Christians have to pursue if they want to bear fruit for God at all. '… If I have a faith that can move mountains, but have not love, I am nothing. If I give all I possess to the poor and surrender my body to the flames, but have not love, I gain nothing,' Paul wrote in 1 Corinthians 13:2–3. Your love for others is expressed by the things you do, and the way you live. And this love must not consist only of words, your actions must correspond.

Jesus Himself commanded us to bear the fruit of love. 'This is my command: Love each other,' He said in John 15:17. You may not hug this Jesus kind of love to yourself either. You have to share it with others. 'Christ's love compels us,' Paul writes in 2 Corinthians 5:14. Jesus' love inspires you to reach out to others, to love them and care for them until this love takes over your whole life and you are eventually able to say with Paul: 'I no longer live, but Christ lives in me' (cf Gal 2:20).

❧ Lord Jesus, let your love compel me to care sincerely for others and show me how I can prove that love by my actions. Amen.

February 16

I no longer live

READ: GALATIANS 2:17–21

And I no longer live, but Christ lives in me.
– GALATIANS 2:20

Paul's whole life was so totally committed to Jesus that he lived only for Him. Nothing else was really important to him. He even professed that he no longer lived, but that Christ lived in him. In Philippians 1:21 and 3:10–11 he says, 'For to me, to live is Christ and to die is gain … I want to know Christ and the power of his resurrection and the fellowship of sharing in his sufferings, becoming like him in his death, and so, somehow, to attain to the resurrection from the dead.'

Usually many things in our lives compete for our attention – and quite frequently we spend more time and money on these things than on God. These things furthermore take up so much of our time that we often have no time left for God. If you are serious about bearing fruit for God, you will have to consider the place Jesus has in your life. Only when He becomes the most important Person in your life, when you are willing to give up your own desires and will and regard your money, security and loved ones as less important than Jesus, will you be where He wants you to be: the place where you can really bear fruit for Him, fruit which will last.

❧ Lord Jesus, It is my desire to be able to declare with Paul that I no longer live, but that You live in me. I pray that You will always be the most important Person in my life. Amen.

February 17

Glorify God

READ: JOHN 15:5-8

This is to my Father's glory, that you bear much fruit,
showing yourselves to be my disciples.
– John 15:8

A farmer who works very hard in his vineyard finds it extremely satisfying to see his vines bearing fruit. Likewise God enjoys seeing his children bearing fruit for Him and being his disciples. When you and I bear fruit for God, He is glorified. 'Ultimately the actions of the believer merely point towards the greatness and power of God. The believer should also see the meaning of his life in this,' reads *Die Bybellennium*.[3]

'You are the light of the world …' Jesus said in the Sermon on the Mount. 'Let your light shine before men, that they may see your good deeds and praise your Father in heaven' (Matt 5:14, 16). When people therefore see the fruit in your life, they will give God the glory.

Being a disciple of Jesus means that you will be his follower; that you will choose to follow Him, and that you will commit yourself to Him. Not all Christians are truly committed to God, but committed children fill his heart with joy. True commitment to God will require that you focus on Him, strive to follow his example, follow in his footsteps, obey his commands and obey Him in every respect. This is no easy task, but commitment to God is always worth it – even when it is hard.

❧ Heavenly Father, I want to glorify You by bearing much fruit for You. Help me, by the power of your Spirit, to be really committed to You. Amen.

February 18

Good works as fruit

READ: TITUS 3:12–15

Our people must learn to devote themselves to doing
what is good, in order that they may provide for
daily necessities and not live unproductive lives.
– TITUS 3:14

When we perform good deeds for the Lord, we bear fruit for Him. The words 'fruit' and 'good works' are used alternately in the Bible to indicate our way of life. And, according to Paul, that is what God has made us for: 'For we are God's workmanship, created in Christ Jesus to do good works, which God prepared in advance for us to do' (Eph 2:10).

It is God's will that you bear fruit for Him – 'visible' fruit, by helping to proclaim the gospel of Jesus throughout the world, and by following his example by doing the things He did, helping people and by really caring for them.

However, you also have to bear 'invisible' fruit – that is, live in such a way that the nine qualities of the fruit of the Holy Spirit will be visible in your life (cf Gal 5:22). According to Bruce Wilkinson, bearing this fruit is the most important earthly reason for your redemption.[4]

God is working in your life at the moment so that you will bring forth more and more of this fruit. A direct translation of the core verse for today in *Die Boodskap* reads, 'You have to be like a tree which bears good fruit in the Lord at all times.' Make sure that you obey this command!

❧ Heavenly Father, Help me to do good works - to bear visible and invisible fruit for You so that others will be able to see You in my life. Amen.

February 19

You are recognised by your fruit

READ: MATTHEW 12:33–37

Make a tree good and its fruit will be good,
or make a tree bad and its fruit will be bad,
for a tree is recognised by its fruit.
– MATTHEW 12:33

Jesus knew that, just as a tree is recognised by the fruit it bears, a believer is recognised by the fruit he bears for God. Your deeds always speak louder than your words. The writer of Proverbs agrees with this: 'Even a child is known by his actions, by whether his conduct is pure and right' (Prov 20:11).

Just as the tree in your garden is clearly a mulberry tree or a lemon tree because it bears mulberries or lemons, unbelievers can see by your actions whether you are serious about being a Christian. If you therefore do things which contradict your confession, your credibility as a Christian can be irreparably damaged. I remember very well how shocked I was one day when I heard the foul language a professing Christian used at a party. Unfortunately sin will always be part of each one of us – Christians too. The devil knows your weak spots much better than you know them yourself, and he will attack you where you are most vulnerable and where you least expect to be attacked. Therefore guard against bearing fruit that does not reflect your confession. When Jesus comes you will have to give an account of the way you lived on earth. Live in such a way that God will be pleased with you.

✿ Heavenly Father, Please forgive me for so often doing things that do not reflect my confession. Grant that I will live in such a way that others will see by my actions that I belong to You. Amen.

February 20

Abundance after testing

READ: PSALM 66

For You, O God, tested us; You refined us
like silver ... we went through fire and water,
but you brought us to a place of abundance.
– PSALM 66:10, 12

God does not exempt his children from hurt and difficult times. We have already determined that God permits hardship in our lives so that we will bear more fruit for Him. Difficult times in your life are like the pruning process for the vines which is intended to ensure a better crop. Likewise a doctor sometimes has to open a festering boil – a very painful process for the patient, but it has to be done to remove the infection and bring about healing.

When God sometimes permits hardship in your life, you do not have to doubt his love for you. He is merely preparing you for a life of spiritual abundance. Ore has to be melted in a furnace before the precious metal can be removed. A vine, a rosebush and a fruit tree have to be pruned correctly before the owner will be rewarded with an abundance of fruit or flowers. A friend told us that a lady who had experienced much hardship had told him: 'God never prunes us to breaking point, only to the point of growth.'

God's pruning process in the life of his child always results in an abundance of fruit. God promises his abundance in your life too if you will permit Him to use his pruning shears.

❧ Heavenly Father, I now realise that my own hardship is merely your pruning shears preparing me for your spiritual abundance in my life. Amen.

February 21

You have to persevere

READ: JAMES 1:2–8

Because you know that the testing of your faith develops perseverance.
Perseverance must finish its work so that you may be mature
and complete, not lacking anything.
– JAMES 1:3–4

The older the vine, the heavier the pruning has to be. Much more dead wood has to be pruned away than in the case of young vines. But, once they have been pruned, the older branches produce many more grapes than the young ones. Although young vines have more leaves than the older ones, they bear less fruit. However, if the older vines are not pruned heavily, the plants become weaker and the yield smaller.

The longer you are a child of God, the more fruit you should produce for Him, and the more you need God's pruning process in your life so that you can produce more fruit. James writes that full spiritual growth will require perseverance, but this perseverance will ensure spiritual maturity. The more God prunes you by permitting difficult times in your life, the more you will become like Jesus and the more things in your life which hamper your relationship with God will be 'pruned away'. Being spiritually mature means that you will eventually be so surrendered to God that you will be willing to give up all other things – even the good ones – so that He can be the King of your life. 'All that remains in your hands is a single passion, one objective, one unhindered opportunity: to bear more fruit,' writes Bruce Wilkinson.[5]

❧ Heavenly Father, Grant that I will have the staying power to persevere to the end, until I am spiritually mature and bear the maximum amount of fruit for You. Amen.

February 22

In accordance with the will of God

READ: MATTHEW 6:9–13

This is how you should pray: Our Father in heaven …
your will be done on earth as it is in heaven.
– MATTHEW 6:9–10

When Jesus taught his disciples to pray, He also taught them to ask that God's will be done on earth as it is already being done in heaven. It was very important to Jesus to do everything in accordance with the will of his heavenly Father. He therefore consulted his Father in everything and spent much time in prayer. Even when He pleaded in Gethsemane that God should remove the cup of inhuman suffering from Him, He concluded his prayer with the words, 'yet not my will, but yours be done' (cf Luke 22:42).

Remaining in Jesus (in order to bear fruit for Him) means that you will be willing to surrender your own way and will. It also means that you will be willing to set God's will above your own. God will make his will known to you if you are really willing to obey Him in everything. 'Seek the LORD while he may be found; call on him while he is near,' the prophet Isaiah wrote (Isa 55:6). This verse includes a warning: It might eventually be too late to obey God. Don't hesitate any longer to find out exactly what God's will means in your life.

🐦 Heavenly Father, I want to obey You - please show me exactly what I have to do to live in accordance with your will. Amen.

February 23

Know the will of God

READ: JEREMIAH 29:10–14

*'You will seek me and find me when you
seek me with all your heart. I will be found by you,'
declares the LORD, 'and will bring you back from captivity.'*
– JEREMIAH 29:13–14

If you really want to bear fruit for God, you will have to be willing to obey Him. Some people find it difficult to determine exactly what God's will involves. In the words of the prophet Jeremiah, God announced his will to his people in captivity: He wanted them to be prosperous, He wanted to give them a future and they would then call upon Him and He would answer their prayers. God promised that He would make his will known to them if they would 'seek Him with all their heart' (v 13).

You could do various things to determine God's will for you. God reveals his will in his Word – make an effort to know your Bible well so that you can know the will of God. You can also ask other Christians for advice and pray that the Holy Spirit reveal God's will through their words to you. The closer you live to the Lord, the easier it will be for you to recognise his will for you and the easier it will be for you to obey Him. May the promise in Hosea 10:12 be fulfilled for you: 'Sow for yourselves righteousness, reap the fruit of unfailing love, and break up your unploughed ground; for it is time to seek the LORD, until he comes and showers righteousness on you.'

❧ Heavenly Father, I want to seek your will with my whole heart - thank you for your promise that You will reveal your will to me and meet me. Amen.

February 24

The branch from the root of Jesse

READ: ISAIAH 11:1–9

A shoot will come up from the stump of Jesse; from his roots
a Branch will bear fruit. The Spirit of the Lord will rest on him –
the Spirit of wisdom and understanding, the Spirit of counsel
and of power, the Spirit of knowledge and of the fear of the Lord.
– ISAIAH 11:1–2

Of all the branches which bear fruit for God, Jesus, 'the branch from the stump of Jesse', bore the most fruit for Him. In Isaiah 11 the prophet Isaiah predicted that a shoot which would bear fruit would sprout from the root of Jesse again. A remnant of God's people would remain which would ensure a new future for them. This prophecy was fulfilled at the birth of Jesus, the promised Messiah. God Himself equipped Jesus, the 'new David' for his task on earth. The Spirit of God gave Him the qualities that a perfect king needed: wisdom and understanding, counsel and power, knowledge and the fear of the Lord. He did indeed find joy in serving his Father, He judged people fairly and was just and reliable in every respect. He also established a new kingdom of Peace: in Christ God reconciled man to Himself and man was reconciled to his fellow-man.

'Whoever claims to live in him must walk as Jesus did,' John wrote (1 John 2:6). If you would like to bear fruit like Jesus did, look at the way He lived and acted – and then do likewise.

❧ Lord Jesus, thank you for establishing a new kingdom on earth - a kingdom where I can be reconciled to God and my fellow-man, because You obtained God's forgiveness for me on the cross. Grant that I will remain in You so that I will bear fruit. Amen.

February 25

God's word brings forth fruit

READ: ISAIAH 55:6–11

As the rain and the snow come down from heaven, and do not return
to it without watering the earth and making it bud and flourish ...
so is my word that goes out from my mouth ... it ... will accomplish
what I desire and achieve the purpose for which I sent it.
– Isaiah 55:10–11

Through the prophet Isaiah, God asks his disobedient people to return to Him. He stretches out his hand of mercy to them and waits
for them to respond to his offer of mercy. Rain and snow which fall
from heaven do not return to it without watering the earth and making the plants grow. Likewise God's words will not return to Him
void, but will bear fruit for Him, do everything He intends to accomplish, and achieve the purpose for which He sends it.

'The fruit of the Spirit must be the key to effective fruit-bearing in
your life. See to it that your relationship with the Lord is sound; focus
your life on Him and strive with all your strength to accomplish God's
will in your life. This will be possible if your remain in the Vine,'
writes John Maxwell.[6] Without God's Word in your life, you cannot
really bear fruit for Him. This Word teaches you how God wants you
to live, what God expects of his children, how He wants to be praised,
honoured and loved. Spend enough time studying your Bible so that
it can teach you about the fruit God requires and how those qualities
can be developed in your life.

❧ Heavenly Father, I praise You for the power of your Word in my life -
thank you that you Word helps me to bear fruit for You. Amen.

February 26

Thirsting for God

READ: PSALM 63

O God, you are my God, earnestly I seek you;
my soul thirsts for you, my body longs for you,
in a dry and weary land where there is no water
My soul clings to you; your right hand upholds me.
– PSALM 63:1, 8

If you love someone very much, it is a joy to be with that person again, and if you have not seen each other for a long time, you have an overpowering desire to feel that person's embrace or hear his voice. Sometimes I miss our son so much – he is working abroad – that I feel I cannot be without him any longer. And if I have not seen my grandchildren for a week, we just have to visit them in Durbanville.

Remaining in Jesus means that you will remain so close to Him that you will develop a thirst for Him which can only be quenched by intimate fellowship with Him. David writes about this thirst in Psalm 63: He thirsts for God like a deer thirsts for water in the desert. He thirsts for the presence of God with all that is within him; he longs with his whole being to worship God.

Is your relationship with God so intimate that you long for his presence this way? Ask the Lord to stir such a desire for Him in you that He will become as indispensable and vital to you as water, until you can say with the psalmist in Psalm 16:5, 'LORD, you have assigned me my portion and my cup …'

❧ Lord Jesus, You know I love You. Stimulate my love so that it will become an all-consuming desire for You, so that You will be my whole life. Amen.

Controlled by the Spirit

READ: GALATIANS 5:13–25

Live by the Spirit, and you will not gratify the desires of the sinful nature.
– GALATIANS 5:16

Fruit does not ripen overnight. It takes a few months from blossom stage until ripe fruit can be picked from the trees or vines. Likewise, spiritual fruit also develops gradually. The fruit of the Spirit develops in our lives as we, as Christians, learn not to respond the way the world normally expects us to. For example, when people annoy us, God expects us to respond in love; He expects us to retain our joy, even in times of sorrow; to have peace in our hearts in the midst of chaos; to be patient when we have to wait a long time for answers to our prayers; to remain good-natured when people are rude; to be kind-hearted towards people who come to us; to be reliable even when others leave us in the lurch; to remain humble even though we actually have reason to feel proud of our achievements; and to be self-controlled even in the face of provocation (see the nine-fold fruit of the Spirit in Galatians 5:22). It is practically impossible to achieve this, but God never asks anything which He cannot fulfil in your life through his Spirit. Before Paul explained the fruit of the Spirit to the church in Galatia, he told them that they had to be controlled by the Holy Spirit so that they would no longer listen to the old sinful nature. By means of the process of sanctification, which lasts all your life, you can eventually become a mature Christian and bear the fruit God expects of you. However, you must always remember that the fruit of the Spirit will take time to develop and mature in your life.

❦ Holy Spirit, make me willing to surrender control of my life to You so that your fruit will be clearly visible in my life. Amen.

February 28

Fruit-bearing and trust

READ: JEREMIAH 17:5–10

Blessed is the man who trusts in the LORD, whose confidence is in him.
He will be like a tree planted by the water ... its leaves are always green.
It has no worries in a year of drought and never fails to bear fruit.
– JEREMIA 17:7–8

The weather plays a very important role in fruit-bearing. If it is too warm out of season, the trees bud too soon and, when it turns cold again, the blossoms drop. The crop will then be smaller than usual. If it rains too little and the fruit trees lacked water, they do not bear fruit. To have a bumper crop, weather conditions have to be just right for the fruit trees to receive enough water and nutrients.

The secret of consistent fruit-bearing in a spiritual sense is found in Jeremiah 17:7: Christians who trust in the Lord are like trees planted by the water: they will always have green leaves, they will not be affected by drought and they will never fail to bear fruit. If you are willing to trust in the Lord, live close to Him and seek refuge in Him, you will be blessed. Then you will also be like a fruit tree planted by a flowing stream. Heat and drought will not affect you, and you will bear fruit for God in abundance season after season, despite factors such as negative physical circumstances and spiritual drought.

At the end of the month in which we studied fruit-bearing, I should like to wish you Colossians 1:10 personally: 'May [you] please him in every way: bearing fruit in every good work, growing in the knowledge of God'.

⚜ Heavenly Father, please help me to trust in You without wavering so that I can be like a tree which is planted by a stream of water, which always has green leaves and never fails to bear fruit for You. Amen.

Lord Jesus,

You are the true vine and I the branch –
I now know that I can only bear fruit
for You if I remain in You.
I pray for the fruit of your Spirit in my life –
help me to be implicitly obedient to You and help me
to live in such a way that others will be able
to see by my conduct that I belong to You.
I now know that difficult times in my life
are merely your pruning process
to enable me to bear more fruit for You
and that the difficult times actually prove
that You are treating me as your child.
I want to remain in You for the rest of my life
and make time to study your Word
and talk to You in prayer frequently.
Please forgive the sin in my life
which sometimes prevents me
from bearing fruit for You.
Help me to be willing to give it up.
Grant that your words will remain in me
so that I will bear fruit in season,
and so that You, Father, can be glorified by it.
I know that I will be recognised by that fruit.
Help me to persevere in faith,
and to know and obey your will.
I now surrender the control
of my life to your Spirit and put my faith in You,
so that I can be like a tree planted
by a stream of water and bear fruit in abundance –
fruit that will last.

Amen

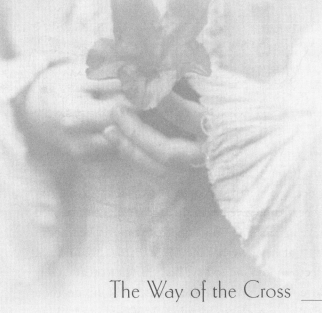

The Way of the Cross

We should think on Jesus' road to Calvary every year, and follow, with his disciples, the events of the last Passover until his resurrection from the dead, so that we will never ever forget how He suffered for us; what God's love for sinners cost Him.

This month we will follow in Jesus' footsteps day after day. The longer you walk the way of the cross with Jesus, the better you will understand what it cost Him to redeem you from sin and the greater the impact the events around Easter will have on your life. I trust that, after the daily readings for March, you will never again see Easter merely as a traditional event.

March

God's decision

READ: ACTS 2:22–28

This man was handed over to you by God's set purpose and foreknowledge …
– ACTS 2:23

It was God's decision to have his Son handed over to the enemy and put to death. Why? Because He loves people. Jesus spells this out very clearly in one of the best known verses in the Bible: 'For God so loved the world that he gave his one and only Son, that whoever believes in him shall not perish but have eternal life' (John 3:16). It could not have been an easy decision for God to have his Son put to death. Only when you have children of your own do you realise what this decision must have cost God. We cannot even imagine sacrificing our child to save the life of a sinner… Therefore, no-one who looks at the cross of Jesus can ever doubt the magnitude of God's love for them.

When Adam and Eve rejected his love in the Garden of Eden, God made this far-reaching decision: He would sacrifice his only Son so that sinners could be adopted as his children. He also promised that the serpent's head would be crushed by Eve's Seed (cf Gen 3:15).

Jesus 'became obedient to death – even death on a cross', even though this obedience to the Father meant indescribable anguish and pain to Him as man.

Although it was God's decision that Jesus should suffer and die, it was our sin which cost Him the agony of death on the cross:

On Calvary's brow my Saviour died
'Twas there my Lord was crucified
'Twas on the cross He bled for me
And purchased there my pardon free
–'Calvary' from Sacred Songs and Solos

❧ Lord Jesus, You bore the punishment for my sin. You died for me - help me to live for You now. Amen.

March 1

Jesus, punished for your sins

READ: ISAIAH 53:2–10

But he was pierced for our transgressions, he was crushed for
our iniquities; the punishment that brought us peace
was upon him, and by his wounds we are healed.
– ISAIAH 53:5

Here the prophet Isaiah tells the story of God's people – his servant – who suffered in exile. Israel's suffering was on behalf of the world. God allowed them to suffer so that other nations could see their faith in God and turn to Him. According to God's divine plan the 'death' of the first Israel would lead to a new birth, a new beginning with his people, at the birth of the Messiah.

In the New Testament this Scripture is applied to Jesus. He is the Servant who had to suffer so that our sins could be forgiven and we could reach God. He bore the punishment for our sins to ensure our peace with God, and by his wounds we are healed. Jesus was willing to die on the cross for you and He therefore paid the full price for your sin. God is now willing to forgive you your sin because Jesus settled your account once and for all. He died for you and you therefore no longer have to fear God's punishment.

Never forget that, indirectly, you were responsible for the suffering of Christ. 'You, with the help of wicked men, put him to death by nailing him to the cross,' Peter said in his speech on the Day of Pentecost (Acts 2:23). This 'you' includes you and me.

Every year, during Holy Week, you should remember this fact once again.

❧ Lord Jesus, please remind me at Pentecost that I, too, was responsible for your suffering. Thank you for bearing the punishment on my behalf. Amen.

March 2

The plot to arrest Jesus

READ: MATTHEW 26:1–5; 14–16

Then the chief priests and the elders of the people assembled
in the palace of the high priest, whose name was Caiaphas,
and they plotted to arrest Jesus in some sly way and kill him.
— *MATTHEW 26:3–4*

The Jewish leaders' suspicions about Jesus (He had, after all denounced their legalistic religion with his new interpretation of the Law), reached a climax when the chief priests and elders assembled in the palace of the high priest to plot the arrest of Jesus. Although the crucifixion of Jesus was in line with God's divine plan, these leaders were nevertheless guilty. However, they could do nothing against the will of God. Jesus had also told his disciples in advance that He would be arrested and crucified during the Passover (cf Matt 26:2). It is very ironical that God used the sly plans of the Jews as the instrument to put into operation his plan (that his son had to be crucified so that our sins could be forgiven). Even here God had the last word – although it looked as if the Jewish leaders were in charge.

Judas played into the hands of the leaders when he offered to betray Jesus at a price. They agreed and offered him thirty silver coins to hand Jesus over to them. From that moment it was a matter of time until Jesus would be handed over to his enemies – Judas was merely waiting for a suitable opportunity to betray him.

God still holds history in his hand. Nothing could happen to Jesus then and nothing can happen to you now without God's knowledge.

❧ Heavenly Father, I praise You for still holding history - and me - in your hand. Thank you that nothing can happen to me unless it forms part of your plan for my life. Amen.

March 3

Anointed for his burial

READ: JOHN 12:1–8

'Leave her alone,' Jesus replied. 'It was intended that she should
save this perfume for the day of my burial. You will always
have the poor among you, but you will not always have me.'
– JOHN 12:7–8

Shortly before the time when Jesus would be crucified, He was invited
to a dinner given in his honour. The disciples and his three friends
from Bethany – Lazarus, Martha and Mary – were also among the
guests. As usual, the capable Martha acted as hostess. While the guests
were reclining at the table, Mary took a jar of very expensive perfume,
spikenard, and poured it on Jesus' feet. Then she dried his feet with
her hair. By this deed she demonstrated her love for Him. The other
guests were rather shocked about this waste, and Judas was particularly indignant, saying that the oil should rather have been sold and
the money given to the poor.

However, Jesus knew that Judas' motives were false – he would
have spent the money on himself. Jesus also knew Mary's heart. He
knew that she sensed his distress about the impending crucifixion. He
also knew that she was actually anointing Him as a sign of her sincere
love for Him. It must have meant so much to Jesus that Mary sensed
his state of mind so clearly. He therefore told the guests to leave her
alone, and said they would always have the poor with them, but they
would not always have Him.

Mary gave Jesus everything she had. Would you be able to be so
extravagant in serving Jesus; would you be able to demonstrate your
love for Him almost recklessly?

❦ Lord Jesus, I want to demonstrate my love for You by offering You myself
and everything I possess. Amen.

March 4

The first Communion

READ: LUKE 22:7–23

And he took bread, gave thanks and broke it, and gave it to them,
saying, 'This is my body given for you; do this in remembrance of me.'
In the same way, after the supper he took the cup, saying, 'This cup
is the new covenant in my blood, which is poured out for you.'
– LUKE 22:19– 20

Jesus planned the celebration of the Passover meal in detail. He explained to Peter and John exactly where the upper room was which had to be prepared for the Passover meal. They followed his directions, found the upper room He had told them about and made the necessary arrangements.

By celebrating the Passover meal with them, Jesus gave a new meaning to this centuries-old Jewish custom. He asked that, whenever they broke bread together, they would remember that He had sacrificed his life for them, and that, whenever they drank the wine, they would remember that the cup symbolised his blood shed for them. The disciples also heard for the first time that one of them would betray Jesus. That evening the traditional celebration of the Passover – which reminded the Israelites of the exodus from Egypt – changed into the Communion which reminds us as Christians of Jesus' death on the cross.

When we come together to partake of the bread and wine in Holy Communion, we still think of Jesus' body broken for us and his blood shed for us on the cross – to save us from our sin. Whenever you put the bread in your mouth and drink the wine, it will remind you of the cruel death Jesus died on the cross so that you can have eternal life.

🌫 Lord Jesus, thank you for being willing to suffer, to give your body to be broken and have your blood shed so that I can have eternal life. Amen.

March 5

Jesus in Gethsemane

READ: LUKE 22:39–45

He withdrew about a stone's throw from them,
knelt down and prayed, 'Father, if you are willing,
take this cup from me; yet not my will, but yours be done.'
– LUKE 22:41–42

Jesus suffered in Gethsemane. Not only was He (as man) deeply distressed and troubled about the suffering awaiting Him, but his three disciples could not even stay awake with Him to pray with Him. Knowing that his crucifixion was looming, Jesus pleaded with his Father to remove the cup of suffering from Him. He nevertheless obeyed the will of his Father implicitly, regardless of the price He would have to pay. For this reason He declared Himself willing to obey God's will.

By his prayer in Gethsemane, Jesus actually shouldered our fear. When you have to face suffering which you cannot bear on your own, think of Jesus and pray like Him: Ask God to take away the cup of suffering, but be willing to obey God's will like Jesus did, even if it means that you would still have to drink the cup of suffering to the last drop. You may ask God anything you wish, but conclude every prayer like Jesus did in Gethsemane by asking that God's will be done, not yours.

❧ Heavenly Father, help me to pray like Jesus in times of trouble. Help me to make my desires known to You, but make me willing to put your will first. Amen.

March 6

Judas betrays Jesus

READ: MATT 26:14–16; 47–50

While he was still speaking, Judas, one of the Twelve, arrived.
With him was a large crowd armed with swords and clubs …
Now the betrayer had arranged a signal with them:
'The one I kiss is the man; arrest him.'
– MATTHEW 26:47–48

We find it incredible that Judas was prepared to betray Jesus after having spent every day with Him for three years; he had experienced the miracles first-hand; he had seen his compassion for people and had experienced his love and friendship. Yet Judas' love for money was stronger than his love for Jesus.

Jesus knew that Judas would betray Him. In fact, He predicted it during the Passover meal: 'The one who has dipped his hand into the bowl with me will betray me' (Matt 26:23).

Although Jesus knew Judas would betray Him, it must have been very hard for Him knowing that one of the twelve He had selected personally to form his core group, was prepared to hand Him over to his enemies. It is incredible, and ironical, that Judas had chosen a kiss (which is a symbol of affection) to identify Jesus to the soldiers. Jesus nevertheless regarded Judas' despicable conduct as part of God's plan for Him. He was still prepared to address him as 'friend'. When Judas kissed Him, He replied, 'Friend, do what you came for!' (Matt 26:50).

Judas' conduct should serve as a warning to you and me. We must make sure that nothing in our lives is more important to us than Jesus.

❧ Lord Jesus, I want to be absolutely faithful to You - so that nothing in my life will come between You and me. Amen.

Jesus is arrested

READ: MATTHEW 26:51–56

'Put your sword back in its place,' Jesus said to him ...
'Do you think I cannot call on my Father, and he will at
once put at my disposal more than twelve legions of angels?'
– MATTHEW 26:52–53

That evening in the garden, the actions of Jesus' other disciples were totally different from the actions of Judas. They were immediately prepared to defend Jesus. Peter even drew his sword and struck the high priest's servant, cutting off his ear. But Jesus commanded him to put back his sword and touched the servant's ear and healed him. He made it quite clear that He was willing to be arrested, that his Father would send twelve legions of angels to save Him should He have asked God. However, Jesus chose a violent death to demonstrate his love for mankind.

Jesus still responded in love towards those who had come to arrest Him. 'Am I leading a rebellion that you have to come out with swords and clubs to capture me?' was his only reproach. Jesus knew that all these things had to happen to fulfil the prophecies of the prophets. When the disciples saw that Jesus had no intention of defending Himself, they left him in the lurch and ran away. With Judas having betrayed Him, and the rest of the disciples having fled, Jesus had been forsaken by everybody – and He had to drink the cup of suffering alone and walk the way of the cross alone.

As Christians you and I should also be willing to act like Jesus when we are treated unfairly; we should also respond in love to the hatred of enemies.

❧ Lord Jesus, please help me to follow your example and respond in love to those who hurt me. Amen.

Jesus before the Sanhedrin

READ: MATTHEW 26:57–68

Then the high priest stood up and said to Jesus,
'Are you not going to answer? What is this
testimony that these men are bringing
against you?' But Jesus remained silent.
– MATTHEW 26:62–63

After Jesus had been arrested, He was taken to the high priest's house. Here, in the courtyard, many false witnesses were brought forward to give false evidence against Him. Although the high priest asked Jesus why He was not answering, He remained silent. He made no effort to defend Himself. However, when He was asked under oath whether He was the Christ, the Son of God, He answered: 'Yes, it is as you say. But I say to all of you: In the future you will see the Son of Man sitting at the right hand of the Mighty One and coming on the clouds of heaven' (Matt 26:64).

This was the last straw. The high priest was so indignant that he tore his clothes and declared that no further witnesses against Jesus were required because He had spoken blasphemy. The rest of the Jews agreed unanimously, 'He is worthy of death!' they cried. They then started hitting Jesus and spitting in his face. Although Jesus had been found guilty by the Sanhedrin officially, this verdict was probably illegal as it happened at night.

'The ways of Jews and Christians are indeed parted by the person of Christ,' *Die Bybellenium* says[1]. Rejoice that you have the opportunity to accept Jesus as your Saviour. Now live as a child of God from this moment.

❧ Lord Jesus, I praise and thank You for having suffered and died for my sake. Thank You that I may be your follower. Amen.

March 9

Peter denies Jesus

READ: MATTHEW 26:69–75

After a little while, those standing there went up to Peter and said,
'Surely you are one of them, for your accent gives you away.'
Then he began to call down curses on himself and
swore to them, 'I don't know the man!'
– MATTHEW 26:73–74

Peter's denial of Jesus became worse. Initially he denied that he knew Jesus (v 70). When another servant girl alleged that she had seen him with Jesus, Peter swore on oath, 'I don't know the man!' (v 72). Then some of the men standing there said that they could hear that he was one of Jesus' disciples because his accent had given him away. He then actually called down curses on himself and swore to them that he did not know Jesus (v 74). Peter therefore denied Jesus in front of all the people gathered at the high priest's house – even though he had vowed that he would never fall away on account of Jesus (cf Matt 26:33).

Immediately a cock crowed and Peter remembered Jesus' words: 'This very night, before the cock crows, you will disown me three times.' Peter realised what he had done and was shattered. He went outside and wept bitterly.

But Peter was given another chance. After Jesus had been raised from the dead, He appeared to his disciples and then asked Peter three times whether he loved Him. Peter responded in the affirmative three times and three times Jesus told him to take care of his sheep – those who followed him. (cf John 21:15–17).

Jesus is always prepared to give us another chance. Even if you sin repeatedly, He is still prepared to forgive you. Always seize this forgiveness like Peter did.

❧ Lord Jesus, thank You for always being prepared to give me another chance. Grant that I will never deny You. Amen.

Jesus before Pilate

READ: JOHN 18:28–40

'What is truth?' Pilate asked. With this he went out again to
the Jews and said, 'I find no basis for a charge against him.'
– JOHN 18:38

Under Roman rule, a Jew, like Jesus, could be sentenced to death only with the permission of a Roman governor. For this reason He had to be tried by Pilate, the Roman governor in Judea. He was therefore taken from the house of the Jewish high priest to the governor's palace. However, Pilate was unwilling to try Jesus and wanted them to judge Him by their own Jewish law. The Jews, however, reminded him that they did not have the right to execute anyone. Thereupon Pilate asked Jesus whether He was really the king of the Jews as the Jews said that He had alleged. Jesus then told him that his kingdom was not of this world, but confirmed: 'You are right in saying I am a king' (John 18:37).

Pilate found Jesus absolutely innocent, and declared Jesus' innocence twice. He even washed his hands in front of the crowd to demonstrate symbolically that he regarded Jesus as innocent. In the gospel of Matthew he said categorically: 'I am innocent of this man's blood. It is your responsibility' (Matt 27:24). When he gave the crowd the opportunity to choose between Jesus and Barabbas, a notorious criminal, they demanded that Barabbas be released and Jesus crucified.

The Jews were immediately willing to accept responsibility for Jesus' death. Jesus was therefore judged by his own people while the Gentiles pleaded to have Him released. Jesus confirmed before Pilate that He is a King – is He the King of your life yet?

❧ Lord Jesus, I worship You as King of my life. Forgive me for my part in your death on the cross. Amen.

March 11

The soldiers mocked Jesus

READ: MATTHEW 27:27–31

[They] twisted together a a crown of thorns and set it on his head.
They put a staff in his right hand and knelt in front of him and
mocked him, 'Hail, king of the Jews,' they said. They spat on him,
and took the staff and struck him on the head again and again.
– MATTHEW 27:29

The soldiers mocked the kingship of Jesus which had been confirmed by Pilate. They put a scarlet robe on Him, set a crown of thorns on his head and put a staff in his hand like the sceptre of a king. Then they 'honoured' Him with the usual greeting for a king, 'Hail, king of the Jews!' Thereupon they spat on Him and hit Him on the head repeatedly.

It is ironic that the soldiers' mockery of Jesus was actually 'proclaiming' the truth: Jesus is the King – not merely the King of the Jews, but the King of the whole universe. Centuries before Isaiah had prophesied the birth of the Child who would be the King of peace: 'Of the increase of his government and peace there will be no end. He will reign on David's throne and over his kingdom, establishing and upholding it with justice and righteousness from that time on and for ever' (Isa 9:7).

That is exactly what Jesus came for. His rule is still a rule of love and righteousness. However, He is also the suffering King who did not hesitate to leave heaven and come to the world as an ordinary human being, to die on a cross so that you and I can be joint heirs with Him.

❧ Lord Jesus, I worship You for having been willing to leave heaven and come to the world so that I could become a joint-heir with You. Amen.

March 12

Jesus crucified

They came to a place called Golgotha (which means
The Place of the Skull). When they had crucified Him,
they divided up his clothes by casting lots.
– MATTHEW 27:33, 35

After the soldiers had mocked Jesus, they took off the robe, put his own clothes on Him and led Him away to be crucified. On the way to Golgotha Simon of Cyrene was forced to carry Jesus' cross. Usually the person to be crucified had to carry his own cross to the place where he was to be executed, but perhaps Jesus was too weak to carry his own cross after the scourging which had preceded the crucifixion.

The crucifixion was a further humiliation which the Son of God submitted to voluntarily. Criminals were crucified naked. For that reason the soldiers divided up his clothes – which were regarded as part of their booty – and they cast lots for his undergarment which was seamless, woven in one piece from top to bottom.

The Jews crucified Jesus by nailing Him to the cross. People who were crucified suffered unspeakable agony. Sometimes it lasted hours before death released them from their suffering. Those who passed by the cross also mocked and blasphemed Jesus. Even the priests and rulers participated in this mockery of Him. However, Jesus' followers and those who loved Him were also at the cross. It must have been terrible for them to see Him suffer in that way. Today, when you read the facts about Jesus' crucifixion it should still stir your heart and underline his love for you.

Lord Jesus, help me to remember the agony You had to suffer so that my sin could be forgiven. Grant that I will remember this every day and not only at Easter. Amen.

Good Friday

READ: MATTHEW 27:35–44

Those who passed by hurled insults at him,
shaking their heads and saying, 'You who are going to
destroy the temple and build it in three days, save yourself!
Come down from the cross, if you are the Son of God!'
– MATTHEW 27:39–40

To those who loved Jesus the Friday on which He was crucified was probably the worst day of their lives. They had to see their dreams of a new kingdom established on earth by Jesus evaporating before their eyes. The Man on whom they had pinned all their hope was hanging on a cross, helpless – and it seemed as if none of his promises would be fulfilled.

Since then Jesus' followers nevertheless call the day on which He died 'Good Friday'. And it was indeed a Good Friday for everyone who believes in Jesus. Although it seemed as if Satan was being victorious, as if the hope of the Christians had been totally dashed, the opposite was happening. If Jesus had not died, you could not have become a child of God. On Good Friday Jesus upset Satan's plans completely. At the very moment when the Son of God seemed at his weakest, He was on the point of revealing the power and love of his Father. Jesus indeed died on the cross, but after three days He was raised from the dead, and in that way death and the devil were finally conquered. God gives you eternal life because of what happened on Good Friday.

❧ Lord Jesus, thank you for turning the darkest day for your followers into Good Friday for your children. I glorify You for revealing to us God's power through the cross. Amen.

March 14

'Father, forgive them ...'

READ: LUKE 23:27–34

Jesus said, 'Father, forgive them,
for they do not know what they are doing.'
– Luke 23:34

While He was hanging on the cross, Jesus spoke seven times. Each time his words sketched a clear picture of his love for sinners and his intimate relationship with his heavenly Father. Even despite the excruciating pain, Jesus noticed other people and tried to help them.

During the period which preceded his crucifixion, Jesus' relationships had also suffered badly. The twelve friends who had accompanied Him for three years deserted Him, Peter denied Him and Judas betrayed Him. The Jewish people for whom He had come, had rejected his offer of salvation and had Him crucified. However, this did not affect his love for them. Despite the agony He was suffering on the cross, Jesus still prayed for those who had rejected Him and had Him crucified. He prayed that his Father should forgive them because they did not understand the impact of their actions: 'Father, forgive them, for they do not know what they are doing,' He prayed.

The unconditional love and forgiveness of Jesus are still available to you. You can confess your sins with confidence, because He is still prepared to forgive them. He will help you to overcome your sins. However, Jesus expects you to forgive others likewise in gratitude for his forgiveness. Are you prepared to do this?

❧ Lord Jesus, thank you for still being willing to forgive me when I sin against You. Help me to be as forgiving towards those who hurt me. Amen.

Together in paradise

READ: LUKE 23:35–43

*But the other criminal rebuked him. 'Don't you fear God?' he said, 'since you
are under the same sentence? We are punished justly, for we are getting what
our deeds deserve. But this man has done nothing wrong.' Then he said,
'Jesus, remember me when you come into your kingdom.'*
– LUKE 23:40–42

Two criminals were crucified with Jesus – one on either side. At first
both criminals hurled insults at Jesus (cf Matt 27:44). However, the
criminal to the right of Jesus apparently had second thoughts. He
asked Jesus to remember him when He came into his kingdom. Jesus
was immediately willing to offer him his mercy and promised: 'I tell
you the truth, today you will be with me in paradise' (Luke 23:43).

Here we see the infinite mercy of God which is never based on
what we deserve. The criminal on the cross could not claim that
mercy at all, he had absolutely nothing to offer in exchange for his
ticket to heaven; there was no reason why his sin should be forgiven
– yet Jesus promised him eternal life. He assured him that he would
be with Him in paradise that same day.

Jesus' love for you does not depend on your achievements or the
things you can offer Him. Only the prayer of the man next to Jesus
is required to unlock the gates of heaven: 'Lord, remember me.' Even
if that is all you can pray, Jesus will tell you too: 'I assure you, heaven
is yours!'

❧ Lord Jesus, please remember me ... Thank you for offering me heaven
and for giving me the assurance that I will one day be with You in paradise.
Amen.

March 16

Here is your son; here is your mother

READ: JOHN 19:25–27

When Jesus saw his mother there, and the disciple whom he
loved standing nearby, he said to his mother, 'Dear woman,
here is your son', and to the disciple, 'Here is your mother.'
– JOHN 19:26–27

Mary and John must have been incredibly brave to have experienced the suffering of her beloved Son and his friend and Teacher on the cross first-hand. Mary must have realised what Simeon had meant when he said many years before that a sword would some day pierce her own heart (cf Luke 2:35).

Despite the agony He was suffering on the cross, Jesus was aware of his mother and his good friend and He tried to alleviate their pain by thinking of them and planning their future. Although Mary had four other sons as well (cf John 7:5), it was Jesus' wish that his beloved disciple take the responsibility for his mother in future. Both of them would be lonely without Him – and they could comfort each other better since they had both loved Him so much. This way Jesus demonstrates his caring love for those who love Him. He is also telling us that the members of our family are sometimes less important than those who share our faith, our 'heavenly family'. 'From that time on, this disciple took her [Mary] into his home,' wrote John (John 19:27).

Remember that the family of God is your real family and that they should take priority.

❧ Lord Jesus, Thank you for showing me that my fellow-believers are not yet important enough in my life. I want to correct that error right now. Amen.

My God, my God ...

READ: MARK 15:29–35

And at the ninth hour Jesus cried out in a loud voice,
'Eloi, Eloi, lama sabachthani?' – which means,
'My God, my God, why have you forsaken me?'
– MARK 15:34

On the cross Jesus was absolutely alone. Different groups of people insulted and mocked Him while He was hanging there. The very people for whom He had come had rejected Him totally. Even his disciples had run away. Only his Father was left ...

After three hours on the cross, Jesus' physical agony reached a climax. However, the spiritual pain brought upon Him as a result of the burden of the sin of the whole world was even worse than the unbearable physical pain. He felt as if even God had forsaken Him. As if even his Father no longer supported Him. He uttered his fear and despair in the words, 'My God, my God, why have you forsaken me?' He found that even the once faithful heavenly Father who had always supported and strengthened Him in the past, was no longer present when his suffering was at its worst.

On the cross Jesus was forsaken by God so that we will never be forsaken. God turned his back on his Son in the hour of his greatest need so that you and I may always approach Him with confidence; so that He will never again have to turn his face away from you; so that you will never again have to be without God. Jesus bore the sin of the whole world on the cross without the support of his Father. Why? Because He loves you so much.

❧ Heavenly Father, You forsook your Son on the cross so that I will never be forsaken by You. Help me to realise and appreciate such love. Amen.

March 18

I am thirsty . . .

READ: JOHN 19:28–29

Later, knowing that all was now completed, and so that
the Scripture would be fulfilled, Jesus said, 'I am thirsty.'
— JOHN 19:28

According to Matthew, Jesus was offered wine mixed with gall which would have numbed the physical pain during the process of crucifixion slightly, but He refused it (cf Matt 27:34). However, on the cross, Jesus said He was thirsty. A jar of wine vinegar stood near the cross. The soldiers then soaked a sponge in the wine vinegar, put it on a stalk of the hyssop plant, and lifted it up to Jesus' lips. This time He received the drink.

This request – for something to quench his thirst – underlined Jesus' humanity. Jesus is God, but on earth He was also man – He was very God and very man - an ordinary human being who became tired and thirsty, who feared and had to suffer indescribable pain. John wrote that the Word became flesh and made his dwelling among us (John 1:14). Although Jesus is truly God, although He is the King of kings, He came to live among us as a human being. The fact that Jesus was a human being like you and me (but without sin), tells us that He understands our human shortcomings perfectly, that He knows what it feels like to resist temptation and suffer pain. He also understands your human worries and fears. You can therefore share everything with Him with confidence – He understands you because He was a human being just like you.

✢ Lord Jesus, It is so easy to talk to You about the ordinary problems of humans because You were also human. Thank you for always understanding me. Amen.

March 19

It is finished

READ: JOHN 19:29–36

When he had received the drink, Jesus said, 'It is finished.'
– JOHN 19:30

Jesus' suffering on the cross had achieved its objective – therefore the second last words spoken on the cross were actually a shout of triumph: It is finished! Not only had his inhuman suffering reached its climax, but the special task God had given Him and the reason why He had come to the world had been completed. He had fulfilled God's will. As Paul wrote to the church in Philippi, He had indeed been 'obedient to death – even death on a cross!' (cf Phil 2:8).

According to *Die Bybellenium*, the Greek word translated as 'finished', implies that He had done everything the Father had expected of Him, that his task had been completed, and that the consequences will never come to an end.[2] In fact, we still live with the positive consequences of Jesus' deed of love. Because He was willing to pay the penalty for your sins and mine in full on the cross, we no longer have to pay the penalty for our sin, and God forgives our sin because Jesus has reconciled us to God by his death on the cross. The death sentence which God metes out for sin was borne by his Son to fulfil the prophecy by Isaiah: 'But he was pierced for our transgressions, he was crushed for our iniquities; the punishment that brought us peace was upon him, and by his wounds we are healed' (Isa 53:5). We can never thank Him enough for this.

❧ Lord Jesus, I praise and thank you for having borne the penalty for my sin on the cross - for completing the task God had given You, so that I could also be saved. Amen.

March 20

In your hands I commit my spirit

READ: LUKE 23:44–49

*It was now about the sixth hour, and darkness came over
the whole land until the ninth hour … And the curtain
of the temple was torn in two. Jesus called out with a
loud voice, 'Father, into your hands I commit my spirit.'*
– LUKE 23: 44–46

Jesus' last words on the cross imply that God had not forsaken Him after all. These words come from Psalm 31:5 where the psalmist says, 'Into your hands I commit my spirit.' At the time of Jesus these words were often prayed by Jewish children as an evening prayer. In Old Testament times people regarded sleeping as similar to dying. By this prayer the children therefore committed their lives to God in the evening and in the morning when they woke up, they thanked Him for restoring life to them. According to Martin Luther you should live according to this prayer throughout your life so that you will be able to pray it with confidence on your deathbed.

The Jews had asked the soldiers to break the legs of the crucified to hasten death so that they could be taken down, because they did not want bodies left on the crosses on the Sabbath. When the soldiers reached Jesus and saw that He was already dead, they did not break his legs. Instead, one of the soldiers pierced his side with a spear to make quite sure that He was dead, and this brought a sudden flow of blood and water – a sign that Jesus had already died (cf John 19:34).

Jesus' death which is sometimes questioned by theologians was therefore a fact.

❧ Lord Jesus, I now know that You really died - that You had died so that I may have eternal life. Amen.

March 21

Jesus dies

READ: MARK 15:33–38

With a loud cry, Jesus breathed his last.
The curtain of the temple was torn in two from top to bottom.
– MARK 15:37–38

After Jesus had drunk the wine vinegar and committed his spirit into the hands of his Father, He breathed his last. The death of Jesus was accompanied by fear-inspiring and supernatural events: the curtain of the temple was rent in two from top to bottom; the earth shook and the rocks split. The tombs broke open and the bodies of many holy people were raised to life. Those who had gathered at the cross saw these happenings and realised that Jesus had not been an ordinary man.

The curtain separated the Holy Place from the Holy of Holies of the temple. When this curtain was torn in two, it symbolised that the separation between the holy God and sinners had been bridged by the death of Jesus. And this bridge had been provided by God – the curtain had been torn from top to bottom. Jesus' sacrificial death provided the way for us to approach God with confidence – He Himself had given us the communication channel. Jesus' death also affected nature visibly – before He died the earth had already been enveloped in darkness for three hours. When Jesus died, light turned into darkness for mankind symbolically (fortunately only temporarily!), reads *Die Bybellenium.*[3]

It is interesting to note that the spectators who had wanted Jesus crucified at all costs, were also shaken by the supernatural events which coincided with Jesus' death: 'When all the people who had gathered to witness this sight saw what took place, they beat their breasts and went away,' Luke wrote (Luke 23:48).

❧ Heavenly Father, thank you that I may communicate with You with confidence because the death of your Son has made it possible. Amen.

March 22

Confession of a soldier

READ: MARK 15:38–41

And when the centurion, who stood there in front of Jesus,
heard his cry and saw how he died, he said,
'Surely this man was the Son of God!'
– MARK 15:39

The testimony of faith of the unknown Gentile centurion who stood in front of Jesus' cross – and who could therefore see and hear everything very clearly – grips our imagination. He had helped to crucify Jesus – he might even have been present when the soldiers divided his clothes among them. However, by looking at Jesus on the cross, hearing his words and also experiencing the supernatural events while He was dying, this man – who had never heard the message which Jesus had brought to mankind – became convinced that Jesus was indeed the Son of God.

This testimony is very important because the Gentile centurion was the very first person to have realised who Jesus was, as a result of his suffering: that He was indeed the suffering Son of God. Jesus' death on the cross was therefore not a tragedy but the absolute proof that He was the Son of God.

Do you acknowledge Jesus as the Son of God and do you believe in Him? Then you may say with John, 'And we have seen and testify that the Father has sent his Son to be the Saviour of the world. If anyone acknowledges that Jesus is the Son of God, God lives in him and he in God' (1 John 4:14–15).

❧ Lord Jesus, I worship You as the Son of God … Thank you for the promise that You live in me and I in You because I believe in You. Amen.

March 23

Jesus is buried

READ: JOHN19:38–42

At the place where Jesus was crucified, there was a garden,
and in the garden a new tomb … Because it was the Jewish day of
Preparation and since the tomb was nearby, they laid Jesus there.
— JOHN 19:41–42

Joseph of Arimathea who had been a disciple of Jesus, but secretly because he feared the Jews, had asked Pilate for the body of Jesus. People who were crucified were usually buried in a mass grave. However, Joseph of Arimathea wanted to give Jesus an honourable burial. When Pilate gave his permission, Joseph and Nicodemus, who had also visited Jesus secretly one night, took Jesus' body away. The love of these two men for Jesus is obvious from the way they handled his body before they laid Him in the grave. They embalmed the body with a mixture of myrrh and aloe and wrapped him in fine linen according to the Jewish custom. According to John they brought about 34 kg of spices to embalm Jesus' body. Such a large amount of spices was used only for important people. This way Nicodemus and Joseph demonstrated that they had regarded Jesus as a very important person.

Near Golgotha was a garden with a new tomb where no-one had ever been laid. It was nearly Sabbath – and since the garden was close, Joseph and Nicodemus laid Jesus in the new garden tomb. When Jesus was raised from the dead, his followers knew exactly where to look for his body. As no-one else had ever been laid in the new tomb, they could not have made a mistake about the place where Jesus had been laid.

❧ Lord Jesus, You are very important to me too. Show me how I can convey this fact to others the way Joseph and Nicodemus did. Amen.

March 24

An empty tomb

READ: JOHN 20:1–13

Early on the first day of the week, while it was still dark,
Mary Magdalene went to the tomb and saw that the stone had
been removed from the entrance. So she came running to Simon Peter
and the other disciple, the one Jesus loved, and said, 'They have taken
the Lord out of the tomb, and we don't know where they have put him!'
– JOHN 20:1–2

Early that Sunday morning Mary Magdalene went to Jesus' garden tomb and discovered that the stone had been removed from the entrance. To her the empty tomb meant that his body had been stolen from the tomb, not that He had been raised from the dead. She immediately went to Peter and John to give them the shattering news and the two disciples ran to the tomb. John outran Peter. He saw the strips of linen but did not go in. The impulsive Peter rushed past John into the tomb despite the fact that a tomb was regarded as unclean. He also noticed the shroud. Only then did John enter and also saw that Jesus' body was gone.

Peter and John must have considered the fact that Jesus had told them that He would rise from the dead. Furthermore the burial cloth that had been around his head was folded up by itself, separate from the linen – a clear indication that Jesus had been totally in control of the events; his rising from the dead therefore differed from that of Lazarus.

The two disciples realised that Jesus' tomb was empty because He had risen from the dead – not because his body had been removed from the tomb.

❧ Lord Jesus, thank you for the proof that You really rose from the dead so that I no longer have to fear death. Amen.

March 25

Jesus is risen

READ: LUKE 24:1–12

*Suddenly two men in clothes that gleamed like
lightning stood beside them … the men said to them, 'Why do
you look for the living among the dead? He is not here; he has risen!'*
– LUKE 24:4–5

On Sunday morning when the women went to Jesus' garden tomb
with the spices they had prepared for the body, they found that the
stone had been rolled away. When they entered the tomb they noticed
that Jesus' body was no longer there. Suddenly two men, in clothes
that gleamed, appeared and asked them why they were looking for the
Living among the dead, and said that Jesus had risen from the dead as
He had told them in Galilee.

Jesus had risen from the dead. Many people were eyewitnesses of
the resurrection: Mary at the tomb, the disciples without Thomas, the
eleven with Thomas, the men from Emmaus … Jesus also appeared
to the disciples at the lake, and He even fried fish for them.

All the senses of the disciples were involved in these appearances
so that they could not doubt the fact that Jesus had risen from the
dead. For example, He told the doubting Thomas to put his finger
into the wounds on his hands and his side. They could also eat the fish
He had prepared for them. Everybody saw Him with their own eyes
and heard his voice with their own ears. We therefore never have to
deny the fact that Jesus rose from the dead even though some modern
theologians would like to deny it. The Biblical facts about the resurrection are far too clear. You therefore never have to doubt the fact
that Jesus rose from the dead.

❧ Lord Jesus, I believe the reality of your resurrection and that I, too, will
one day rise from the dead and be with You for ever. Amen.

March 26

Crucified with Jesus

READ: GALATIANS 2:15-21

For through the law I died to the law so that I might
live for God. I have been crucified with Christ
and I no longer live, but Christ lives in me.
– GALATIANS 2:19-20

Paul wrote to the church in Galatia saying that he had been crucified with Christ – that he no longer lived, but that Jesus lived in him. The translation in The Message reads as follows: 'I have been crucified with Christ. My ego is no longer central. It is no longer important that I appear righteous before you or have your good opinion, and I am no longer driven to impress God. Christ lives in me'.

You have also been crucified with Jesus. Your old sinful body was nailed to the cross with Him and should now be dead. And just as He was raised from the dead, you must be raised to a new life and live for Jesus only. In Colossians 3:5 and 8 Paul lists the things in your life which have to be crucified: 'Put to death therefore, whatever belongs to your earthly nature: sexual immorality, impurity, lust, evil desires and greed; anger, rage, malice, slander and filthy language …' A formidable list – and few of us have none of the above in our lives. Read Paul's list of sins to which you have to die and tick those which still rear their ugly heads from time to time. Then ask Jesus to release you from them once and for all.

❧ Lord Jesus, I know I have been crucified with You - but I also know I still have sin in my life. Please forgive me and release me from these sins. Amen.

March 27

Being raised to a new life

READ: COLOSSIANS 3:9–17

You have taken off your old self with its practices and
have put on the new self, which is being renewed
in knowledge in the image of its Creator.
— COLOSSIANS 3:9–10

If you have been crucified with Jesus, you must also be raised with Him and live like a brand-new person from this moment. In Colossians 3:9–17 you can read what the 'new you' should look like. You will become more like Jesus every day. The Message uses a practical image of this new person – you are like someone who has stripped off a filthy set of ill-fitting clothes and put it in the fire. Now you are dressed in a new outfit. Every item of your new way of life is custom-made by the Creator, with his label on it. Paul also explains exactly what the life of a resurrected Christian should look like: 'Dress in the wardrobe God picked out for you: compassion, kindness, humility, quiet strength, discipline. Be even-tempered, content with second place, quick to forgive an offence. Let the peace of Christ keep you in tune with each other, in step with each other. None of this going off and doing your own thing. And cultivate thankfulness. Let every detail in your lives – words, actions, whatever – be done in the name of the Master, Jesus, thanking God the Father every step of the way' (cf Col 3:12–15, 17, The Message).

Study these new qualities just as carefully as you studied the list of 'carnal qualities' yesterday. Then ask the Lord to help you to cultivate these qualities in your life.

❧ Lord Jesus, I want to become more and more like You - please help me to put on my new wardrobe and keep it on. Amen.

March 28

Take up your cross

READ: LUKE 9:23–27

Then He said to them all: 'If anyone would come after me,
he must deny himself and take up his cross daily and follow Me.
For whoever wants to save his life will lose it,
but whoever loses his life for me will save it.'
– LUKE 9:23–24

Long before his crucifixion Jesus told his disciples that whoever would follow Him would have to be willing to deny himself, take up his cross and follow Him. All of us should be perfectly willing to do this now that we know what it cost Him to die for us.

It is still not easy to be a Christian. A cross awaits every Christian in the world. And to follow in the footsteps of Jesus, you would have to be willing to sign your own death sentence by taking up your personal cross day after day and following Jesus. If you choose to live for yourself and satisfy your own selfish desires, you will eventually lose everything. However, if you are willing to set Jesus first and follow his lead, He offers you eternal life.

It will not be easy for you while you are in the world. Like Jesus you will have to lift your cross on your shoulders. However, Jesus assures you that you will never have to bear your cross alone. On the cross Jesus was forsaken by God so that He can now always be with you to assist and help you.

✣ Lord Jesus, I am willing to take up my personal cross every day and follow You. Thank you for the promise that You Yourself will help me to bear my cross. Amen.

March 29

The power of death has been broken

READ: ACTS 2:22–28

But God raised him from the dead, freeing him from the agony
of death … Therefore my heart is glad and my tongue rejoices;
my body also will live in hope, because you will not abandon
me to the grave, nor will you let your Holy One see decay.
– ACTS 2:24, 26–27

Peter made it very clear in his speech at Pentecost that God Himself had raised his Son from the dead. For this reason he rejoiced and praised God – because Jesus had conquered death, he, Peter, would not be abandoned to the grave either. We have already heard that many eyewitnesses had seen Jesus after his resurrection. We know that He had conquered death and the devil. And this is why we celebrate Easter Sunday.

The good news is that you never have to fear death again. Death no longer has authority over you. In 1 Corinthians 15:35–57 Paul writes about the resurrected body which will be yours one day. Your earthly body will be replaced by an imperishable body. And in this glorified body you will live happily ever after with Jesus in heaven. For this reason we can confess with Paul: 'Death has been swallowed up in victory' (1 Cor 15:54).

Since Jesus died for you on the cross, you now have the assurance that you will conquer death with Him and one day, after your death, be with Him in heaven for ever.

❧ Lord Jesus, I praise You for having made it possible for me to conquer death and one day live with You in heaven for ever. Amen.

March 30

God loves you so much

READ: JOHN 3:1–16

For God so loved the world that he gave his one
and only Son, that whoever believes in him
shall not perish but have eternal life.
– JOHN 3:16

John 3:16 tells us how God's love for people was put into action. He gave his Son so that whoever believes in Him no longer has to suffer the fatal consequences of the original sin, but have eternal life with Him. God not only gave Jesus to die on a cross, but He also gave Him to come into the world, to be born in a humble stable, to live on earth as an ordinary human being for 33 years and ultimately to pay the price which would set us free. The Greek word which is translated as 'perish' actually means 'being separated from God's presence for ever'. He would be without God's love, his gifts and his mercy for ever. And that is what we actually deserve, because we are born into sin.

But God loves us too much to permit this. He cannot face sin and has to punish it, but He chose his Son to bear the penalty for your sin. God loves you so much that, should you choose to love and serve Jesus, God will forgive your sin on the basis of Jesus' death on the cross and make it possible for you to live for ever one day.

🍃 Heavenly Father, I am completely overwhelmed by your unmerited love for me. Thank you for accepting your only Son's sacrifice for my sin so that I will never have to be without You. Amen.

March 31

Lord Jesus,

this month I followed the way of the cross

every day and what You suffered for me

was once again impressed on my mind.

I once again realised that I, too,

was responsible for your agony,

that your body was broken for me

and that your blood was shed for me.

Help me to become more like You every day:

to set the will of your Father before mine;

to respond to hate with love,

never to deny or betray You,

but to be absolutely faithful to You.

I want to worship You as the King of my life.

Thank you for having been willing

to come to this world so that I will one day

be able to go to heaven; for having been forsaken by God,

so that I will always have Him with me;

for understanding me perfectly

because You became flesh like me;

that You passed through death

to give me eternal life;

that You were buried and rose again

so that I could conquer death for ever with You

and be raised to a new life in You.

I now want to take up my personal cross

and follow You every day of my life.

You love me so much

that You were willing to die for me,

grant that I will now be willing to live for You.

Amen

Glorify God!

G od creates everything for one purpose only: to glorify Him. As his children, all of us should learn how to love God with our whole being and how to glorify Him in everything we do and say.

To glorify God means serving Him as Lord of our life; acknowledging Him as our Master, and acknowledging Him as King in every sphere of our lives. Each Person of the Divine Trinity plays a specific role in interpreting the glory of God. God the Father radiates this glory; Jesus came into the world to illustrate it because He was the visible representation of this glory, and the Holy Spirit teaches you and me how to reflect that glory.

This month we will focus on the different ways in which God can be glorified in our lives.

April

Five ways to glorify God

READ: REVELATION 4:6–11

You are worthy, our Lord and God, to receive glory
and honour and power, for you created all things, and
by your will they were created and have their being.
– REVELATION 4:11

We know quite well that we should glorify God – however, we do not always understand how to do this. In his book *The Purpose Driven Life*, Rick Warren says that we can glorify God in five ways, i.e. by worshipping Him, by really loving other believers, by becoming more like Jesus every day, by serving others with our gifts, and by telling others about Him.[1]

Try to commit yourself to doing these five things from now on. God is worthy to be glorified by you: To Him, the Creator of everything, be honour and praise and glory for ever. According to John, Jesus is also 'Worthy … to receive … honour and glory and praise … To Him who sits on the throne and to the Lamb be praise and honour and glory and power for ever and ever.' (Rev 5:12–13).

Commit yourself to glorifying God in your prayers and with your life. Ask Him to key in a Jesus-love for others into your life; commit yourself to living like Jesus did; be prepared to make your God-given gifts available to others; and be a witness wherever you are. In this way others will see that God is truly the Lord of your life.

❧ Heavenly Father, please teach me to glorify You so clearly in my prayers and by my way of life that others will notice it. Amen.

April 1

Nature glorifies God

READ: PSALM 19:1–7

The heavens declare the glory of God;
the skies proclaim the work of his hands.
– PSALM 19:1

In June 2006 my husband and I visited our son in the United States. During this visit he took us to five of the national parks. I have never been so aware of God's absolute glory as I was in those parks. Whether it was among the fantastic illusions created by the incredibly delicate rock formations of Bryce Canyon; travelling along the towering red sandstone cliffs of Zion; or marvelling at the boiling geysers of Yellowstone, I was constantly aware of the glory of the Creator God who had created these natural wonders. In Yellowstone National Park the words on the T-shirt of a young American said it all: 'The earth is the Lord's and the fulness thereof' (Ps 24:1, KJV). In the midst of all these natural wonders God's presence was so overwhelming that I could almost touch Him.

That night I read Psalm 111:2 in my Bible: 'Great are the works of the LORD; they are pondered by all who delight in them. Glorious and majestic are his deeds …' God did indeed make the world incredibly beautiful.

Always guard against becoming blasé about his creation; of becoming blind to the evidence of his glory which is visible in every flower and insect, in every baby and cobweb, in every mountain range and cloud formation. Try to be really aware of his glory in nature around you in future.

❧ Father, thank you that your glory is reflected in even the minutest detail of your creation. Help me to really see the work of your hands. Amen.

April 2

Acknowledge his glory

READ: 1 CHRONICLES 16:23–36

For great is the LORD and most worthy of praise ...
The LORD made the heavens. Splendour and majesty
are before him; strength and joy in his dwelling place.
– 1 CHRONICLES 16:25–27

The more we read about God in his Word and the more we look at
the work of his hands, the more we become aware of his greatness
and majesty. It also becomes even more incredible that He should
love sinners. Although God is so great and wonderful, He loves you
dearly – He loves you so much that He sent his only Son into the
world to save the world through Him. Whenever you remember
this, you should acknowledge the glory of God and praise Him for
this sacrifice.

Unfortunately many people run to God only when they need Him
– just as the Israelites, his chosen people, used to do time and again.
When we prosper, we pay little attention to Him, but as soon as we
run into trouble, we hurry back to God to ask his help. Although God
is so merciful that He helps us time and again, this is not fair. You
should follow David's example in 1 Chronicles 16, and focus on giving God the glory and honour which is his due; on glorifying Him in
everything you do. And when you talk to Him in prayer, be conscious
of to Whom it is that you are talking. Honour and glorify the Lord as
you should.

❧ Father, I want to bow low before You and give You all the honour and
glory in my heart. Keep me from only remembering You when I need You,
and teach me to glorify You in everything I do and say. Amen.

April 3

Jesus, image of God's glory

READ: HEBREWS 1:1–6

The Son is the radiance of God's glory
and the exact representation of his being,
sustaining all things by his powerful word.
– HEBREWS 1:3

In the Old Testament no-one could see God's glory and live. However, God sent his Son into the world to enable his children to see his glory face to face. John puts it very clearly: 'The Word became flesh and made his dwelling among us. We have seen his glory, the glory of the One and Only, who came from the Father, full of grace and truth' (John 1:14). Jesus came to live among us, and God therefore became accessible to mankind in the person of Jesus – a situation which differed totally from the past. By his life on earth everybody who met Him could see the glory of God.

Since He came into the world as an ordinary human being, we are inclined to forget that Jesus is God, that He is the radiance of God's glory. However, just read the first verses of the letter to the Hebrews to see the error of such thinking: Jesus created the world together with God, He is heir to everything, He is the exact representation of God's being, He sustains all things by his powerful word. He is the radiance of God's glory. When you get to know Him better and read about Him in the Bible, you once again realise how wonderful God is. If you want to see God's glory first-hand, look at Jesus.

🦋 Lord Jesus, I praise You for having been willing to come into the world as a human being so that I can see the glory of God face to face. Amen.

April 4

One in glory

READ: JOHN 17:20–26

I have given them the glory that you gave me, that they may
be one as we are one … Father, I want those you have given me
to be with me where I am, and to see my glory, the glory you have
given me because you loved me before the creation of the world.
– JOHN 17:22, 24

Jesus, who was the exact representation of God's glory, wants to pass this glory on to his children. In his high-priestly prayer in John 17, Jesus specifically asked that God should make his disciples one so that they would be able to see his glory and so that this glory would be visible in them. In *Die Boodskap* the word *glory* is translated as 'status'. Jesus therefore prays that his disciples would enjoy the same status before God as He did, so that they would be joined together and work as a team – just as He and his Father worked together as a team. As a result of this unity people could see that He had been sent by God Himself. When we as believers work together as God's team, exactly the same happens: People who observe us will be able to see God's love in our lives, and that way they will understand this love better.

By your interaction with other believers, you glorify God in your own life – provided you reflect Jesus by your actions, live as He did, and love others in the way He loves you. Others will then be able to see God's glory in your way of life.

❧ Lord Jesus, please help me to live in such a way that others will catch a glimpse of the glory and love of God in my way of life and cooperation with other believers. Amen.

April 5

God's new world

READ: REVELATION 21:10–23

[The city] shone with the glory of God, and its brilliance was like that of a very precious jewel … The city does not need the sun or the moon to shine on it, for the glory of God gives it light, and the Lamb is its lamp.

– REVELATION 21:11, 23

When we look at the world around us we often become very despondent because we cannot see God's glory in the people and events around us. It often seems as if sin has the final say in the world; that murder and violence, theft and fraud are still the order of the day. We sometimes wonder why God permits all these things, why He doesn't intervene and improve everything.

Fortunately the children of God know this will indeed happen eventually. In the new Jerusalem which God is preparing for his children, his glory will be visible in a new way. This glory is described beautifully in Revelation 21. The walls of the new Jerusalem will be of opal, the city itself as well as the streets will be of pure gold, the foundations of the city wall will be decorated with precious stones and the twelve gates will be twelve pearls. The sun and moon will no longer be required because the glory of God will be the source of light (cf Rev 21:18–23). Nothing impure or evil will enter this city – the citizens will be those whose names are written in the Book of the Lamb.

What a beautiful promise to hold on to. Live in such a way that you will not miss this glory!

❦ Heavenly Father, how wonderful to be able to look forward to your new world where your glory will be reflected perfectly. Help me to live in such a way that I will be part of it one day. Amen.

April 6

Mirrors of his glory

READ: 2 CORINTHIANS 3:7–18

The Government of Death, its constitution chiselled on stone tablets,
had a dazzling inaugural … And so we are transfigured much
like the Messiah, our lives gradually becoming brighter and more
beautiful as God enters our lives and we become like Him.
– 2 CORINTHIANS 3:7, 18, THE MESSAGE

Everything God touches takes on the radiance of his glory. When Moses came down from Mount Sinai after God had given him the tables of the law, his face was so radiant that the Israelites could not look at him (cf Exod 34:33–35). God's law still reflects his glory here on earth today.

God chooses ordinary human beings to mirror his all-transcending glory! The more we are changed to be like Jesus, the greater the glory becomes that we radiate. When you look at the night sky it is difficult to see which of the heavenly bodies are stars and which are planets. Only stars have their own light – planets do not have light of their own but reflect the light of stars in such a way that we find it difficult to distinguish them from stars. Like the planets which reflect the light of the sun, we have to reflect God's glory in our lives. And we have to do it in such a way that others will find it difficult to distinguish between God's glory and the glory we reflect.

God wants you to reflect his glory. God lives in you through the Holy Spirit, and this Spirit enables you to become more like Christ so that you will radiate God's glory.

✢ Lord Jesus, change me, make me more and more like You until I radiate God's glory. Amen.

April 7

The glory must increase

READ: 2 CORINTHIANS 3:16–18

And we, who ... reflect the Lord's glory, are being
transformed into his likeness with ever-increasing glory,
which comes from the Lord, who is Spirit.
– 2 CORINTHIANS 3:18B

Once we see and understand God's glory, the Holy Spirit transforms us gradually until we radiate the same glory. This glory which God's children radiate should increase in intensity. However, this cannot happen unless our lives have been surrendered to the control of the Holy Spirit. Only the Spirit of God can let the glory of God increase in our lives. 'And we, who ... reflect the Lord's glory, are being transformed into his likeness with ever-increasing glory, which comes from the Lord, who is the Spirit,' Paul wrote to the church in Corinth (2 Cor 3:18b). If you are willing to allow the Holy Spirit to control your life, you will increase in holiness. This is the sole task of the Holy Spirit who lives in you.

All of us know people who radiate the glory of God. They cannot hide the fact that they belong to God and that they are filled with his glory. One can see it on their radiant faces. In Acts 6:15 we read that the face of Stephen was 'like the face of an angel'. If you are serious about your love for Christ and the glory which you radiate increases daily, others will be able to see that glory in you. However, that would mean that you would have to entrust the control of your life to the Holy Spirit.

❧ Holy Spirit, help me to be so committed to You that the glory which I radiate will increase day by day. Amen.

April 8

Do everything to his glory

READ: 1 CORINTHIANS 10:23–11:1

So whether you eat or drink or whatever you do,
do it all for the glory of God.
– 1 CORINTHIANS 10:31

God's children should live in such a way that they will do absolutely everything to glorify Him. Unfortunately not many of us manage to do this!

Paul could honestly say that to him, to live was Christ. He did everything for the glory of God. He therefore confessed in Philippians 1:20–21: 'I eagerly expect and hope that I will in no way be ashamed, but will have sufficient courage so that now as always Christ will be exalted in my body, whether by life or by death. For to me, to live is Christ and to die is gain.' Throughout his ministry, Paul always tried to accommodate everybody so that they could be won for God's kingdom.

And this is what Christ expects of you: that you will in future try to do everything for his glory; to glorify Him with your whole being, so that you will be able to confess like Paul that for you to live is Christ. Then you will no longer fear death but you will understand that it is merely crossing over to real life where you will see God's glory face to face.

Try to follow in Paul's footsteps in future. And accept his invitation in 1 Corinthians 11:1: 'Follow my example, as I follow the example of Christ.'

Heavenly Father, help me to follow Paul's example in future - to do everything for your glory - so that for me, to live will be Christ, and to die will be gain. Amen.

April 9

Glorify God's Name

READ: MATTHEW 6:9–13

Our Father in heaven, hallowed be your name …
– MATTHEW 6:9

In Jesus' model prayer, God's glory is referred to twice. At the beginning He prays that God's Name should be hallowed, or revered – and in the New King James version the Lord's Prayer is concluded with the words, 'For Yours is the kingdom and the power and the glory forever' (Matt 6:13). Unfortunately these words have been omitted from the NIV because they do not form part of the original text. The words nevertheless conclude the Prayer beautifully – the kingdom, power and glory belong to God after all – and we should therefore glorify his name.

When his disciples asked Him to teach them to pray, Jesus taught them the Lord's Prayer. Base your own prayers on this model prayer if you would like to pray like Jesus. In the Lord's Prayer Jesus teaches you how God wants to be worshipped. In your own prayers you should therefore make room to glorify God intentionally. He did after all create you specially to honour and glorify Him. God Himself said through the prophet Isaiah: 'Everyone who is called by my name, whom I created for my glory, whom I formed and made.' (cf Isa 43:7). As the crown of God's creation you should be attuned to living to his glory every day and to glorifying his Name in everything you say and do.

❧ Heavenly Father, help me to glorify your Name and to honour You with my life. Amen.

April 10

Glorify God with your gifts

READ: EPHESIANS 4:7–16

But to each one of us grace has been given as Christ
apportioned it ... to prepare God's people for works of
service, so that the body of Christ may be built up ...
– EPHESIANS 4:7, 12

God gives us gifts so that we can use those gifts to his honour to glorify Him. It is very obvious when an artist is dedicated to the honour
of God rather than his own. In the paintings of Father Claerhout, the
Flemish priest – particularly in his paintings based on Biblical themes
– you can also see that he painted to the glory of God. While we were
in England and visited the beautiful cathedral in Canterbury, we were
fortunate enough to hear a visiting youth choir from America practising for their performance that evening. It was an incredible experience. The reverent atmosphere of the magnificent cathedral, together
with the clear young voices blended in perfect harmony to glorify
God, was an experience which we will always remember. This choir
practice was a striking example of people using their gifts to glorify
the Creator of those gifts.

One of the best ways to glorify God is to use your own gifts to his
glory. Usually people use their gifts to their own advantage, or to earn
money. However, never forget that your gifts are from God and that
you were blessed with them in order to glorify Him.

❧ Father, I praise You for the gifts You gave me. Please show me how I can
use them to glorify your Name. Amen.

Glorify his Name

READ: PSALM 66

Sing the glory of his name; make his praise glorius! Say to God,
'How awesome are your deeds! … your enemies cringe before you.'
— PSALM 66:2–3

Another way in which God's glory can be honoured is by telling others of his miracles in your life. This is what the psalmist does in the beautiful Psalm 66. The very first line is an invitation to everybody, 'Shout with joy to God, all the earth!' Then he invites the people: 'Come and see what God has done, how awesome his works on man's behalf!' (cf v 5). Then he gives a description of how God had led his people out of Egypt; how He had turned the sea into dry land so that they could pass through the waters without getting their feet wet. 'We went through fire and water, but you brought us to a place of abundance,' he says in v 12.

Have you ever told fellow-believers about what God has done in your life? It's not so difficult to talk to others about God's grace in your own life. Take the bull by the horns and tell a friend about the things God has done in your life. Even if you are going through a difficult time at the moment, you will probably discover that, as soon as you start counting your blessings, you will be able to say with the psalmist, 'I cried out to him with my mouth; his praise was on my tongue' (v 17). Although your life's journey might also take you through fire and water, God promises to lead you to a place of abundance eventually.

❧ Heavenly Father, I want to praise and honour You for what You have done for me in the past. Please help me to share my testimony with my friends. Amen.

April 12

Willing to change

READ: GALATIANS 1:11–24

*They only heard the report: 'The man who formerly persecuted
us is now preaching the faith he once tried to destroy.'
And they praised God because of me.*
– GALATIONS 1:23–24

It is very ironic that of everything God had created, only two types of creatures do not glorify Him, that is, man and the fallen angels. Although God had made man in his image, man is contaminated with evil from birth as a result of the original sin, and God has to transform us and make a new creation before we can glorify Him. However, you and I have been created for this purpose – to glorify God. And if you do not yet glorify God, it is high time that you try to perform your God-given duty.

Paul is an excellent example of someone who did his best to persecute the church, but who eventually accepted God's offer of mercy. Instead of persecuting the church he became the greatest missionary ever, and it is primarily as a result of his ministry that scores of Gentiles received Jesus as their Saviour. In the Scripture reading for today, Paul tells us how he became an apostle. When he returned to the churches which he had persecuted previously, people could see that his life had been completely transformed. They therefore glorified God because of him.

Do you live in such a way that others can glorify God when they look at you? If not, you should try to change so that others will see your good works and glorify God because of you (cf Matt 5:16).

❧ Heavenly Father, please change me so that others will also praise You because of me. Amen.

April 13

Glorify God by your obedience

READ: JOHN 17:1–8

I have brought you glory on earth by
completing the work you gave me to do.
– JOHN 17:4

Obeying God's commandments – which are found in his Word – is one of the best ways of glorifying Him. This is exactly what Jesus did. In his high-priestly prayer Jesus testified that He had glorified God on earth by completing the work God had given Him. When He sent Jesus into the world, God gave Him a specific task to do. He sent Him to make the Name of his Father known and to recruit followers for Him. And Jesus never considered the cost of this obedience to his Father – He was prepared to obey God's command to the letter. 'He became obedient to death – even death on the cross,' Paul said in Philippians 2:8. Just before He died, Jesus said, 'It is finished' – He had completed his task (John 19:30).

Jesus had been obedient to death, therefore He was glorified by God. 'And now, Father, glorify me in your presence with the glory I had with you before the world began,' He asked in John 17:5.

God still has a specific task for each of his children. He wants you to be a witness for Him and recruit disciples for Him. You can also glorify God by obeying his command. Ask the Holy Spirit to help you to achieve this.

❧ Holy Spirit, help me to make disciples for Jesus so that I will be able to glorify your Name by sharing the good news of Jesus with others. Amen.

April 14

Glorify God by bearing fruit

READ: JOHN 15:1–8

This is to my Father's glory, that you bear much fruit,
showing yourselves to be my disciples.
– JOHN 15:8

Like her husband, Bruce Wilkinson, Darlene Marie Wilkinson also wrote a book on John 15. In this book she says that we would bear more fruit for God by doing less and being more with God. Jesus also says, 'If a man remains in me and I in him, he will bear much fruit; apart from me you can do nothing' (John 15:5).[2]

You need God's power if you want to glorify Him in your life by bearing fruit for Him – just as the branch needs the strength of the vine to bear grapes. If you are serious about glorifying Christ, you should make enough time for God in your life. Just as the branch cannot bear fruit unless it is attached to the vine, you cannot bear fruit for God on your own.

The secret of how you can glorify God by bearing fruit for Him is to remain in Jesus. 'Whoever claims to live in him must walk as Jesus did,' John wrote (1 John 2:6). Therefore, live close to God every day, consult Him before you do anything, make Jesus the most important Person in your life and try to spend more time with Him every day. The better you get to know Him, the easier it will be to become more like Him in everything you do and say.

❧ Heavenly Father, I want to glorify You by bearing much fruit for You. Help me to remain in Jesus and become more like Him day after day. Amen.

April 15

Glorify God by your love for others

READ: 1 PETER 4:7–11

Above all, love each other deeply, because love covers a multitude of sins.
In all things [let] God be praised through Jesus Christ. To Him
be the glory and the power for ever and ever. Amen.
– 1 PETER 4:8, 11

We have already said that we should glorify God with our gifts. (See 11 April.) Although we did not receive the same number of gifts or the same exceptional talents, all of us have one particular gift with which we can glorify God; one gift which everybody should have, that is, love. In 1 Corinthians 13 you can read what this love should look like. The love with which God should be glorified is a love which is patient and kind; a love which does not boast and which is not jealous; a love which is not self-seeking and which keeps no record of wrongs. It is a love like God's, which protects, trusts, hopes and perseveres (cf 1 Cor 13:4–7). It is a love which will never pass, which will remain until we see God face to face.

When you see the exceptional talents of your friends, you may perhaps feel God stinted you when He handed out gifts. Focus on loving others unselfishly like Jesus did. Copy the love for others set out in 1 Corinthians 13. This will be very difficult, but the Holy Spirit will enable you to do it if you ask Him for this gift, because it is God's will that we should love one another.

Lord Jesus, I want to love like You and glorify God with my love for others. Thank you for the promise that You will pour out this love into my heart by the Holy Spirit. Amen.

April 16

Glorify God with your body

READ: 1 CORINTHIANS 6:12–20

Do you not know that your body is a temple of the Holy Spirit,
who is in you, whom you have received from God?
You are not your own; you were bought at a price.
Therefore honour God with your body.
– 1 CORINTHIANS 6:19–20

Corinth was a prosperous commercial centre with the result that prostitution was a profitable occupation there. Paul wrote to the Christians in Corinth that they could not do with their bodies as they pleased – God had redeemed them from sin and they (and their bodies) therefore now belonged to Him. Unlike the Gentiles they had to live in such a way that they would glorify Him with their bodies. 'Don't you know that you yourselves are God's temple and that God's Spirit lives in you? If anyone destroys God's temple, God will destroy him; for God's temple is sacred, and you are that temple,' Paul wrote in 1 Corinthians 3:16–17.

If you belong to Christ, your body is his temple, his sanctuary; the Spirit of God lives in you. You do not belong to yourself and you therefore cannot satisfy physical lusts at will. All other sins are outside a person's body, but sexual sins are sins committed against his or her own body. It is your duty as a Christian to glorify God with your body, that is, to act in such a way that others will see by your actions and words that you belong to God. Since you live in a permissive society, it is also your responsibility to talk to others about this.

❧ Heavenly Father, I now realise that my body is your temple and that this temple is sacred. Please help me to glorify you with my body. Amen.

April 17

The future glory

READ: ROMANS 8:18–30

*I consider that our present sufferings are not worth
comparing with the glory that will be revealed in us.*
– ROMANS 8:18

God's glory should be acknowledged in all areas of your life even, and particularly, when you are experiencing problems. The way Christians handle hurts and problems actually reveals to others the glory of God in their lives. You are also able to look to God and radiate joy despite your troubles, because you are assured of the fact that your hope will not be disappointed. You have God's promise that even if everything on earth should go wrong, He will save you out of all your troubles (Ps 34:6).

Nothing can take away this excitement about the glory which awaits you in heaven. This is a promise given by God Himself. This is the reason for Paul's joy in the core verse for today: Your present sufferings, he says, are not worth comparing with the eternal glory which awaits you in heaven. If you are struggling at the moment, fix your expectation on that glory, focus on it and believe it. Take God's promise in Romans 8:30 as encouragement: 'And those he predestined, he also called; those he called, he also justified; those he justified, He also glorified.'

✤ Lord Jesus, I praise and honour You for the promise that my present sufferings are not worth comparing with the glory that awaits me in heaven. Hold me in the hollow of your hand until then. Amen.

April 18

Sharing his glory

READ: COLOSSIANS 3:1–17

When Christ, who is your life, appears,
then you also will appear with him in glory.
– COLOSSIANS 3:4

As God's children we already share Jesus' glory on earth if we serve Him, but one day, when He returns, this glory will reach a climax. Only then will we really understand what God's glory involves and discover with joy that we share this glory. For this reason Christians already live as if Jesus is coming today. We should be ready and expect his second coming any day.

Paul wrote to the church in Colossae that, while they were waiting for the second coming, they should get rid of those things which were part of their way of life before they met Jesus. Negative qualities like anger, hatred, filthy language and jealousy should no longer be part of them. Instead they should live as people who had been redeemed. They should clothe themselves with compassion, kindness, humility, gentleness and tolerance towards one another. They should be forgiving and, above all, love one another in perfect unity (cf Col 3:12–17).

Consider your life and see whether certain aspects of your old carnal nature have remained in your life – habits which prevent you from glorifying God with your life. Then read Colossians 3:12–17 in your Bible again and underline the qualities which you should like to have in your life. By doing this you can share in the glory of Jesus even now – while you are looking forward to this glory reaching a climax at his second coming.

✤ Lord Jesus, please help me to be loving, tolerant, kind, humble, gentle and forgiving so that I can share in your glory even now. Amen.

April 19

The crown of glory

READ: 1 PETER 5:1–5

Be shepherds of God's flock that is under your care,
serving as overseers … And when the Chief Shepherd appears,
you will receive the crown of glory that will never fade away.
– 1 PETER 5:2, 4

Here the elders of the church are requested to look after God's flock so that the believers to whom Peter is writing, will be motivated to carry out the instructions in the letter. Peter promises his readers that, when Jesus appears, the elders who have performed the task which God has entrusted to them will receive the crown of glory that will never fade away. Jesus is the real Shepherd of God's flock, therefore Peter calls Him the Chief Shepherd.

It is interesting that Peter gives the elders the same instruction which Jesus had given him. After he had denied Jesus three times, Jesus asked him three times whether he loved Him and then gave him three instructions: feed my lambs; take care of my sheep and feed my sheep (John 21:15–17). Peter also describes in detail how this instruction has to be carried out: they have to oversee the Christians, not because they have to, but because they are willing; they must not be greedy for money, but eager to serve; not lord it over the others, but be examples (cf 1 Pet 5:2–3).

Here on earth all God's children have the responsibility to reach out to one another. If you are willing to care spiritually for other Christians in your congregation, you can also claim the promise that, when He comes, you will receive his crown of glory that will never fade away.

❧ Lord Jesus, Make me willing to serve in your kingdom by caring for your sheep so that I will receive your crown of glory when You come. Amen.

April 20

Jesus glorified

READ: JOHN 12:20–36

Jesus replied, 'The hour has come for the Son of Man to be glorified.
I tell you the truth, unless a grain of wheat falls to the ground and dies,
it remains only a single seed. But if it dies, it produces many seeds.'
– JOHN 12:23–24

According to John 12, a group of Greeks had enquired about Jesus. This was the sign to Jesus that his task on earth had nearly been completed. He Himself said that the hour for Him to be glorified was near and used the example of the grain of wheat to explain to his disciples that He had to die before mankind could be saved.

In verse 25 Jesus applies this image to believers. 'The man who loves his life will lose it, while the man who hates his life in this world will keep it for eternal life,' He promised.

We must also be willing to die for Jesus' sake in order to live for ever one day. If we want to serve Him with our whole heart we must be willing to follow in his footsteps and follow his example. You can glorify Jesus with your life by making everything else subordinate to Him, by making sure that nothing in your life is more important than He is. Make quite sure whether you are willing to surrender everything for the sake of Jesus. If you still have doubts, He cannot be glorified by you. However, if you are prepared to follow and serve Jesus to the end, you may claim the promise in verse 26: 'My Father will honour the one who serves me.'

❧ Lord Jesus, I want to love You above all else, I want to honour and glorify and serve You to the end so that I will also have eternal life. Amen.

April 21

On the mountain of transfiguration

READ: MATTHEW 17:1–6

After six days Jesus took with him Peter, James
and John the brother of James, and led them up a high
mountain by themselves. There he was transfigured before them.
His face shone like the sun, and his clothes became as white as the light.
– MATTHEW 17:1–2

Jesus' disciples did not always understand that He was as much God as He was man. During the transfiguration on the mountain God gave them a glimpse of the glory Jesus would again have after his resurrection. Jesus was changed before them: His face shone and his clothes became white as light, Matthew said. Just then Moses and Elijah also appeared and started talking to Jesus. The impulsive Peter immediately suggested that they should put up three shelters on the mountain: one for Jesus, one for Moses and one for Elijah. While he was speaking, a voice came from a cloud saying that they should listen to Jesus.

The disciples were terrified, but Jesus came and touched them, saying that there was no need for them to be afraid. During the difficult time which lay ahead this transfiguration would definitely have comforted and strengthened the three disciples.

As believers we sometimes have 'mountain-top' experiences – times when God feels very close to us. If you experience a difficult time in your life, do read the transfiguration on the mountain again and remember that Jesus is still the Glorified One – that He wants to touch you in the midst of your suffering and tell you not to be afraid.

❧ Lord Jesus, I worship You as the glorified Lord. Thank you that I never have to be afraid because You are with Me. Amen.

April 22

The hope of the glory of God

READ: ROMANS 5:1–11

Through [our Lord Jesus Christ] we have gained access
by faith into this grace in which we now stand.
And we rejoice in the hope of the glory of God.
– ROMANS 5:2

People who believe in Jesus are people whose hearts are filled with hope. They hope that they will one day be in heaven. And this hope about which Paul is writing to the church in Rome is the same hope to which the writer of the letter to the Hebrews is referring when he says: 'Now faith is being sure of what we hope for and certain of what we do not see'.

If you believe in Jesus you not only hope you will be in heaven one day, you know it and you know your hope will not be disappointed because you already know that you can claim God's mercy. Jesus earned this mercy for you on the cross – all you have to do is to accept his sacrifice. Once you have done this, heaven is yours! You then share the promise of hope which Paul writes about in Romans 8:24–25: 'For in this hope we are saved. But hope that is seen is no hope at all. Who hopes for what he already has? But if we hope for what we do not yet have, we wait for it patiently.'

Even when you are struggling, you can cling to this hope so that God can be glorified in your life. 'However, if you suffer as a Christian, do not be ashamed, but praise God that you bear that name,' Peter writes (1 Pet 4:16).

✢ Lord Jesus, I praise You for enabling me to wait patiently for that glory which will one day be mine in heaven. Amen.

April 23

Jesus, our hope of glory

READ: COLOSSIANS 1:24–29

To them God has chosen to make known among
the Gentiles the glorious riches of this mystery,
which is Christ in you, the hope of glory.
– COLOSSIANS 1:27

Jesus not only enables us to hope for the heavenly glory which God promises his children, He Himself is that hope! In his letter to the Colossians, Paul writes that this 'hope of glory' which we referred to yesterday is actually a Person: Jesus Christ. He lives in us, therefore He enables us to receive God's glory. He is, as it were, our hope of glory.

Paul was even prepared to risk everything he had to ensure that this glory which God promised his children would one day be his. 'To this end I labour, struggling with all his energy, which so powerfully works in me,' he said in Colossians 1:29.

Jesus is your hope of glory. Without a relationship with Him, you can never find God. However, if you remain in Him and if you are serious about your relationship with Him, He makes it possible for God to forgive all your sin, and you then know that you will one day have eternal life. Resolve to labour like Paul, to struggle like him with all your energy to grow spiritually every day until you are able to receive that glory.

❧ Lord Jesus, I worship You as my Hope of glory. Thank you that You made eternal life possible for me through your death on the cross. Amen.

April 24

The way to glory

READ: HEBREWS 2:5–13

In bringing many sons to glory, it was fitting that God,
for whom and through whom everything exists,
should make the author of their salvation
perfect through suffering.
– HEBREWS 2:10

The way to God's glory often passes through the wilderness of suffering. Here on earth no-one is exempt from difficult times, but God sometimes uses hurt and problems in the lives of his children to lead them to glory. He did this with Jesus too. Jesus suffered on the cross and paid the price for our sin, so that we could be redeemed. God made Him perfect through suffering.

Sometimes God permits suffering in your life because He wants to make you perfect and holy. When Lazarus was ill, Jesus Himself said, 'This sickness will not end in death. No, it is for God's glory so that God's Son may be glorified through it' (John 11:4). Jesus did not heal Lazarus when he was ill, but He allowed him to die, and then raised Lazarus from the dead. Raising Lazarus from the dead was a far greater revelation of his power and glory than merely healing him would have been.

We can never understand God because He is so much greater than we are. If you wonder why God permits so much suffering in your own life, remember that this very suffering could eventually lead to the revelation of God's glory in your life. Trust God to make you spiritually stronger through your difficult times.

❧ Lord, I have often wondered why You permit so many problems in my life. Thank you for your answer that You can reveal your power in my life through these problems. Amen.

April 25

God is glorified by good works

READ: MATTHEW 5:13–16

Let your light shine before men,
that they may see your good deeds
and praise your Father in heaven.
– MATTHEW 5:16

By your doing good deeds, others who look at you and see the things you do for God, might glorify God for what you have done.

In the world where we live opportunities to do good abound. Jesus says clearly in the very next chapter (Matt 6:3–4) that our left hand must not know what our right hand is doing when we do things for Him. However, it is impossible to hide what you are doing when you spread God's light in the world (cf Matt 6:3). In Isaiah 58:7–11 God speaks through the prophet Isaiah and gives a whole series of promises to those who reach out to people in need. He promises that if you share your food with the hungry, provide shelter and clothes, your light will break forth. God Himself with go before you and answer your prayers, your light will rise in the darkness and your night will be like the noonday. The Lord Himself will guide you and satisfy your needs; you will be like a well-watered garden, like a spring whose waters never fail.

Don't wait any longer to attend to the needs of those who are less fortunate than you. Let your light so shine before men that they will see your good deeds and glorify God.

❧ Heavenly Father, please show me how I can help others so that people will glorify You for what I have done. Amen.

April 26

An all-surpassing glory

READ: 2 CORINTHIANS 4:16–5:5

For our light and momentary troubles are achieving
for us an eternal glory that far outweighs them all.
– 2 CORINTHIANS 4:17

When Paul wrote this letter to the church in Corinth, he was already on the way to his death. Physically he was not at all well, but Paul was not put off by his physical circumstances. He was able to remain courageous and to trust in God because God was renewing him inwardly day by day. He knew that his daily sufferings in this life were temporary and would pass to make room for the heavenly glory that would never fade away.

If I had to choose only one verse from the thousands of Bible verses to encourage others, I would choose this verse. It is extremely comforting to hold on to God's promise that this suffering which you are experiencing at the moment cannot be compared to the glory which God is preparing for you. Paul implies that it is actually almost insignificant and only temporary, while the glory which will follow will never end.

Paul invites us to look at the invisible things, because the things which are not seen are eternal while the suffering which you have to face at present, is only temporary (2 Cor 4:18).

Memorise the core verse for today so that you can be encouraged by it when you experience problems again.

❧ Heavenly Father, I praise You for the promise that You are preparing an all-surpassing glory for me in heaven. Thank you that I may know that my suffering will soon be over. Amen.

April 27

Raised in glory

READ: 1 CORINTHIANS 15:42–55

*[That which] is sown in dishonour, [it] is raised
in glory … For the perishable must clothe itself with
the imperishable, and the mortal with immortality.*
– 1 CORINTHIANS 15:43, 53

The Bible not only promises that the glory which awaits us in heaven
one day will make all suffering on earth look insignificant, but we are
also assured that our mortal bodies which are subject to sickness and
pain will also be renewed; that we will receive glorified bodies when
Jesus returns.

Some people find it difficult to understand that our mortal bodies
will one day be resurrected when Jesus returns. Paul explains it by
using the example of planting a seed. When the original seed germi-
nates, the husk decays but a new plant with a new shape grows from
the seed. Although our mortal bodies decay when we die, they are like
small seeds which will germinate and change into our new glorified
bodies. At the resurrection all of us will receive new bodies which will
be totally different from our mortal bodies. These new resurrected
bodies will no longer be mortal. According to *Die Bybellennium*, 'God
Himself gives people the 'robes' to wear when they meet Jesus; the
robe of immortality.'[3] For this reason you no longer have to fear death.
Paul writes, 'Death has been swallowed up in victory.' And then he
quite rightly asks, 'Where, O death, is your victory? Where, O death,
is your sting?' (1 Cor 15:54–55). If you belong to Jesus you already
have the victory over death. Like Jesus you will one day rise from the
dead and be with God for ever.

❦ Lord Jesus, thank you for having conquered death and for having promised your children a new immortal resurrected body in which we will meet You.
Amen.

April 28

To Him be the glory for ever

READ: ROMANS 11:33–36

Oh, the depth of the riches of the wisdom and knowledge
of God! For from him and through him and to him
are all things. To him be the glory for ever! Amen.
– ROMANS 11:33, 36

Here Paul wrote a beautiful song of praise about the glory of God. He praised God's unfathomable wisdom, knowledge and riches. He exclaimed exuberantly that the glory belongs to God for ever and ever.

The fact that the glory belongs to God is emphasised so many times in the Bible that we must never doubt it. 'Our God and Father, to whom be glory for ever and ever,' Paul repeats in Galatians 1:5 and Jude also wrote, 'To the only God our Saviour be glory, majesty, power and authority, through Jesus Christ our Lord, before all ages, now and for evermore' (Jude 1:25).

What is so incredible is the fact that the Bible also tells us that we may share God's glory. 'He called you to this through our gospel, that you might share in the glory of our Lord Jesus Christ,' Paul wrote to the church in Thessalonica (2 Thess 2:14). 'When Christ, who is your life, appears, then you also will appear with him in glory,' he promised the Colossians (Col 3:4).

Although it is therefore a Divine command that you have to give God the glory which is his due, it is also a promise that you will one day share in that glory when Jesus comes again.

❧ Heavenly Father, I want to glorify and praise You because all praise and glory is yours now and for evermore. It is wonderful that I will one day be able to share in that glory! Amen.

April 29

The riches of God's glory

READ: ROMANS 9:19–26

What if he did this to make the riches of his glory
known to the objects of his mercy, whom he prepared
in advance for glory – even us whom he also called … ?
– ROMANS 9:23–24

In the Old Testament, God chose the people of Israel and set them aside to be the recipients of his glory and his glorious promises. To us it sounds unfair that only certain people should be chosen by God to be his children. However, God is always perfectly just. '… in order that God's purpose in election might stand: not by works but by him who calls …' Paul wrote in Romans 9:11–12. When you think about it, the mystery of God's election also merely proves God's tremendous mercy for mankind. After all, all human beings are sinners and deserve death. Although only the Jews were reckoned as God's chosen people in the Old Testament, the coming of Jesus paved the way for everybody who believes in Jesus to become God's children, to share in God's glory. You therefore never have to wonder whether you have been elected by God. The choice is yours. 'Yet to all who received him, to those who believed in his name, he gave the right to become children of God,' John writes very clearly (John 1:12).

If you believe in Jesus, if God has already elected you, then you are also an 'object of his mercy'. 'Even us, whom he also called, not only from the Jews, but also from the Gentiles,' Paul wrote to the Christians in Rome. Are you sure that you are one of the elect? Don't wait any longer to entrust your life to Jesus.

❧ Lord Jesus, thank you for having chosen me to belong to You; that I may believe in You, and so receive the riches of your glory. Amen.

April 30

Heavenly Father,

I worship You as the Lord of my life,
I acknowledge your Kingship and glory
in every area of my life.
I want to glorify your Name
in everything I say and do.
Help me to see your glory in your creation.
Teach me more about your glory every day
so that it can be reflected clearly in my life
and so that others will honour You for it.
I praise you for the promise that my suffering on earth
will one day be turned into a heavenly glory
which will exceed all suffering.
Lord Jesus, Thank you for coming into the world
to make God's glory visible to me.
Grant that I will become more like You day after day,
that nothing in my life will be more important to me than You,
that I will glorify You by loving like You
and bearing fruit for You.
Thank you that I could choose
the riches of your glory and
that I know that I will receive
this crown of glory when You come again.
Holy Spirit, I pray that the glory
which comes from You will increase,
that it will become more in my life every day
until I glorify your Name in everything I do and say,
because yours be the power and the glory for ever.

Amen

In the footsteps of Hosea

In the book written by Hosea, the prophet, we have a picture of the unfaithfulness of God's people, and of God's steadfastness, despite their unfaithfulness. God's faithfulness is contrasted with Israel's unfaithfulness and inability to serve and obey the Lord with their whole heart (which is our problem too.)

On studying this book in depth, we discover our own unfaithfulness to God and we are motivated to return to Him. We will follow in the footsteps of Hosea[1] and it is my prayer that you will rediscover God's burning love for you during this series of Bible studies. It is also my prayer that you will return to the Lord and, through the power of the Holy Spirit, remain faithful to Him for the rest of your life.

May

A shocking command

READ: HOSEA 1:1–3

When the LORD began to speak through Hosea, the LORD said to him,
'Go, take to yourself an adulterous wife and children of unfaithfulness,
because the land is guilty of the vilest adultery in departing from the LORD.'
– HOSEA 1:2

The Lord ordered Hosea to do something shocking: He had to marry a prostitute with illegitimate children. By means of this extraodinary 'marriage' God wanted to illustrate to his people exactly how unfaithful they were to Him. Hosea's life therefore became a living metaphor of Israel's unfaithfulness to God. Just as a prostitute is unfaithful to her husband, the people were unfaithful to the God of the Covenant. They left Him time and again to worship heathen idols.

Hosea did not merely convey the Lord's message to his people verbally; the Lord wanted him to demonstrate his message to the Israelites in detail, physically. Gomer, the prostitute whom Hosea married, fell pregnant and a child was born.

It is interesting to note that God expected Hosea to obey Him before He made his message known to him. Hosea first had to do something, i.e. marry Gomer, and then the Lord gave him the message he had to convey to the people. By this appalling command the Lord subjected his servant Hosea to pain and rejection. However, this is the same pain and rejection which God experiences when we reject Him and worship idols instead of Him. Consider carefully whether you have things in your life which have gradually become 'idols', that is, things which have become more important than God. If so, then Hosea's message is addressed to you.

❧ Lord, Forgive me for not always serving You with my whole heart, and show me exactly how I grieve You when I reject your love for me. Amen.

May 1

Three children for Hosea

READ: HOSEA 1:4–9

Then the LORD said to Hosea, 'Call him Jezreel (no more mercy) …
Gomer conceived again and gave birth to a daughter.
Then the LORD said to Hosea, 'Call her Lo-Ruhamah (not loved) …
After she had weaned Lo-Ruhamah, Gomer had another son. Then the
Lord said, 'Call him Lo-Ammi (not my people), for you are not my people …'
– HOSEA 1:4, 6, 8–9

By means of the rather odd names which He commanded Hosea to give his children, the Lord highlighted the magnitude of Israel's unfaithfulness. They had rejected Him to serve Baal, the Canaanite god of fertility. Hosea's first son was called Jezreel. This was also the name of the city where Jehu had shed so much blood – a part of Israel's history which they preferred to forget (cf 2 Kings 9–10). By means of this name God wanted to remind Israel that He would not merely ignore their sins of the past.

After the birth of their first child, Hosea discovered that Gomer was unfaithful to him. The name of the second child was Lo-Ruhamah (not loved). The Lord's message by means of this name was that He would no longer treat the house of Israel with love, but would withdraw his care and love from them.

Hosea's second son was called Lo-Ammi (not my people), a name which said that God no longer acknowledged the unfaithful Israel as his covenant people. They had forfeited God's covenant promises as a result of their unremitting sin and unfaithfulness.

God loves his children unconditionally, but He expects us to be faithful to Him. If you regularly reject Him for other gods, He might also withdraw from you until you repent.

❧ Lord, thank you for loving me. Help me to be absolutely faithful to You so that You will never have to withdraw Yourself from me. Amen.

May 2

God is merciful

READ: HOSEA 1:10–12

Yet the Israelites will be like the sand on the seashore,
which cannot be measured or counted. Say of your brothers,
'My people', and of your sisters, 'My loved one'.
– HOSEA 1:10; 2:1

Although Israel had disappointed Him deeply, God nevertheless offered them his mercy once again. He offered to renew his covenant promises and promised Hosea that the Israelites would be like the sand on the seashore. With this promise the names of Hosea's children were turned around completely: The Battle of Jezreel is won by God's people, so that it became a name of salvation; 'Without mercy' now became, 'Those who receive mercy'. And 'Not my people' were promised that they would be children of the living God. God offered his people a new beginning. He would heal the breach between them and the illegitimate children would become children of the covenant.

God's mercy is still unchanged, it is still the same as at the time of Hosea. Even when we persist in rejecting his mercy and continue sinning, He is always prepared to give us another chance. He loves you despite your sin. What are you doing with that mercy? Have you embraced it, or not? Don't hesitate to accept the invitation in Hebrews 4:16: 'Let us then approach the throne of grace with confidence, so that we may receive mercy and find grace to help us in our time of need.'

❧ Heavenly Father, I praise You for offering me your mercy once again. I accept it so that I can be sure that I belong to You. Amen.

May 3

When we take advantage of God

READ: HOSEA 2:1–13

'I will punish her for the days she burned incense to the Baals;
she decked herself with rings and jewellery, and went after
her lovers, but me she forgot,' declares the LORD.
— HOSEA 2:13

Here the prophet called his children together and instructed them to rebuke their mother, the prostitute Gomer, for her unfaithfulness which had caused a rift in the marriage. She was not prepared to accept the reconciliation which God had offered, and therefore had to be punished for her unfaithfulness. God was simultaneously accusing Israel of unfaithfulness to Him. He promised to punish them for rejecting Him for heathen idols.

In the day of Hosea the people were quick to turn to God as soon as things went wrong. They knew He was always prepared to help them again. We often do exactly the same. While all is well, we are inclined to forget God, because we think we are coping on our own. However, as soon as things go wrong, we do what Israel did and return to Him for help. We therefore use God only when we cannot cope without Him. But although God loves us unconditionally, He is a holy God who will not permit his children to take advantage of Him. Therefore, if you are one of those Christians who only knows God in times of trouble, be warned. Confess your sin and return to God.

❧ Heavenly Father, I confess that I have also taken advantage of You in the past - that I pray much more in times of trouble than when all is well. Please forgive me and hold me in the hollow of your hand. Amen.

May 4

A second chance

READ: HOSEA 2:14–22

Therefore I am now going to allure her;
I will lead her into the desert and speak tenderly to her.
There she will sing as in the days of her youth …
– HOSEA 2:14–15

God's mercy on his disobedient children amazes us! He actually asked Hosea to take his unfaithful wife into the desert again to woo her and give her another chance. This way He is telling us that He will always give his unfaithful children another chance to accept his offer of mercy. God enabled Hosea and Gomer to start over again. The prophet took her into the desert and assured her of his love. When Gomer discovered that Hosea still loved her, she promised to remain faithful to him.

God wants to offer you a second chance as well. Perhaps He will take you into the wilderness of suffering so that you will discover your dependence on Him and then accept your second chance.

God always gives his children another chance. Listen to the beautiful words He uses to assure you of his love: 'I will betroth you to me for ever; I will betroth you in righteousness and justice, in love and compassion. I will betroth you in faithfulness, and you will acknowledge the LORD' (Hos 2:19–20).

Confess your own unfaithfulness and sin before God and turn around, because you can be sure that God will enable you to return to Him. Don't wait any longer to seize this opportunity.

Perhaps you will not have another chance.

❧ Father, thank you for a second chance. I want to accept your offer of love and commit my life to You. Amen.

May 5

Seek the will of God

Afterwards the Israelites will return and seek the LORD their
God and David their king. They will come trembling
to the LORD and to his blessings in the last days.
– HOSEA 3:5

The Lord commanded Hosea marry his unfaithful wife again. He also expected the prophet to love her again. She had apparently deserted him and he now had to buy her back. After he had taken her back, she undertook to be faithful to the prophet. Like Gomer, Israel also repented of their sin, undertook to turn away from the heathen gods and to return to the Lord. They promised to be faithful to the Lord, to obey Him and serve Him with all their heart in future.

It must have been very hard for Hosea to take his unfaithful wife back after she had hurt him so deeply, and to love her as before – despite her unfaithfulness to him. However, God expected this of Hosea to illustrrate that this is exactly what He does for us. He is always willing to receive us back as his children, despite the fact that we have rejected Him in the past. He also wants you to forgive others as He has forgiven you. In this way you reflect his unconditional love for sinners.

If you are willing to do this, God offers you his abundance in future.

❧ Lord, I want to return to You and obey You, like Israel. I praise You for always being prepared to take me back. Please help me to forgive and love like You. Amen.

May 6

The Lord accuses his people

READ: HOSEA 4:1–4

There is no faithfulness, no love, no acknowledgment of God in the land.
There is only cursing, lying and murder, stealing and adultery;
they break all bounds, and bloodshed follows bloodshed.
But let no man bring a charge, let no man accuse another,
for your people are like those who bring charges against a priest.
– HOSEA 4:1–2, 4

The Lord accused his people and said that they lacked three things: faithfulness, love and acknowledgment. And the lack of these three qualities resulted in the irreversible increase of corruption and violence in the country. The Lord now called Israel to account and made them realise that they could not go on without his mercy.

While I read the above verses, I involuntarily recognised the same evil in our country. Crimes such as murder, theft, adultery and corruption are on the increase and the papers report daily about the shedding of innocent blood. Most citizens in South Africa lack the 'faithfulness, love and acknowledgment of God' which He demands of his children. Perhaps we should examine our own love, faithfulness and acknowledgment of God and our fellowman. We often act in exactly the same way as the unfaithful Israel. Like Israel we also have to realise that we cannot continue without God's mercy. If the Christians should repent and return to God so that our personal relationship with Him could be renewed, He promises to restore our country. Are you prepared to take the first step yourself?

❧ Father, Please forgive my own lack of faithfulness, love and acknowledgment of You and my fellow-man. In your mercy, restore my relationship with You so that our country can be healed. Amen.

May 7

A lack of commitment

READ: HOSEA 4:4–14

My people are destroyed from lack of knowledge.
Because you have rejected knowledge, I also reject you as my priests;
… because they have deserted the Lord … they consult a wooden idol …
– HOSEA 4:6, 10–12

The Lord not only accused the inhabitants of the land, but also the spiritual leaders. Here He addressed the priests, the church leaders, who were supposed to spread the word of God and proclaim his message. They not only lacked commitment but they had failed to lead the people spiritually. The priests were even guilty of temple prostitution; they sacrificed to the very idols against which they had to warn the people – at Gilgal and Bethel, the places where they used to serve God. Consequently the people were also unfaithful to God and had started to serve idols. As the prophet puts it: '[My people] consult a wooden idol and are answered by a stick of wood.' God pronounced a curse on priests who did such things, and warned that He would reject them.

If the spiritual leaders of our day fail to remain faithful to God and his Word, the judgment poured out upon the priests in Hosea's day might also be poured out on them. Church leaders should therefore search their hearts to determine whether they are really living close to God; whether they are leading their congregations spiritually, or whether they are perhaps guilty of those things judged in the Bible. Pray that the ministers in your congregation will be faithful to God.

❧ Heavenly Father, I pray for the spiritual leaders in my congregation. Please make them committed to You, faithful to the instructions in your Word and willing to give guidance to your children. Amen.

May 8

A stubborn people

READ: HOSEA 4:15–19

The Israelites are stubborn, like a stubborn heifer.
How can the LORD pasture them like lambs in a meadow?
— HOSEA 4:16

In Psalm 23 David calls God the Shepherd who sees to it that all the needs of his sheep are met. However, in the book Hosea, God is portrayed as the One who refuses to continue caring for his people because they have become as 'stubborn as a stubborn heifer'. The original sin of God's people is identified here by Hosea: they were stubborn, they refused to listen to God because they wanted to do their own thing. The prophet warned that the Lord would leave them to their own designs and without his protection so that they would be free to destroy themselves. The 'whirlwind' Hosea referred to in 4:19 indicated the spirit of unfaithfulness and apostasy that was rife among them.

If we were honest we would recognise ourselves in this description of Israel as a stubborn and disobedient people. We do not like being led by the Lord either; we prefer to have our own way. Israel's lack of commitment reminds us of ourselves. Most of us also regard the law of the Lord as a string of 'don'ts' instead of realising that it is the Lord's guideline to show us how to be really happy.

If you persist in rejecting God's covenant of grace, you might find yourself in the same position as Israel in Hosea's day.

❧ Lord, the more I learn about Hosea, the more I recognise myself. Please forgive me for being so stubborn and make me willing to be led by You and to obey your commandments. Amen.

May 9

The period of grace could pass

READ: HOSEA 5:1–7

Their deeds do not permit them to return to their God ...
they do not acknowledge the LORD. When they go with
their flocks and herds to seek the LORD, they will not
find him; he has withdrawn himself from them.
– HOSEA 5:4, 6

In this third warning in the book of Hosea, the leaders of Israel are addressed: the kings, the leaders of the people and the priests. Like the Israelites, these people who were supposed to be the leaders, had completely forgotten that they were supposed to obey the Lord. They were no longer committed to the Lord. However, the Lord saw what they were doing – they could not hide anything from Him, therefore He was going to withdraw Himself from them. Even if they wanted to return to Him, He was not going to answer them because his patience with his unfaithful people had reached a cutoff point.

This Scripture includes a serious warning to us as well: God knows us through and through; He knows exactly when we reject Him for other gods – we cannot hide anything from Him. And God's patience with you and me might also reach a cutoff point; a time might come when He will no longer respond to our prayers when we call to Him in an emergency. Follow the advice of the prophet Isaiah and sort out your relationship while his grace is still available to you: 'Seek the LORD while he may be found; call on him while he is near' (Isa 55:6).

❧ Lord, I want to seek You and ask your will for my life while You are still near me. Please forgive my sin and accept me as your child again. Amen.

May 10

Quarreling among brothers!

READ: HOSEA 5:8–14

Judah's leaders are like those who move boundary stones.
I will pour out my wrath on them like a flood of water ...
I will be like a lion to Ephraim, like a great lion to Judah.
I will tear them to pieces ...
— HOSEA 5:10, 14

There was civil war between Judah and Israel. Because Ephraim had rejected God and gone to the heathen Assyria for help instead of turning to God, they were now being punished severely. They were losing the war against Judah. However, Judah was not exempt from God's punishment. God had become like a disease destroying them from the inside and like a predator tearing them to pieces from the outside. There was only one hope: They would have to repent and ask God's forgiveness. God never rejects his children when they want to return to Him.

Another danger which affects us as well is highlighted here. Many modern Christians have so many differences that very little of the unity proclaimed by Jesus is visible in their lives. We will have to learn to love and tolerate one another again and return to God together. Then He will remove our differences so that Jesus' prayer for his disciples will be fulfilled in us: 'I pray that all of them may be one, Father, just as you are in me and I am in you ... to let the world know that you sent me and have loved them even as you have loved me' (John 17:21, 23).

🐾 Lord, please forgive our pettiness which causes so much division among us. Help us to be one in You and to love You as one. Amen.

May 11

Return to the Lord!

READ: HOSEA 6:1–6

Let us acknowledge the LORD; let us press on to acknowledge him.
As surely as the sun rises, he will appear; he will come to us like
the winter rains, like the spring rains that water the earth.
– HOSEA 6:3

The prophet Hosea called the people to return to the Lord. He asked them to recommit themselves to God, and assured them that the Lord would appear and refresh them as surely as the sun rises every morning. Unfortunately the people's promises to the Lord meant very little. The Lord Himself said that their love was like the morning mist, like the early dew that disappears (cf Hos 6:4). He desired mercy from them, not sacrifices, acknowledgment rather than burnt offerings.

God's promises of new life are available to us as well. We have to be willing to recommit ourselves to the Lord; He will meet and restore us. However, our love must be steadfast and not like early dew. As in the day of Hosea, God can still renew us and enable us to turn away from our sin and return to Him. But we have to ask Him to do this for us. What is your love for God like? Can He rely on it? Are you a new creation because you believe in Him, or do you still have doubts about really being committed to God? Don't hesitate any longer. God wants to renew you. Allow Him to do so. Emphasise your decision to be born again by a life of commitment in future.

❧ Heavenly Father, I want to return to You and recommit myself to You. Help me to do so. Thank you for the promise that You want to make me a new creation. Amen.

May 12

Sin upon sin

READ: HOSEA 6:7–7:2

Whenever I would restore the fortunes of my people,
whenever I would heal Israel, the sins of Ephraim
are exposed and the crimes of Samaria revealed …
they do not realise that I remember all their evil deeds.
Their sins engulf them; they are always before me.
– HOSEA 7:1–2

After the war the whole Israel was sick because their relationship with God had been broken. People were committing murder, even on their way to the temple, they were lying, burgling houses, robbing one another in the streets – they apparently did not even realise that they could not hide their sin from God. According to the core verse for today, He knew all their sins – 'they were always before (the Lord)'. Even the king and the princes were guilty of immorality.

These desperate conditions once again remind us of conditions in our own country. We no longer feel safe anywhere, not even in our own homes. And these conditions are probably also related to the fact that our relationship with God leaves much to be desired. If every Christian in South Africa should return to the Lord, these conditions would definitely change. If every criminal should be aware of the fact that God is aware of all sin, our country would perhaps be in better shape. Let us, you and I, start with ourselves. Let us take the first step to change our attitude and to obey God. And, when you are tempted to sin, remember that God is aware of all sin.

Father, I realise how many wrong things I still cherish in my own life. Please reveal my secret sins to me and help me to take the first step to serve You with my whole heart from now on. Amen.

A blazing oven

READ: HOSEA 7:4–7

They are all like adulterers, burning like an oven whose fire the baker need not stir from the kneading of the dough till it rises. All of them are hot as an oven; they devour their rulers. All their kings fall, and none of them calls on me.

– HOSEA 7:4, 7

This is a vivid description of the extent to which the people had been corrupted by sin: The prophet warned that the people were like a blazing oven. They were rebellious, unreliable and refused to consult God. When the will of God is no longer considered, things inevitably go wrong. And God makes it abundantly clear that He will not tolerate corruption and injustice. Israel would ultimately be called to account for their wrongdoing.

Here in South Africa, as in the case of Israel of old, people also often fail to consider the will of God and merely go their own way and follow their own selfish desires. Small wonder, therefore, that things are going wrong in our country, that violence and corruption are the order of the day. If all Christians – those in leadership as well as ordinary citizens – in all walks of life, should undertake to ask God's will and return to Him again, a positive change is assured. Let's respond to God's invitation in 2 Chronicles 7:14: 'If my people, who are called by my name, will humble themselves and pray and seek my face and turn from their wicked ways, then will I hear from heaven and will forgive their sin and will heal their land.'

❧ Heavenly Father, please forgive my sin and the sin of my people. We want to know your will - please hear from heaven and heal our land. Amen.

May 14

Judgment of Israel

READ: HOSEA 7:8–16

Woe to them, because they have strayed from me!
Destruction to them, because they have rebelled against me!
I long to redeem them but they speak lies against me.
They do not cry out to me from their hearts …
– HOSEA 7:13–14

Here God pronounced judgment on his unfaithful people and He did not beat about the bush regarding his feelings. Since God's people had been acting like the heathen nations, they also looked like them. They were like the same batch of dough, like a burnt, flat cake which had not been turned over, like dough which had become mouldy. Heathen nations robbed them of their wealth without their noticing it. God compared them to a silly dove, without sense, and a faulty bow – they were absolutely useless to Him and their fall was imminent. Everything was their own fault because they refused to obey Him and wanted to do everything their own way.

The irony of it all was that Israel was totally unaware of this gradual deterioration. They were still proud and were still using God for emergencies when they needed Him.

However, before we judge Israel too harshly, we must consider whether we are perhaps guilty of the same attitude. Many Christians are so proud that they do not realise their own sinfulness. Like Israel they also use the Lord merely as a safety net and are focused on going their own way. Ask the Lord to reveal your sin to you and then make a U-turn and return to Him!

❧ Heavenly Father, please forgive me for not realising the magnitude of my own sin, and make me more committed to You. Amen.

May 15

Declaration of war

READ: HOSEA 8:1–7

Israel cries out to me, 'O our God, we acknowledge you!'
But Israel has rejected what is good; an enemy will pursue him.
– HOSEA 8:2–3

Although Israel had rejected the Lord for heathen gods and had broken their covenant, they still turned to Him in emergency situations. In the past they were used to running to God when danger threatened – and they continued this practice even though they no longer followed the Lord. They even alleged that they were still committed to the Lord; that they were his people. However, God no longer listened to them and instead declared war against them: Since they had done wrong in the eyes of the Lord, they would be pursued by their enemies. The prophet Hosea listed their sins in detail: they had set up kings and leaders without God's consent; they had made idols for themselves and worshipped them. And God was going to punish them for this. Israel had 'sown the wind' by worshipping heathen idols, and they would reap God's 'whirlwind' (Hos 8:7).

Like Israel of old, we are also inclined to rely on God's intervention in times of danger, but when we are prosperous, we live as if God does not exist. And God is indeed patient with us – like He was with Israel – but only up to a point. Do take Hosea's warning to heart if you are also inclined to know God only when you need Him. Eventually all 'sowers of wind' will reap God's 'whirlwind'.

❧ Heavenly Father, I have to confess once again that I am guilty; that I know You best when I need You most. Please forgive me. Amen.

May 16

Religion for personal gain

READ: HOSEA 8:8–14

Israel has forgotten his Maker and built palaces;
Judah has fortified many towns. But I will send fire
upon their cities that will consume their fortresses.
– HOSEA 8:14

Here two negative images are used to describe Israel. In the eyes of the other nations they were like 'a worthless thing' (8:8) and 'like a wild donkey wandering alone' (8:9). The Lord furthermore accused them of a useless form of religion: 'They offer sacrifices given to me and they eat the meat, but the LORD is not pleased with them' (8:13). Israel was guilty of practising a form of religion to their own advantage and to honour themselves – not God. And God does not tolerate this kind of religion. God therefore announced that they would be punished for their transgressions by being exiled to Egypt. Their cities would be destroyed and their beautiful houses burnt down because they no longer paid any attention to God and his commandments.

Israel had used their religion to their own advantage. Sometimes we fall into the same trap as they did. We are religious so that we can benefit from it. We even offer our assistance in our congregation and serve on various committees because they are seen as status symbols. Examine your motives. If you maintain a high profile in your congregation, seek God's glory, not your own glory and status.

❧ Heavenly Father, thank you that I can be of service in my own congregation. Please help me to practise my religion to your glory and never as a status symbol for myself. Amen.

God gives his children a life of celebration

READ: HOSEA 9:1–4

Do not rejoice, O Israel; do not be jubilant like the other nations.
For you have been unfaithful to your God.
– HOSEA 9:1

Hosea was standing on a threshing-floor during the harvest festival and told Israel that they should not celebrate unless they were glorifying the Lord. Indeed, they no longer thanked the Lord for their harvest, but instead followed all the heathen customs, like temple prostitution. The Lord therefore announced that they would have no further harvests. 'Threshing-floors and winepresses will not feed the people; the new wine will fail them,' the prophet prophesied in 9:2. The Israelites would furthermore be carried away in exile: Ephraim would be taken to Egypt and they would have to eat the unclean food of the Assyrians. This was an incredibly severe punishment because the religious rituals were very important to the Israelites. God also said that they would not have the joy of celebrations again because there would not be another harvest.

God wants his children to be filled with joy, He wants them to radiate happiness. The writer of Proverbs says, 'All the days of the oppressed are wretched, but the cheerful heart has a continual feast' (Prov 15:15). Do you want a continual feast? Your life cannot really be a continual feast unless you know and honour God. The joy He keys into your life does not depend on your circumstances but comes from Him. Therefore, only the Lord can give you a continual feast. Ask Him to give you this feast.

❧ Heavenly Father, I praise You for a continual feast in my heart because I know and love You. Help me to remember that the continual feast comes from You only. Amen.

May 18

The day of reckoning

READ: HOSEA 9:5–9

The days of punishment are coming,
the days of reckoning are at hand. Let Israel know this …
God will remember their wickedness and punish them for their sins.
– HOSEA 9:7, 9

God was going to punish Israel for their deliberate transgressions because it was the only way to bring them to repentance. Here Hosea announced their punishment: Israel's harvest festivals would in future become festivals of judgment. Their country would be destroyed and they would be taken to Egypt, the country of slavery from which God had delivered them. As they had refused to listen to the prophets and did not heed God's warnings, they were now going to reap the fruit of their disobedience.

On reading the history of Israel in the days of Hosea, we are once again amazed at God's great mercy. If we were honest, we would have to admit that we are also disobedient to God. However, instead of being punished like Israel, He sent Jesus to bear our sin. When the prophet Isaiah describes the servant of the Lord, New Testament Christians see it as a prophecy which applies to Jesus: 'He was pierced for our transgressions, he was crushed for our iniquities; the punishment that brought us peace was upon him, and by his wounds we are healed' (Isa 53:5). Jesus bore God's punishment for your sin on the cross, therefore you may now claim God's forgiveness!

❧ Lord Jesus, thank you for having been prepared to take my place and for bearing the penalty for my sin so that God no longer holds my sin against me. Amen.

May 19

God rejects Israel

READ: HOSEA 9:10–17

My God will reject them because they have not obeyed him;
they will be wanderers among the nations.
– HOSEA 9:17

The Lord has always loved his chosen people passionately. He forgave their unfaithfulness time and again. Whenever they wanted to return to Him, He took them back as his people and renewed his covenant with them. They were as precious to Him as grapes found in the desert, as the early fruit on the fig-tree (cf 9:10). However, this time his people had gone too far – they had not realised his expectations and had become despicable to Him as a result of their constant un-faithfulness. They could therefore no longer avoid his punishment. God announced that He would make the people of Israel barren – there would be no births or pregnancies, and their children would die. Children were very important to the Israelites and this was probably the worst punishment God could mete out to them. God also said that He would no longer love them but that He would reject them because they refused to listen to Him.

God is also extremely patient with you and me. He is willing to forgive our unfaithfulness to Him time and again. He loves us so much that He even let his Son die on the cross to pay the penalty for our sin. We therefore dare not persist in our sin, like Israel, but we should try, with God's help, to live in such a way that others will see that God is our Lord and King.

🦋 Heavenly Father, I am trying so hard to live your way, yet I sin again and again. Please transform my life by your Spirit so that I will be able to obey your commandments. Amen.

May 20

The danger of prosperity

READ: HOSEA 10:1–8

Israel was a spreading vine; he brought forth fruit for himself.
As his fruit increased, he built more altars; as his land prospered,
he adorned his sacred stones … The Lord will demolish
their altars and destroy their sacred stones.
– HOSEA 10:1–2

Initially Israel prospered because they served the Lord and He blessed them. They were like a spreading vine which bore fruit in abundance, says Hosea. However, this prosperity eventually led to their destruction. This prosperity actually led to their building altars dedicated to heathen gods and they worshipped these gods instead of God. However, God is a jealous God who demands faithfulness (Exod 20:5), and who does not tolerate idolatry. The Lord therefore said He would demolish their altars and the sacred stones dedicated to their idols.

Their prosperity, which had led Israel to be unfaithful to God, therefore eventually destroyed them. When we start prospering financially, we should also see warning lights flickering. The more money and possessions one gathers, the more important those possessions become and the easier it becomes to let prosperity take the place of God in one's life. 'No-one can serve two masters. Either he will hate the one and love the other, or he will be devoted to the one and despise the other. You cannot serve both God and Money,' Jesus warned in his sermon on the mountain (Matt 6:24). If you have many possessions, see to it that Mammon does not take God's place in your life.

🌿 Heavenly Father, thank you for blessing me with so many material things. Grant that my money and securities will never become more important to me than You. Amen.

May 21

Call to repentance

READ: HOSEA 10:9–15

Sow for yourselves righteousness, reap the fruit of unfailing love,
and break up your unploughed ground; for it is time to seek the LORD,
until he comes and showers righteousness on you.
– HOSEA 10:12

Although God pronounced his judgment on Israel time and again, He nevertheless invited his unfaithful people repeatedly to start over again. He asked them to prepare a new field and sow according to his will. If they would be willing to do this, if they would ask his will, they would again reap his covenant love; God Himself would then pour out his blessings upon them like rain.

Here God asked Israel to return to Him and live according to his will again. However, the people refused to listen and were taken away in exile – as the Lord had warned them. It is ironic that, in exile, they eventually started serving the Lord again.

Israel forfeited the grace of God because they waited too long to respond to his invitation and rejected his grace. Don't let this happen to you. You can also wait too long to respond to the Lord's grace – the period of grace might eventually run out for you too, as in the case of Israel.

Fortunately you still have a chance to accept God's invitation. He loves you so much that He sent his Son into the world to give you another chance. Don't hesitate any longer to respond to his offer of grace. Come to Him today!

❧ Heavenly Father, thank you that your period of grace for me has not yet run out. I now want to respond to the unmerited grace which You are offering me. Thank you for your blessings which You pour out upon me. Amen.

May 22

God's loving care

READ: HOSEA 11:1–5

When Israel was a child, I loved him … It was I who taught Ephraim to walk, taking them by the arms; but they did not realise it was I who healed them.
– HOSEA 11:1, 3

God has always loved Israel. Hosea 11 sketches the picture of a loving father who teaches his little boy to walk and carries him about in his arms. After God had delivered his people from slavery in Egypt, He protected and cared for them in the desert. Yet Israel rejected God's caring love time and again because they felt they did not need Him. They refused to acknowledge that He was the One caring for them.

God's caring love is also available to you. 'The eternal God is your refuge, and underneath are the everlasting arms,' Deuteronomy 33:27 promises. And this love lasts all your life. In the beautiful promise in Isaiah 46:3–4 God Himself says, 'I have upheld [you] since you were conceived, and have carried [you] since your birth. Even to your old age and grey hairs I am he, I am he who will sustain you. I will sustain you and I will rescue you.'

This is a wonderful promise: God has his arms around you from before your birth to your old age, and He promises that He will carry you when you cannot go on. If life knocks your feet from under you again, hold on to this promise.

❧ Heavenly Father, You are so good to me. You offer me your love repeatedly. I praise You for this love which will sustain me day after day for the rest of my life. Amen.

May 23

God's burning love

READ: HOSEA 11:6–11

How can I give you up, Ephraim? How can I hand you over, Israel …
My heart is changed within me; all my compassion is aroused …
For I am … the Holy One among you. I will not come in wrath.
– HOSEA 11:8–9

Israel was guilty of numerous transgressions; they therefore deserved to be destroyed by God, but God's love for them burned so strongly that He could not find it in his heart to destroy them. When Israel refused to turn back to God, God undertook to turn to them. He promised to be merciful to Israel and not punish them; to control his wrath about Israel's unremitting unfaithfulness and to take them back to their country. He was prepared to forgive his people and to forget their sin.

God's love for his children has never changed. Throughout the Bible we are assured of this unfathomable, unconditional, eternal love of God for sinners. This love is as great as the distance between heaven and earth, David wrote in Psalm 103:11. And Paul wrote in Romans 8:38–39, 'For I am convinced that neither death nor life, neither angels nor demons, neither the present nor the future, neither height nor depth, nor anything else in all creation, will be able to separate us from the love of God that is in Christ Jesus our Lord.' If you should ever doubt the love of God for you, look at Jesus on the cross.

❧ Heavenly Father, I cannot grasp your love for me, but I want to receive it with both hands. Thank you for the assurance that nothing can separate me from your love. Amen.

May 24

God's punishment

READ: HOSEA 12:1–6

The Lord has a charge to bring against Judah;
He will punish Jacob according to his ways
and repay him according to his deeds …
The LORD God Almighty, the LORD is his name of renown!
– HOSEA 12:2, 5

Throughout the history of God's people deceivers appeared on the scene from time to time. One of the best known deceivers was Jacob who deceived his father, Isaac, and his twin brother, Esau, and then his father-in-law, Laban (cf Genesis 27 and 30). And their patriarch's tendency to being dishonest came to the fore in Israel time and again! Like Jacob they would say one thing and then do something else. They even tried to deceive God. They confessed their love for God and their willingness to keep his commandments, but then continued to worship their idols. Here God accused them of being just as unreliable as their forefather Jacob, and warned that they would be punished.

Just as the history of Israel could not save them, our religious traditions of the past cannot save us either. God knows all your sins – you cannot hide them from Him. And according to God, sin always deserves the death penalty. But we who are in Christ have been delivered from that death penalty because Jesus bore the punishment for our sin on Golgotha! God now asks you, as He asked Israel, to obey Him and live according to his will. Do not wallow in your sins - confess your sins before God and ask Him to forgive you. He will do so for Christ's sake. Then live according to the will of God.

❧ Heavenly Father, I know I cannot hide my sin from You. I therefore ask You to forgive me my sin, and enable me to live as your child from now on. Amen.

May 25

Return to your God!

READ: HOSEA 12:7– 15

But you must return to your God;
maintain love and justice, and wait for your God always.
– HOSEA 12:6

God's people could gain God's favour in one way only: They had to be willing to return to God personally; they had to decide to love Him again, obey his commandments in future, and build their hope on Him. However, Israel refused – they still felt they had done nothing wrong. God now announced that He was still the same God who had delivered them from Egypt and who had given them his law. Throughout Israel's history He had revealed Himself to them in various ways, through the prophets and historical events.

The Lord also expects us to return to Him if we have strayed from Him, to love Him again and obey his law, and to believe his promises. And He still speaks to us through his messengers and through history. Like Israel of old, many people still ignore God's message – they continue sinning yet feel they are doing nothing wrong.

Perhaps it is time for you to leave behind the wrong things in your life and to return to God. Like the father in the parable of the prodigal son, He is waiting for you with outstretched arms, waiting to pour out grace and mercy!

❧ Heavenly Father, I want to return to You; I want to love You and keep your commandments. Thank you that I can believe your promises. Amen.

May 26

The mortality of man

Therefore they will be like the morning mist, like the early dew
that disappears, like chaff swirling from a threshing-floor,
like smoke escaping through a window.
– HOSEA 13:3

Israel continued sinning while they still held on to the Lord with one hand. (We often do the same!) Although they were still regarded as God's chosen people and still called on Him when they were in trouble, they had been far removed from total commitment to the Covenant God for a long time. Their religion had gradually degenerated to a form of religion. Their hearts were no longer devoted to God either. They not only worshipped Baal, but even had silver idols made which they distributed and worshipped (13:2).

God was fully aware of this situation. He said Israel's love was as unstable as morning mist and the early dew which disappears as it becomes warmer (cf Hos 6:4). This image is used to emphasise the mortality of mankind as referred to elsewhere in the Bible as well. People will blow away like chaff on the threshing-floor and disappear like smoke escaping through a window, Hosea wrote. God the Creator of the world, the eternal God for whom nothing is impossible is contrasted with this fragility and mortality of man.

We must never lose sight of our own mortality. Compared with the Creator God, we are indeed 'dust on the scales' although we may regard ourselves as very important! (cf Isa 40:15). When you consider God, never forget how small and insignificant you are and how great and glorious He is.

❧ Heavenly Father, I worship You as the eternal God, the almighty Creator of the earth and everything in it. Make me aware of my own mortality every day. Amen.

May 27

God is always faithful

READ: HOSEA 13:4–11

I am the LORD your God who brought you out of Egypt.
You shall acknowledge no God but me, no Saviour except me.
I cared for you in the desert, in the land of burning heat.
– HOSEA 13:4–5

After the exodus from Egypt, and during the years in the desert, Israel was totally dependent on God. He provided them with food and water and protected them against their enemies. During those years when they could not survive without his intervention, Israel served God faithfully. However, now that they were prospering they had forgotten Him and had exchanged Him for useless idols, despite his caring love in the past. Instead of being the caring shepherd, He now said, 'I will come upon them like a lion, like a leopard I will lurk by the path' (Hos 13:7). God threatened that He would tear his people to shreds – that He who used to help them would now destroy them because they were unfaithful.

Hosea 13 has a warning for each of us. When we are prospering and are independent, it is easy to forget the Lord and depend on our own abilities. Lost in the desert, when we need Him, we turn to Him again. However, God will not tolerate such a 'yo-yo religion'. He wants his children to be faithful to Him and to acknowledge their dependence on Him – at all times.

The sooner you realise that you cannot do anything without God, the better. Then He will be your Shepherd again and He will see to it that you will not be in want.

❧ Lord, forbid that I should turn away from You. Keep me close to You so that I will always realise my dependence on You and serve You faithfully. Amen.

May 28

The final announcement of judgment

READ: HOSEA 13:12–14:1

I will have no compassion, even though [Ephraim]
thrives among his brothers. An east wind from the Lord
will come blowing in from the desert; his spring will fail and
his well dry up. His storehouse will be plundered of all its treasures.
– HOSEA 13:14–15

The people of Israel themselves were responsible for the punishment which God pronounced upon them. When they refused to listen and repent, God left them to their own designs. However, Israel would no longer be able to avoid punishment. God announced that Israel would be destroyed by an east wind which would dry up the wells. All their treasures and supplies would therefore be destroyed.

I understood this image in a new way a few years ago, when severe water restrictions in the Western Cape prevented us from watering our gardens and our flowers, shrubs and lawns shrivelled up while we looked on and were helpless!

We deserve the death penalty for our sinfulness, just like the ancient Israelites did, but when Jesus died for our sin, He settled our account. Paul assured the church in Colossae (cf Col 2:14) that 'He forgave us all our sins, having cancelled the written code, with its regulations, that was against us; he took it away, nailing it to the cross.' Israel was judged because their sin had become too much, because they had chosen to turn away from the Lord. The choice is still yours. What are you going to choose? Are you going to choose the death penalty, or are you going to accept Jesus who paid the price for you?

✦ Lord Jesus, thank you for nailing the written code that stood against me, to the cross, and for taking it away for ever. Amen.

May 29

Recipe for conversion

READ: HOSEA 14:1–6

Return, O Israel, to the Lord your God.
Your sin has been your downfall! …
I will heal their waywardness …
– HOSEA 14:1, 4

God's mercy triumphs in the last chapter of the story of Hosea. The Lord promised that He would take away the unfaithfuness of the people. Although they had come to a fall as a result of their sin, He would forgive that sin. In fact, He would heal their tendency to be unfaithful! In the words of the prophet, God gave them this beautiful promise: 'I will heal their waywardness and love them freely, for my anger has turned away from them. I will be like the dew to Israel; he will blossom like a lily. Like a cedar of Lebanon he will send down his roots; his young shoots will grow. His splendour will be like an olive tree, his fragrance like a cedar of Lebanon' (Hos 14:4–6).

This promise is still valid today and it is also addressed to you. This is the main thrust of Hosea's message: Although we sin and are unfaithful, the Lord loves us unconditionally, and He is still ready to forgive our sin and unfaithfulness time and again. He also undertakes to do so for you in future. He Himself will heal your unfaithfulness, forgive your sin and make you strong in Him. In gratitude for this mercy the least you can do is to straighten out your relationship with the Lord, confess your sin and leave it behind you. Once your unfaithfulness has been healed, you can be faithful to the Lord for the rest of your life.

❧ Heavenly Father, I want to accept your offer of mercy. Thank you for healing my unfaithfulness through Christ's reconciliation. Make me strong and faithful to You. Amen.

May 30

Everything comes from the Lord

READ: HOSEA 14:8–10

I ... will care for him ... your fruitfulness comes from me.
Who is wise? He will realise these things. Who is discerning?
He will understand them. The ways of the LORD are right ...
– HOSEA 14:8–9

People who confess their sin and return to the Lord, discover time and again that He has forgiven their sin and that they now live under the protecting wings of God. God promises his people that He will look after them, provided they realise that everything they possess comes from Him, and that they have not earned any of the good gifts and that nothing is the result of their own achievement.

This is a lesson each of us has to remember daily. Everything you have and are, is yours by the grace of God. It is very easy to develop a swollen head when you are successful and well-to-do. Perhaps you think your financial prosperity is the result of your business acumen or quick brain. 'You may say to yourself, "My power and the strength of my hands have produced this wealth for me. But remember the LORD your God, for it is he who gives you the ability to produce wealth,"' reads the warning in Deuteronomy 8:17–18. Rather be sincerely grateful for everything the LORD gives you in his mercy, and give Him the glory for your achievements and success.

'The ways of the LORD are right; the righteous walk in them, but the rebellious stumble in them,' reads the last verse of Hosea. That is something else you should take to heart: God always knows best – even when it does not feel like that to you.

❧ Heavenly Father, I acknowledge that everything I have comes from You. I therefore want to give You all the glory for all my abilities and achievements. Thank you that You always know best. Amen.

May 31

Heavenly Father,

thank you for the lessons I could learn this past month:
You confronted me with my own sinfulness
and unfaithfulness time and again.
I recognised myself in Israel's actions
and I realised your love and grace in a new way.
Please forgive me for neglecting You at times,
yet knowing You so well when I need You,
for taking advantage of You in times of crisis
and then forgetting You again when all is well.
I want to return to You, I want to seek your will
and obey your commands.
Please reveal my secret sins to me
and help me to leave them behind.
Lord, I also pray for the people in our country,
particularly for our spiritual and political leaders.
Grant that those who know You will love and obey You.
Please heal our land and bless us again.
Forgive the disunity among Christians –
give us a spirit of unity so that we will serve You as a family
and commit ourselves to You anew.
Lord, forbid that I will use my religion to my own advantage.
Thank you for promising me a life of celebration,
thank you for giving me financial security,
thank you for never changing and for being immortal.
I praise You for your incomprehensible love for me
which is so strong that You refuse to give me up,
and that You are prepared to give me
another chance time and again.
Grant that I will always remember
that everything I have and am
is by your unmerited grace.

Amen

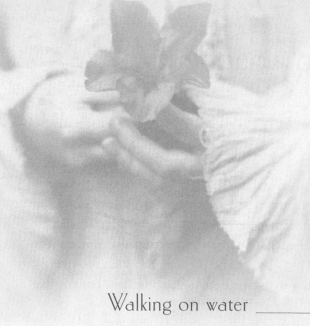

Walking on water

John Ortberg wrote a moving book entitled: *If You Want to Walk on Water, You've Got to Get Out of the Boat!*[1] This month we will be studying the same theme – so, if you haven't yet experienced the miracles of God, you should be convinced by the end of this month.

And you will also have participated in such miracles.

You are invited to take a walk that will last thirty days and after this walk, your life should have been changed for ever. You will be asked to deny yourself, to take up your cross and to follow Jesus. Toss your fears overboard, prepare yourself for an adventure: Step out of your safe little boat and walk on the water with Peter – towards Jesus.

June

Step out of your boat!

READ: PHILIPPIANS 4:13

I can do everything through him who gives me strength.
— *PHILIPPIANS 4:13*

The story of Peter who walked on the water has gripped the imagination of Christians for centuries. I am sure all of us have wondered whether we would have had the courage to accept this challenge. Peter's act of faith is an invitation to each of us who, like him, want to experience more of God's power and presence. Walking on water is, after all, doing something which is humanly impossible – but possible with the help of God.

There is a fixed pattern in the lives of people who are used by God in this way, writes Ortberg:

- There is always a calling – God asks an ordinary person to perform an act which requires unusual faith – to exchange his or her safe boat for a stormy sea.
- There is always an element of fear – you may fear your inadequacy and that you will fail.
- There is always reassurance – God promises you that He will be with you and that He Himself will help you to succeed in what He asks of you.
- There is always a decision – sometimes people say yes to God's call; sometimes they refuse.
- There is always a changed life – Those who say yes to God learn to grow – even through their failures. Those who say no to God, also grow: They will find it slightly easier to say no the next time they hear his voice – until they no longer hear his voice.[2]

❧ Lord Jesus, I want to step out of my safe little boat so that You will be able to use me to the maximum in your kingdom. Please give me the courage to step out! Amen.

June 1

Take courage! It is I.

READ: MATTHEW 14:22–27

When the disciples saw him walking on the lake, they were terrified.
'It's a ghost,' they said, and cried out in fear. But Jesus immediately
said to them: 'Take courage! It is I. Don't be afraid.'
– MATTHEW 14:26–27

While the apostles were crossing the lake in a storm, someone approached the boat, walking on the water. They were terrified, thinking that it was a ghost. However, Jesus spoke to them and allayed their fears. It's odd that the disciples had not recognised Jesus. By that time they had known Him fairly well, they had worked with Him for a long time and were often present when He performed miracles. Surely they must have realised that He was the only person who could walk on water! However, instead of being relieved when He approached their boat – they had after all experienced his calming storms before – they were terrified and thought He was a ghost.

When our own little boats of life are storm-tossed, we too often fail to recognise Jesus in the midst of the negative events in our lives. We are so busy trying to find reasons for the catastrophe that we fail to see the lessons the Lord wants to teach us.

If your life becomes storm-tossed again, try to see Jesus' presence. And listen to what He is saying to you: 'Take courage! It is I. Don't be afraid.'

❧ Lord Jesus, help me to recognise You and your voice when my life is storm-tossed. Thank you that I never have to be afraid when You are with me. Amen.

June 2

Lord, if it is You ...

READ: MATTHEW 14:28–29

'Lord, if it's you,' Peter replied, 'tell me to
come to you on the water.' 'Come,' he said.
– MATTHEW 14:28–29

After Jesus had reassured the group of terrified disciples in the boat that He was not a ghost, Peter immediately reacted in his usual impulsive way. 'Lord, if it is You, tell me to come to You on the water,' he replied. Peter actually asked Jesus to prove Himself. People have cherished the dream to walk on water for centuries. In ancient times only gods were supposed to be able to walk on water. However, Jesus did not tell Peter that it was impossible for him – He immediately invited him to come to Him.

We have already determined that Jesus sometimes approaches the boat of our life. In crisis situations we often do not recognise Him, because we focus on our problems. Long afterwards, when we see what we have gained through that particular situation, we discover that He was in fact there. When you experience a storm in your life again, study your circumstances carefully and you will recognise Jesus. It really is Jesus – and He is asking you to come to Him.

Perhaps it seems impossible to you, but step out of your safe boat and tackle the challenges of life by the power of Jesus. And respond to Him when He tells you to step out of the boat and come to Him!

❧ Lord, I want to come to You, but I lack the courage. Help me to obey your command. Amen.

June 3

Are you prepared to follow Jesus?

READ: MATTHEW 16:24–28

Then Jesus said to his disciples, 'If anyone would come after me,
he must deny himself and take up his cross and follow me.
For whoever wants to save his life will lose it,
but whoever loses his life for me will find it.'
— MATTHEW 16:24–25

Your 'boat' is that safe place where you feel cherished, where you are safe, writes Ortberg. While life outside your boat teems with danger, in your boat nobody and nothing can 'touch' you. However, if you never take the risk of stepping out of your boat, you will never experience the excitement of walking on water.

Don't hesitate any longer, take the risk and step out of your boat of life and follow Jesus. It might be a dangerous trip – Jesus warns that if you want to follow Him, you will have to be prepared to deny yourself, take up your cross and follow Him. He also says that whoever wants to save his or her life would perhaps lose it. Following Jesus therefore involves risk, but risk which will always be worthwhile. You cannot gain eternal life unless you are prepared to lose your own.

And if you tend to turn a deaf ear to Jesus' voice which encourages you to follow Him, you will eventually no longer hear it. Eventually you will no longer have the courage to step out of your safe little boat and then you will never know what it feels like to live victoriously.

Lord Jesus, help me to be willing to deny myself, to take up my cross and to follow You for the rest of my life. Amen.

June 4

What about failure?

READ: MATTHEW 14:29–32

*Then Peter got down out of the boat and walked on the water and came
towards Jesus. But when he saw the wind, he was afraid and,
beginning to sink, cried out, 'Lord, save me!'*
– MATTHEW 14:29–30

Peter obeyed Jesus and began to walk on the water. But then the situation was not quite what he had expected. When he felt the strong wind and saw the high waves, he was afraid and began to sink. The other disciples who were safe in the boat were probably relieved that they had not been so daring. However, although Peter failed, eleven bigger failures were in the boat.

All of us experience failure in life. Failure is unavoidable, but only those who have failed, experience success. Before Jonas Salk developed the polio vaccine which eventually saved the lives of millions, he had about two hundred unsuccessful efforts. 'What does it feel like to have failed two hundred times?' one of his friends asked him. 'I have never failed two hundred times,' Salk replied, 'I merely discovered two hundred vaccines which had not worked!'

Do not lose courage as a result of failure. Try again if things do not work out the way you had expected. The biggest failure is not beginning to sink, but remaining in the boat. Jesus immediately reached out and took Peter's hand and He helped him back into the boat. He will also be there to help you when your plans fail.

❧ Lord Jesus, I want to walk towards You on the water - thank you for the assurance that You will help me immediately, should I start to sink. Amen.

June 5

Gifts from God

READ: 1 CORINTHIANS 12:4–11

There are different kinds of gifts, but the same Spirit ...
Now to each one the manifestation of the Spirit is given for the
common good ... All these are the work of one and the same Spirit,
and he gives them to each one, just as he determines.
— 1 CORINTHIANS 12:4, 7, 11

My Mom had a special dinner service, edged with gold, which she did not want to use. My Dad always said he and his second wife would some day use it every day! Your God-given gifts are gifts from God, Ortberg says. There are two things you can do with gifts. You can decide they are too precious to use, or you can use and enjoy them despite the risk that they might be broken or spoiled. A gift which is never taken out of its gift wrap is a tragedy, says Ortberg.[3]

God gives each of his children a special gift which they have to use in his service and to his glory. You also received such a gift, because He does not omit anybody. However, it is your choice to open the gift and use it or to bury it like the servant in Jesus' parable (Matt 25:24–25). The disciples who remained in the boat buried their gifts. They were afraid to use their gifts and therefore played safe. What about you? Have you unwrapped your gift from God yet, even if it involves risk?

❦ Lord, thank you for the gifts which I received from You. Forbid that I should bury them, Lord, but help me to use them in your service. Amen.

June 6

Different gifts

READ: ROMANS 12:3–8

We have different gifts, according to the grace given us.
– ROMANS 12:6

God does not give everyone the same number or the same kind of gifts. In the parable which Jesus told in Matthew 25:14–30, one servant received five talents of money, the other two and the last one only one. One of these coins was equivalent to about 15 years' wages of a servant. In those days even one year's salary was an enormous amount of money – because the people lived from day to day, and no-one actually saved money.[4] Even the servant who therefore received only one talent, still received a huge sum of money which he could have used, while the servant who had been entrusted with five talents had unheard of wealth at his disposal. He and the servant who had received two talents seized the once-in-a-lifetime opportunity and used the wealth they had received. However, the man who received the one talent of gold buried his wealth.

God calls all of us to be active in his kingdom with the specific gifts He has entrusted to us. You should estimate the true value of your gifts, and not compare them with the gifts others have received. Seize every opportunity to use your specific gifts in God's kingdom as if it is the opportunity of a lifetime. The Lord has a way of increasing one gift when it is used – He will do it for you too.

❧ Heavenly Father, forgive me for often being dissatisfied with the gifts You have entrusted to me. Make me willing to use them in your kingdom. Amen.

Account and reward

READ: MATTHEW 25:14–30

His master replied, 'Well done, good and faithful servant!
You have been faithful with a few things; I will put you in charge
of many things. Come and share your master's happiness!'
– MATTHEW 25:21

The first two servants in the parable which we read today, worked hard to increase the money entrusted to them. Both doubled the amounts which their master had initially entrusted to them. However, the third servant buried the talent entrusted to him. He forgot a very important detail: his master would return one day. On his return, the master was very impressed with the first two servants. He praised them and promised them that he would put them in charge of much more since they had been faithful with a few things. However, he was not impressed with the third servant who had buried his talent. He gave instructions that the worthless servant should be thrown outside, into the darkness (cf Matt 25:30).

If you are still burying the gifts God has given you, you must realise that you will have to give account to God some day. It is interesting to note that the third servant had actually done nothing wrong – he had not stolen his master's money, wasted or embezzled it. He was punished because he had not used it, while the hardworking servants 'shared in the happiness' of their master (Matt 25:21).

God does not expect you to work with gifts you have not received. However, He will ask you what you have done with the gifts you did in fact receive. Live in such a way that you will share in your Master's happiness!

❧ Heavenly Father, forgive me for having done so little for your kingdom with the gifts You have entrusted to me. Help me to be so responsible with the gifts You have entrusted to me that it will give You joy. Amen.

June 8

God's special assignment

READ: ISAIAH 49:1–6

…my God has been my strength – he says:
'… I will also make you a light for the Gentiles,
that you may bring my salvation to the ends of the earth.'
– ISAIAH 49:5–6

Those who want to know when and how to step out of the boat need courage as well as wisdom to ask the right questions, the ability to identify the Master's voice and the patience to wait for his command,[5] says Ortberg.

Have you ever wondered what God does with his time? In John 5:17, Jesus said, 'My Father is always at work to this very day, and I, too, am working.' The creation and maintenance of the world form part of God's work, and since you and I were made in the image of God, it was his intention that we should also work. God gives you certain gifts which you have to identify, develop and use with joy to serve Him and his creation.

It is your task to identify God's special assignment and calling for you. This calling is not something you choose at random, but is something given to you – for example, a unique gift, or abilities with which God has specially blessed you. Consider carefully: What kind of work gives you joy? What is your passion? Don't feel stressed because you cannot do everything but do that which God has created you for.

❧ Lord, I want to discover my calling in life so that I can develop and use the special gift You have given me. Please help me and give me the strength to do this. Amen.

Task and equipment

Therefore go and make disciples of all nations, baptising them
'in the name of the Father and of the Son and of the Holy Spirit,
and teaching them to obey everything I have commanded you.
– MATTHEW 28:19–20

The specific task God has assigned to you is practically always beyond your capabilities. In his book, *If You Want to Walk on the Water, You've Got to Get out of the Boat,* Ortberg quotes Henry Blackaby as follows: 'I have reached a stage in my life where the following happens: If I get the impression that God has a task for me, and it's something I can handle, then I know it's probably not from God. In the Bible God always gave people 'God-sized' tasks. In other words, far greater than an ordinary human being can handle. However, God then gives that person his supernatural power to do it, and in that way He demonstrates his nature, his power, his provision and his love for his people to those who are watching.'[6]

Jesus gave his small group of disciples the formidable task of confronting the whole world with his gospel message. It must have seemed an overwhelming task! However, when God calls people, He also equips them to fulfil their calling. Together with his practically impossible task, Jesus promised his disciples: 'All authority in heaven and on earth has been given to me' and 'I am with you always …' (Matt 28:18, 20).

If God calls you, He will also equip you. You never have to tackle God's task in your own strength. He will provide his own power to make the impossible possible for you. As soon as you are willing to accept your calling, you will discover the secret that there is absolutely nothing you cannot achieve with God's help.

❧ Father, how great You are: You provide the supernatural power with the impossible assignment. Amen.

Career versus calling

READ: JEREMIAH 1:4–10

Before I formed you in the womb I knew you; before you were
born I set you apart; I appointed you as a prophet to the nations …
You must go to everyone I send you to and say whatever I command you.
– JEREMIAH 1:5, 7

The Lord has a special calling for each of his children. Your calling is the task for which God placed you on earth. And there is a huge difference between one's calling and one's job, says John Ortberg.[7]

- You yourself decide what your occupation will be, but your calling comes from God. A calling is something you do for God, while your job is something you do for yourself.
- Your occupation usually guarantees your status, money and power, while your calling often involves problems and suffering but it also gives you the opportunity to be used by God.
- Your occupation usually ends at retirement and you then receive a golden handshake, while your calling ends at your death.
- The reward of your occupation is therefore temporary, but that of your calling eternal.

Read the four differences between your occupation and your calling again carefully and decide for yourself whether you are working at your occupation or your calling at the moment. Then ask God to show you what specific calling He has in mind for you – and know that He Himself will equip you for it.

❧ Heavenly Father, please reveal to me what specific calling You have in mind for me here on earth. Make me willing to fulfil that task and equip me for it. Amen.

June 11

The first step

Then Peter got down out of the boat
and walked on the water and came towards Jesus.
– MATTHEW 14:29

Peter began to walk on the water. However, before he could do that, he had to step over the side of the boat and take the first step on the water. To do this must have cost tremendous courage. It was a dark, stormy night. He probably could not swim or even see far. However, Peter looked at Jesus and risked the first step. And then a miracle happened! Peter did the impossible: He succeeded in walking on water! The only way he could have done this was for God to have taken over. Nothing is impossible for God. When the Israelites were delivered from Egypt, they also experienced God's miracle-working power, but before they could cross the Red Sea, they had to take the first step through the sea, with a wall of water on either side (Exod 14:22).

All of us know that God is omnipotent; that He is with his children day after day, and that He can protect us under all circumstances. It is nevertheless a risk to take the first step. Are you perhaps facing a challenge at the moment which you cannot overcome without God's help? All God asks of you is to be willing to take the first step. Remember that nothing is impossible for God: He can let Peter walk on water, and also defuse your impossible crisis of the moment. Trust Him and risk the first step!

❧ Lord, at the moment darkness surrounds me and I cannot see ahead of me at all. Yet I want to risk the first step on the water. Thank you that nothing is impossible for You. Amen.

June 12

In all things God works for your good

READ: ISAIAH 41:8–14

So do not fear, for I am with you; do not be dismayed, for I am your God.
I will strengthen you and help you; I will uphold you with my
righteous right hand … For I am the Lord your God,
who takes hold of your right hand and says to you,
Do not fear; I will help you.
– ISAIAH 41:10, 13

When Peter noticed the strong wind, he was afraid. He forgot how he had enjoyed walking on the water; he even forgot that Jesus was only a few steps away from him. When he felt the water under his feet, it felt as if he was losing control. And we hate losing control!

One of the characteristics of people who are in control of themselves and their situation, is the ability to process stress. People who tend to become depressed have a major problem because they usually lose control – they cannot handle their negative circumstances. If you feel as if you have lost control of your circumstances at the moment, just remember that God is still in control.

When Peter started sinking, Jesus was there immediately and reached out to draw him to safety. You do not have to panic either, even if your situation is critical. God is always there for you. He is able to save you and to protect you. Even though you cannot do anything about it, if you are met with a series of disasters, you may still depend on the promise in Psalm 138:8, 'The LORD will fulfil his purpose for me.'

🌱 Heavenly Father, I praise You for the promise that You are always with me to help and protect me, and that I can rely on You to fulfil your promise to me. Amen.

June 13

Fear not!

READ: ISAIAH 43:1–7

*Fear not, for I have redeemed you; I have summoned you by name;
you are mine. When you pass through the waters, I will be with you;
and when you pass through the rivers, they will not sweep over you.*
— *ISAIAH 43:1–2*

Most people are weighed down by dozens of fears. The older I become, the more fears I have! Fear, according to John Ortberg, is the number one reason why people hesitate to step out of the boat. However, Peter did, and it went well for a while, but then fear hit him a second time. When Peter saw the strong wind, he succumbed to his fear – and that was the beginning of the end. Peter looked away from Jesus and started sinking!

It is interesting to note that 'Fear not' is the command which occurs most frequently in the Bible. I have read somewhere that 'Fear not' occurs 366 times in the Bible – once for every day of the year and one more for leap year. Fear has a way of making our faith disappear – it is indeed the major stumbling block in our trusting God completely. Those who are afraid, yet risk stepping out of the boat in the power of God, are really courageous.

What do you fear? Share your fears with God. He will help you to overcome that which you fear most. Fear and faith go hand in hand – choose not to fear any longer, but trust God.

❧ Lord Jesus, You know I still have many fears in my life which keep me in the boat. Help me to overcome my fears because I know You are with me. Amen.

June 14

In the cave of suffering

READ: PSALM 142

When my spirit grows faint within me ...
Look to my right and see; no-one is concerned for me.
I have no refuge; no-one cares for my life.
– PSALM 142:3–4

At some stage or other every Christian lands in a place where he or she does not want to be – a place where he or she has a hard time and where there is no way out. David's 'cave of suffering' is the cave of Adullam where he once hid from Saul. He wrote Psalm 142 during this difficult time in his life (cf v 1). In this dark cave he felt no-one could help him, no-one cared about him – not even God.

The worst thing about such a cave experience, says John Ortberg, is that you eventually start wondering whether God still remembers where you are. Caves are nevertheless often the places where God shapes his children best. When all the other crutches in your life have disappeared and you only have God left, you often discover that God is enough. Often your cave is the place where you encounter God in a special way, because you have to depend on Him alone.[8]

David also called to God in these difficult circumstances: 'I cry to you, O LORD; I say, "You are my refuge,"' he wrote in Psalm 142:5. For this reason he ended this psalm on a positive note: 'Then the right-eous will gather about me because of your goodness to me.'

❧ Lord, this cave experience is very unpleasant. Thank you for the new insight that You want to use it to shape me; that You do some of your best work in caves! Amen.

June 15

With God as your refuge

READ: PSALM 42

Why are you downcast, O my soul? Why so disturbed within me?
Put your hope in God, for I will yet praise him, my Saviour and
my God … all your waves and breakers have swept
over me. By day the Lord directs his love …
– PSALM 42:5, 7–8

Saul marched against David with 3 000 soldiers in an effort to capture him. He entered the same cave where David and his men were hiding. When Saul entered, David and his men were deep inside the cave, and David's men urged him to kill the king, but David refused. He was willing to allow God to let things happen as they should. In this cave David discovered that it was more important to obey God than to become king. Success was less important to him than pleasing God (1 Sam 24:3–7).

Although we know the rest of the history and know that David eventually became king, David did not force the issue. However, he knew that God was his refuge. In difficult situations where you do not know what awaits you, learn from David. Acknowledge God as your refuge and be willing to wait on Him and do not take the situation into your own hands. God knows best, and his will for your life is always to your advantage.

You do not have to be able to see into the future – rather trust God to let all things work together for your good at the right time. For you it is enough to know God is your refuge.

❧ Father, please help me to trust You and not to do things my way. Thank you for being my refuge. Amen.

June 16

Dogged does it!

READ: PHILIPPIANS 3:7–14

Forgetting what is behind and straining towards what is ahead,
I press on towards the goal to win the prize for which
God has called me heavenwards in Christ Jesus.
– PHILIPPIANS 3:13–14

In the film Chariots of Fire the English sprinter, Harold Abrahams, lost a race for the first time in his life – a race against the Scottish sprinter, Eric Liddell. Abrahams found it so hard to handle his defeat that he vowed never to compete again. 'If you cannot lose, it is perhaps the best thing to do,' Cybil, his girlfriend told him. 'I do not run to lose, I run to win! If I cannot win, I refuse to run,' Abrahams answered. 'Well, you cannot win unless you run,' Cybil responded.

You will often be on the losing side in the race of life. Losing is never pleasant, but losing does not mean you have failed. You only fail if you refuse to run, Ortberg writes.[9]

There is one race where you will always be the winner if you are prepared to run according to the rules and if you refuse to become discouraged. This is the race of faith which Paul refers to in our core verse. Forget what lies behind and strain towards what is ahead, the finishing line. Run the race in such a way that the heavenly prize will be yours.

❦ Lord, I want to run the race of life in such a way that the heavenly prize will one day be mine. Help me to forget what is behind and to strain towards what lies ahead. Amen.

Focus on Jesus

READ: HEBREWS 12:1–3

Let us run with perseverance the race marked out for us.
Let us fix our eyes on Jesus, the author and perfecter of our faith.
– HEBREWS 12:1–2

While Peter fixed his eyes on Jesus, he did the impossible – he walked on the water. However, as soon as he looked away from Jesus, he was in trouble. As soon as he felt the force of the wind and saw the high waves, Peter was afraid and began to sink. 'Hope made Peter step out of the boat, faith made him walk on the water, and fear made him sink,' Ortberg says.[10] Everything depended on whether his attention was focused on Jesus or the storm.

In the race of life it is very important to focus our eyes on the right Person. Athletes who run looking over their shoulders, will never win a race. When you are in a crisis, condition yourself not to look away from Jesus. Fix your eyes on the One Person who is the author and perfecter of your faith. Our ability to remain focused on Jesus is related to what goes on in our thought life. Your thinking patterns influence everything you do. Therefore, focus your thoughts on Jesus. Follow Paul's advice in Romans 12:2: 'Be transformed by the renewing of your mind.' Then decide, once and for all, whether you are going to live with fear or by faith.

When your problems become too much for you again, look away from them and fix your eyes on Jesus. Focus on his promises for you. There is nothing you cannot handle with his power.

❧ Heavenly Father, How wonderful to know that I can handle everything with your power if I focus my thoughts and eyes on You! Amen.

June 18

Focus your thoughts on Jesus

READ: PSALM 1

Blessed is the man ... [whose] delight is in the law of the LORD,
and on his law he meditates day and night. He is like a tree
planted by streams of water, which yields its fruit in season ...
— PSALM 1:1 – 3

Meditation is the best way in which you can focus your thoughts on Jesus. If you have not yet tried it, it is actually quite easy to teach yourself to meditate. 'If you can worry, you can also meditate,' Ortberg says.[11] Meditating actually means thinking about something over and over again. And we already know how tremendously important our thoughts are in our spiritual life. 'Above all else, guard your heart, for it is the wellspring of life' warns the writer of Proverbs (Prov 4:23). Follow Paul's winning recipe in Philippians 4:8: 'Finally ... whatever is true, whatever is noble, ... whatever is lovely, whatever is admirable – if anything is excellent or praiseworthy – think about such things.'

Memorising Scripture is important if you wish to focus your thoughts on Jesus. When you have your devotions, select one particular verse which speaks to you, think about it, focus on it the rest of the day and share it with your family. Then write it on a slip of paper and put it up where you can see it often. If you memorise only one verse per week, you will know 52 verses of Scripture by the end of the year – verses which you will be able to take with you wherever you go – even when your Bible is not within reach.

❧ Father, thank you for my Bible through which You speak to me every day. I want to make the truths in your Word part of my life; meditate on them day after day. Amen.

June 19

Learn to wait

READ: MATTHEW 14:22–32

Immediately Jesus made the disciples get into the boat and go on
ahead of him to the other side ... the boat was ... buffeted by the
waves because the wind was against it. During the fourth watch
of the night, Jesus went out to them, walking on the lake.
– MATTHEW 14:22–25

Matthew said that the wind died down after Peter and Jesus were back in the boat (Matt 14:32). However, the storm was not over immediately and they had to wait until the sea was calm.

Nobody enjoys waiting. We become impatient in a long queue, at a red traffic light, in a doctor's waiting-room ... Jesus went out to the disciples 'during the fourth watch of the night, walking on the lake' (between three and six in the morning). The disciples who had been in the boat since the previous day (Matt 14:23–25) must have been exhausted by then.

We read in different places in the Bible about people who had to wait a long time before God's promises to them were fulfilled. Abraham waited many years for his promised heir – so long that it was physically impossible for him to have a child when God eventually fulfilled his promise. The Israelites had to wait four hundred years in slavery in Egypt before they were delivered by God; they also had to wait many centuries for the coming of the Messiah. And at the moment Christians are awaiting the second coming of Jesus.

You and I have to learn to wait patiently until God's promises are fulfilled. Sometimes we find it difficult to wait, but this suffering actually produces perseverance. Waiting forms part of God's process to make you the person God wants you to be.

❧ Lord, I hate waiting! But I realise that You always know best. Please give me the patience to wait with perseverance until your promises to me have been fulfilled. Amen.

June 20

Waiting on the Lord with perfect trust

READ: PSALM 131

I have stilled and quietened my soul; like a weaned child
with its mother, like a weaned child is my soul within me ...
Put your hope in the Lord both now and for evermore.
— PSALM 131:2–3

God often asks us to wait on Him. Peter and the other disciples had to wait in the boat until the storm had died down. While one has to wait, time passes very slowly. In Psalm 90 the psalmist explains that the Lord is not slow in fulfilling his promises, his timing merely differs from ours. 'A thousand years in your sight are like a day that has just gone by, or like a watch in the night' (v 4). We should trust God to fulfil his promises and realise our dreams at the right time. Be prepared to wait: for the right marriage partner; for the long desired baby; for God's answer to your prayers.

You must also be willing to wait without interfering in God's plan or timing. Abraham's wife Sarah did the latter when she felt she had waited long enough for an heir. Henri Nouwen uses the beautiful picture of a trapeze artist to illustrate this act of 'waiting patiently'. This is, he says, like when the 'flyer' hangs motionlessly in the air for a fraction of a second after he has let go of the trapeze so that the 'catcher' can grasp his wrists. Perfect trust is required for this action. And this is how God wants to be trusted. He expects you to let go of everything else and to wait on Him, even if his promises to you have not yet been fulfilled.

🌸 Heavenly Father, teach me to wait for your intervention in my life with perfect trust. Enable me to exchange my timing for yours. Amen.

Strength to wait

READ: ISAIAH 40:27–31

*Even youths grow tired and weary and young men stumble
and fall; but those who hope in the Lord will renew their strength.
They will soar on wings like eagles; they will run and not grow weary…*
– ISAIAH 40:30–31

When we are waiting for something, we realise time and again that we are not in control. In fact, in a doctor's waiting-room, you cannot insist that it's long past your original appointment. At the supermarket you cannot push in front of a long queue of heavy-laden trollies just because you have only one loaf of bread! You simply have to wait your turn.

However, when you have to wait for the Lord, it is different. You now wait for Someone. You are not merely waiting for something to happen. And since you know God, you know waiting for the Lord is never in vain. Your prayers are always answered in his own time and in his own way – even when it is not exactly the way you had asked. He is absolutely faithful, you may trust Him completely to help you at the right time.

Those who are prepared to wait for the Lord will receive new strength, the prophet Isaiah promises. They will soar on wings like eagles, they will run and not grow weary, they will walk and not be faint. If you are sitting in the Lord's waiting room at the moment, take courage and ask Him to give you his strength.

❧ Heavenly Father, please fulfil your promise in my own life that those who wait for You will receive new strength. Amen.

June 22

How big is your God?

READ: JOB 37:14–24

Listen to this, Job; stop and consider God's wonders …
The Almighty is beyond our reach and exalted in power;
in his justice and great righteousness, he does not oppress.
– JOB 37:14, 23

The disciples were eye-witnesses of Jesus walking on the water (and of Peter also risking it!). As soon as He and Peter got back into the boat the storm died down. Then the disciples worshipped Him saying, 'Truly you are the Son of God' (Matt 14:33). If they had considered Jesus' power before, they would probably not have been so scared to step out of the boat.

Bible scholars say that when Jesus said to his disciples, 'It is I', in Matthew 14:27, He used the Greek version of the Name by which God had introduced Himself to Moses from within the burning bush: 'I am who I am' (cf Exod 3:14). With these words He wanted to assure the disciples that He was omnipotent – that they could trust Him because He could change their circumstances.

One of the reasons for our fear is indeed that we feel the God we worship is not really powerful enough to intervene in our circumstances. We remain worried because we fear that everything will depend on us. It is therefore important that you consider God's omnipotence from time to time and, like his disciples, once again realise the greatness of God; that you will see his wonders in nature and his miracles in your own life and glorify Him.

How big is your God? Is He big enough to make each of your worries disappear?

🦋 Heavenly Father, You are great and omnipotent. Please forgive me for disregarding your greatness and omnipotence by my unbelief and persistent worrying. Amen.

Believe in God

READ: MATTHEW 14:28–34

And when they climbed into the boat, the wind died down.
Then those who were in the boat worshipped him,
saying, 'Truly you are the Son of God.'
– MATTHEW 14:32–33

When Peter began to sink and he cried out to Jesus, Jesus reached out and caught his hand, saying, 'You of little faith, why did you doubt?' (Matt 14:31). The reason for Peter's fear and doubt was that he had not trusted Jesus enough; his faith was not strong enough. However, the events which followed strengthened his own faith as well as the faith of the other disciples. Peter's story ended with the disciples kneeling before Jesus in the boat and worshipping Him as the Son of God. 'To worship God sincerely, we have to begin by listening to his voice and doing what He tells us,' the well-known reformer John Calvin said.

When you experience a storm in your own life, remember that you do not have to doubt like Peter, but that you may believe in God and trust Him. Make worshipping Him a habit – even when no crisis is threatening in your life – praise and thank Him for everything He does for you and gives you. Kneel before Him regularly during your quiet times and worship Him as the Son of God. Praise Him for his love and mercy for you personally, and realise anew every day that you do not have to fear anything when He is with you in your boat of life.

Lord Jesus, I praise You as the Son of God, You who are also God. Help me never to doubt You. I praise You for the assurance that I do not have to fear anything because You are with me in my boat of life. Amen.

Do everything to God's glory

READ: 1 CORINTHIANS 10:31; 11:1

So whether you eat or drink or whatever you do,
do it all for the glory of God … Follow my example,
as I follow the example of Christ.
– 1 CORINTHIANS 10:31; 11:1

'Worship is much more than praise, singing and prayers to God. Worship is a lifestyle of delighting in God, of loving Him and of giving ourselves to Him so that we can be used for his purposes. When you commit your life to glorifying God, everything you do becomes worship,' Rick Warren writes.[12] You can turn everything you do into worship if you do it to glorify and please God. For this reason Paul advises the church in Corinth to do everything – even the most mundane things like eating and drinking – to God's glory.

Once you discover this secret of doing everything to God's glory – not only reading your Bible and praying – you have found the secret of true worship. You can worship God in your kitchen, at the stove while cooking; you can worship Him while you clean your house, when you are ironing the washing or taking the children to school. In this way your whole life will be a life of worship – and you will be aware of God's presence in your life all day. You will be connected to Him by a golden thread of prayer and you will consult Him in everything. You will also glorify and praise Him for everything He does for you.

❧ Heavenly Father, I want to worship You in everything I do. Help me to do even the most mundane things to your glory. Amen.

The God you worship

READ: JOHN 3:27–33

He must become greater; I must become less.
The one who comes from above is above all; the one
who is from the earth, belongs to the earth, and speaks as
one from the earth. The one who comes from heaven is above all.
– JOHN 3:30–31

When John the Baptist testified about Jesus, he said, in no uncertain terms, that Jesus was much bigger than he was. He also said plainly that Jesus would become greater, and he would become less. In CS Lewis' well-known Narnia books Jesus is portrayed as the lion, Aslan. When Lucy met Aslan again after a very long time, she said, 'Aslan, you're bigger.' And Aslan responded, 'That is because you are older, little one. Every year you grow, you will find me bigger.'

This is also true about us. The more you grow spiritually, the greater God will be to you, and the easier it will be for you to worship Him, to trust Him totally, and to give Him full control of your life. And eventually you will be able to say like Paul, 'I no longer live, but Christ lives in me' (cf Gal 2:20).

The great Triune God is present in your life every day: God the Father, the Almighty, the Creator God; Jesus who triumphed over death, and the Holy Spirit who lives in you. His power is infinite – and this power is available to you every day. When you come to the end of your own strength, you have not yet touched God's reserves. Remember that you can do all things through Christ who empowers you.

❧ Heavenly Father, How great You are! I want You to become greater in my life every day. Thank you for your infinite power which You make available to me. Amen.

June 26

Grow spiritually!

READ: 2 PETER 3:14–18

But grow in the grace and knowledge of
our Lord and Saviour Jesus Christ.
– 2 PETER 3:18

If you have reached the stage where you are willing to entrust your whole life to God, allow Him to steer your life. He asks you to grow spiritually and become stronger every day. Peter learnt this lesson well. In the above verse he says that the believers have to grow in the grace and knowledge of our Lord and Saviour Jesus Christ (2 Pet 3:18). In the first chapter of his second letter, he explains how we will be able to do this: 'For this very reason, make every effort to add to your faith goodness; and to goodness, knowledge; and to knowledge, self-control; and to self-control, perseverance; and to perseverance, godliness; and to godliness, brotherly kindness; and to brotherly kindness, love (2 Pet 1:5–7).

Are you sure that you are growing spiritually as desired: That you are becoming more like Jesus, that you are getting to know God better and that you are really increasing in grace and knowledge day after day? If you really want to become spiritually mature, look carefully at the different qualities which Peter highlights in the above three verses, and see to it that each of them forms part of your life in future. You will not be able to do this yourself, therefore pray that the Lord will give you faith, goodness, knowledge, self-control, perseverance, godliness, brotherly love and love by the presence of the Holy Spirit in your life.

🙏 Heavenly Father, forgive me for being so slow in growing spiritually. I pray that each of the qualities which Peter mentions in his letter will be manifested in my life so that I will become stronger spiritually day by day. Amen.

Thirsting for the Word

READ: AMOS 8:4–14

'The days are coming,' declares the Sovereign LORD, 'when I will send a famine through the land – not a famine of food or a thirst for water, but a famine of hearing the words of the LORD.'
– AMOS 8:11

The people who lived in the days of the prophet Amos, kept the outward form of religion faithfully, but their hearts were far from God. They transgressed the law of God in various sly ways, exploited the poor and pursued dishonest business practices. The Lord pronounced judgment upon his disobedient people, and warned them that He would punish them. People who try to live without his Word, always pursue their own destruction. God announced that there would come a time when He would send a famine of hearing his word throughout the world.

If you want to grow spiritually, you have to develop such a hunger for the word of God that you will set aside enough time to study your Bible in-depth. In fact, it is between the pages of your Bible that you will get to know God better, that you will 'increase' in knowledge and become stronger spiritually. When you read your Bible, God speaks to you directly and personally. You learn how He wants you to live; you become aware of your sin and your life changes. 'The word of his grace (which) can build you up and give you an inheritance among all those who are sanctified,' Paul told the elders in Ephesus (Acts 20:32). See to it that you make these words inextricably part of your own life.

❧ Father, thank you for your Word, the light for my path. Please help me to comply with the guidelines in your Word. Amen.

June 28

A committed life

READ: 1 THESSALONIANS 5:16–24

May God himself, the God of peace, sanctify you through and through.
May your whole spirit, soul and body be kept blameless at the coming of
our Lord Jesus Christ. The one who calls you is faithful and he will do it.
– 1 Thessalonians 5:23–24

If you study the Word, you will inevitably change when you discover your own sinfulness in the mirror of that Word. 'The Scriptures are able to make you wise for salvation through faith in Christ Jesus. All Scripture … is useful for teaching, rebuking, correcting and training in righteousness,' Paul wrote (2 Tim 3:15–16). The Bible therefore tells you what to do to live the way God wants you to. By obeying the instructions in your Bible, you will become more and more committed to God.

Commitment requires a willingness to surrender your whole life to God; to make time for Him: time to pray, time to listen to what He says in his Word. However, it also means that you will live a committed life. This means that you live in such a way that others will see by your way of life that you are different, that your whole life is a sacrifice to God. You will be full-time in his service, 24 hours a day. You will be expected to love others sincerely, to help people in need, to really care for others, to be humble and forgiving, to live your faith with enthusiasm!

❧ Lord, I confess that I fall so far short in my commitment to You. Please make me more committed through the power of your Spirit. Amen.

A life of commitment to God

READ: COLOSSIANS 2:6–15

*So then, just as you received Christ Jesus as Lord, continue to live
in him, rooted and built up in him, strengthened in the faith
as you were taught, and overflowing with thankfulness.*
– COLOSSIANS 2: 6–7

Paul explained to the church at Colossae what the life of someone
who lives close to Christ looks like. In the above verses the Christian
is compared with a tree and a building. First of all the believer
should be rooted in Christ like a tree which is anchored to the
ground by a strong root system and, secondly, we have to be built up
in Him – like a building built on a strong foundation. Jesus is indeed
the foundation of our faith, because without Him in our life we have
no true security. *Die Boodskap* says it beautifully: 'Your relationship
with Him should be as strong and as intimate as the bond between
a tree and the soil from which it grows. Like a house which is built
on a strong foundation you have to build your life on Jesus. Be
steadfast in what you believe … (directly translated). Paul continued and said that we share the fulness of Christ if we remain close
to Him (Col 2:10).

If you really want to be serious about your own spiritual growth
so that you will have the courage to step out of your safe boat of life
and walk on the water towards Jesus, you will have to be willing to
work on your relationship with Him every day. Live in the fulness of
God from now on and thank Him for having paid the penalty for
your sin on the cross once and for all.

❧ Lord Jesus, thank you that I may remain close to You and that I may
share in your fulness. I want to be rooted and built up in You for the rest of
my life. Amen.

June 30

Lord Jesus,

please give me the courage to
step out of the safe boat of my life
and to walk towards You on the water like Peter.
Help me to recognise your voice in the midst of storms,
to be prepared to deny myself
and to follow You for the rest of my life.
And when the storm becomes too much for me,
thank you that I know You will be there
to take my hand and save me.
Lord, I want to use the gifts of grace
which you have given me to your honour and in your service
and the service of others.
Please show me your calling for me,
equip me for it, and give me the strength to carry it out.
Thank you that I do not have to fear anything
if You are in my boat of life.
Help me to overcome the fears
which are still part of my life.
Use the negative experiences in my life
to shape me as a Christian.
I want to trust in You,
and wait patiently until your promises have been fulfilled.
I want to run the race of my life in such a way
that I will win the prize.
I now decide to focus on You only,
to live close to You, to study my Bible
and to become stronger spiritually day after day.
How great You are, Lord Jesus!
Nothing is impossible for You.
I glorify You as the Son of God,
who is God Himself.

Amen

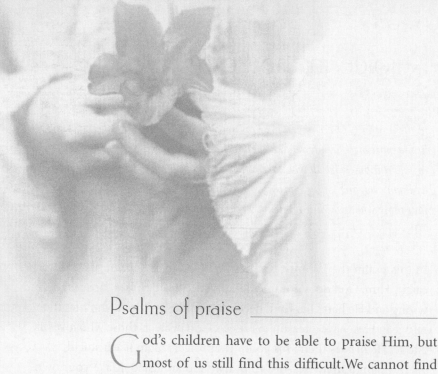

Psalms of praise

God's children have to be able to praise Him, but most of us still find this difficult. We cannot find the right words to praise Him or to tell Him how good He is to us and how much we love Him.

It is God's will that we praise Him: 'Praising God is the highest calling the Lord has for us: we are called to praise the living God, to praise Him together with the whole creation,' Johan Cilliers wrote.[1]

If you still struggle to praise God in your own words, the best way to do so is to turn to the psalmists.

It is my prayer that, in the coming month, you will find in the psalms of praise which we will discuss, exactly the right words with which to praise God for the rest of your life.

July

Rejoice in the Lord!

READ: PSALM 5

In the morning, O LORD, you hear my voice;
in the morning I lay my requests before you and wait
in expectation ... let all who take refuge in you be glad;
let them ever sing for joy. Spread your protection over them,
that those who love your name may rejoice in you.
– PSALM 5:3, 11

In this psalm the psalmist testifies that God listens when his children call to Him. God does not tolerate injustice. He despises those who do wrong and He hates liars and deceivers. But his children who find their refuge in Him have a reason to rejoice. God protects those who love his Name. He blesses them; his goodness protects them like a shield.

In Psalm 5 many reasons to praise God are listed. Make your own list and thank God for each: He loves you and you know He listens when you speak to Him. He protects you from dangers. You may approach God's throne of grace with confidence because Jesus earned you that privilege on the cross. He paid the price for your sin once and for all – and now God has forgiven you the sin which would have cost you your life if it had not been for Jesus' mediation. Because you believe in Jesus, you are welcome in his presence. By his love for you, you can enter his house and bow before Him in his holy temple with the respect which is his due. His goodness will protect you like a shield for the rest of your life.

❧ Heavenly Father, thank you that I may take refuge in You, that You will protect me and bless me. Thank you for listening to my voice and that I may receive your grace all my life. Amen.

July 1

Praise to the Creator

READ: PSALM 8

O LORD, our Lord, how majestic is your name in all the earth!
You have set your glory above the heavens. O LORD, our Lord,
how majestic is your name in all the earth!
– PSALM 8:1, 9

When we spend our holidays at Struisbaai, we always read Psalm 8 on our first night. This psalm verbalises our family's personal amazement about God and his creation. Can anyone see the azure blue sea, the snow-white cumulus clouds, the mountains, the moon and the stars without feeling small and insignificant before the great Creator God? Who can appreciate the beauty of nature without being amazed once again that God has appointed insignificant man to rule the work of his hands?

Only when we acknowledge that we are nothing have we reached the right place where we can praise God for his omnipotence and greatness. Only when you realise your own insignificance can God's infinite grace become a reality to you. Consider the fact that God made you just a little lower than the angels (although He is fully aware of each one of your many sins); that He crowned you with glory and honour; that He subjected to you everything He has created. The more you think about this, the more you realise his mercy. God is so great! To Him be all the glory!

❧ Heavenly Father, I want to praise You because your Name is wonderful. I want to praise You for the wonder of your creation, and I want to praise You because I am wonderfully made. Thank you for your great mercy which You poured out upon me. Amen.

July 2

Praise God for seeing your trouble

READ: PSALM 10

But you, O God, do see trouble and grief;
you consider it to take it in hand ... You hear, O LORD,
the desire of the afflicted; you encourage them, and you listen to their cry.
– PSALM 10:14, 17

Sometimes when we are really struggling, it feels as if the Lord does not hear our prayers; as if we are no longer aware of his presence; as if He is not aware of our struggles. Sometimes we even wonder whether He still loves us. This is exactly what the psalmist feels at the beginning of Psalm 10. 'Why, O Lord, do you stand far off? Why do you hide yourself in times of trouble?' he wanted to know.

However, in the second part of the psalm, the psalmist realised that he was wrong: that God had been aware of his suffering and grief all along. That He will put an end to that as well. God listens when his children cry to Him – He gives the helpless courage again and hears their prayers.

Should you again feel as if God is not listening to you, as if He is not aware of your suffering, praise Him for knowing about your suffering. Nothing can be hidden from God – He knows all about you. He is also available to you every moment of the day, because He is only a prayer away. And when you are struggling, He is even closer to you to assist and help you, even if you can't feel it at that moment.

❧ Heavenly Father, I praise and glorify You because I know that You are aware of all my suffering, all the grief in my life. Thank you for promising that it will not last for ever. Amen.

July 3

Praise God for saving you

READ: PSALM 14

The fool says in his heart, 'There is no God.' They are corrupt,
their deeds are vile; there is no-one who does good ... Oh,
that salvation for Israel would come out of Zion! When the LORD
restores the fortunes of his people, let Jacob rejoice and Israel be glad!
– PSALM 14:1, 7

When God looks down from heaven at his people, He finds that all
have sinned and that no-one does good. 'All have turned aside, they
have together become corrupt; there is no-one who does good, not
even one,' the psalmist complains in verse 3.

When we look at the world in which we live, we are inclined to
agree with this verdict. Indeed, we see mostly crime and violence
around us. Apparently the small group of people who serve God and
who are still prepared to praise Him is becoming smaller by the day.
And we are faced daily with fools who maintain that God does not
exist (v 1).

We nevertheless still have reason to praise God. He remains faithful to his children, and although we have to live in a world teeming
with violence and danger, we know He is already preparing heaven for
us. God is still our refuge today as He was to his people then.

Even you may praise God because He will intervene in your life
and eventually make all things work together for your good. Together
with ancient Israel, you may rejoice because God will change your
situation. He is able to change your negative circumstances and save
you. Trust Him to do this!

❧ Lord, thank you that You will deliver me despite my negative circumstances. I know that my suffering on earth will never weigh up against the glory
which You are preparing for me in the future. Amen.

July 4

Praise God because He cares for you

READ: PSALM 16

LORD, you have assigned me my portion and my cup;
you have made my lot secure. The boundary lines have fallen
for me in pleasant places; surely I have a delightful inheritance …
You have made known to me the path of life; you will fill me with
joy in your presence, with eternal pleasures at your right hand.
– PSALM 16:5, 6, 11

In Psalm 16 the psalmist is filled with joy about what God does for him. God protects him; He cares for him; everything he possesses comes from the hand of God. God instructs him – even at night; he is kept from stumbling because the Lord is with him. God does not abandon him to the grave; He teaches him how to live. In God's presence he is filled with abundant joy; He fills his life with good things. For this reason the psalmist does not even consider idols – God is the One he worships and praises. He confesses that he belongs to God and that he has no good thing apart from God.

Your relationship with God gives you numerous reasons to praise Him all your life. God undertakes to care for you – not only now, but also after your death. God gives you everything you need. Your joy comes from God. You may take refuge with God because He will protect you all your life. There is only one thing you must never forget: Always give God the glory for everything you have.

❧ Heavenly Father, I praise You because You are my life, because You care for me and protect me day after day, because everything I have comes from You. Thank you that my life is filled to overflowing with your joy. Amen.

July 5

Praise Jesus because He has delivered you

READ: PSALM 17

May my vindication come from you; may your eyes see what is right ...
And I – in righteousness I shall see your face; when I awake,
I shall be satisfied with seeing your likeness.
– PSALM 17:2, 15

Psalm 17 is the prayer of someone who is pursued despite his innocence. David asks God to protect him from his enemies like the apple of his eye, to hide him in the shadow of his wings (v 8). David is in mortal danger, therefore he calls to God for protection. He requests God to destroy his enemies and to save him because he is innocent.

Unlike David who felt he was innocent, we are not innocent before God. We have been received and born in sin. We all sin from birth. However, God did not leave it at that. He sent his Son to deliver us because He loved us so much. When Peter was brought before the Jewish Council, he testified about Jesus in glowing terms: 'Salvation is found in no-one else, for there is no other name under heaven given to men by which we must be saved (Acts 4:12).

On the cross Jesus brought about your deliverance. Because Jesus has saved you, you are delivered from the penalty for your sin, if you believe in Him. God forgives your sin time and again because his Son has paid the penalty for your sin on the cross. And for this reason you should praise Him all your life.

❧ Lord Jesus, thank you for loving me so much that You were prepared to die for me and that the penalty for my sin has now been paid for ever. Amen.

July 6

Creation glorifies God

READ: PSALM 19

The heavens declare the glory of God;
the skies proclaim the work of his hands …
The law of the LORD is perfect, reviving the soul.
– PSALM 19:1, 7

Not only mankind should praise God – all creation praises God by proclaiming his power; his Word is perfect and points us in the right direction. When we consider everything God has created, we cannot but praise and glorify Him. If you look at the multitudes of stars and consider that God has named everyone of them; if you look at the sun and realise that nothing can escape its glow, you cannot but praise the Creator of the sun and the stars together with the whole creation.

You should also praise God for the wonder of his Word – for the Word which is perfect and reliable and which gives life; for the precepts of the Lord which are right and give joy to the heart; for his commands which are radiant and give light to the eyes. The ordinances of the Lord are sure and altogether righteous, says the psalmist. He uses beautiful imagery to express his praise: 'They are more precious than gold, than much pure gold; they are sweeter than honey, than honey from the comb' (v 10). The psalmist concludes this psalm by asking that God should keep him from wilful sins – that what he says and does would be pleasing to God (v 13, 14).

❧ Heavenly Father, together with nature I want to glorify your greatness; I want to praise You for your Word which is precious to me. Teach me to live in such a way that everything I say and do will be acceptable to You. Amen.

July 7

Praise God with other believers

The LORD is my light and my salvation – whom shall I fear?
The LORD is the stronghold of my life – of whom shall I be afraid? ...
My heart says of you, 'Seek his face!' Your face, LORD, I will seek.
– PSALM 27:1, 8

When David wrote this psalm, he was struggling. However, he trusted the Lord to help him as before. He therefore verbalised his trust in the Lord: The Lord was the stronghold of his life, therefore he was not afraid. He asked the Lord to allow him to live in the house of the Lord all his life and to seek Him in his temple and meditate on his goodness. He also remembered that the Lord had commanded the people to serve Him, and therefore he reported for duty. He praised God for hiding him in the shelter of his tabernacle in the day of danger and that he was safe in the house of the Lord. David's faith was strengthened by the presence of other believers.

God wants you to praise Him with other believers. When you attend services you have the opportunity to praise Him in song and prayer with the rest of the congregation. And Jesus Himself promised: Where two or three come together in my name, there am I with them' (Matt 18:20).

Attend services regularly; get together with your fellow-believers so that, like the psalmist, you will be able to praise God for his goodness to you with the other believers.

❧ Heavenly Father, I praise You for being my light and my deliverer, and that I may meet with other believers to worship You. I also praise You for hearing my prayer and for having mercy on me. Amen.

July 8

Praise God because He helps you

READ: PSALM 28

Praise be to the LORD, for he has heard my cry for mercy. The LORD is my strength and my shield; my heart trusts in him, and I am helped. My heart leaps for joy and I will give thanks to him in song.
— PSALM 28:6–7

At the beginning of this psalm, the psalmist asked God not to turn a deaf ear to his cries. He also prayed that the Lord should punish his enemies and the godless. He was in such a desperate state, that he confessed that he would surely die unless God helped him. The second part of the psalm was a song of praise because God had heard his prayer and delivered him. He praised the Lord for his help, and also for helping his people.

In times of temptation you may ask God's help with confidence. He is there for you, He is merciful and He loves you. He also wants to reach out to you in your need. You may rely on Him – and his deliverance – totally. You can therefore say with the writer of the letter to the Hebrews: 'The LORD is my helper; I will not be afraid. What can man do to me?' (Heb 13:6). God not only helps his children, He also undertakes to help your people and country in difficult times. He saves those who belong to Him, because He loves us and has delivered us from sin.

❧ Heavenly Father, I praise You as my Helper, the One who is always there for me. Thank you that I do not have to be afraid. I pray that You will also help and protect the people in South Africa in times of danger. Amen.

July 9

Praise God in times of trouble

READ: PSALM 34

My soul will boast in the LORD; let the afflicted hear and rejoice.
Glorify the LORD with me; let us exalt his name together ...
Those who look to him are radiant; their
faces are never covered with shame.
– PSALM 34:2, 3, 5

When all is well, it is not difficult to praise God. However, when you are struggling, when it feels as if no-one cares about you, it becomes more difficult. The psalmist nevertheless managed to sing about the greatness of God and to praise his Name, particularly while he was battling. He could even be radiant with joy while he was suffering. The reason for this joy is found in verse 4: 'I sought the Lord, and he answered me; he delivered me from all my fears.' When God is with you, no trouble will be too much to bear. Joy in the midst of suffering can only come from God, because the joy which God gives is the only kind of joy which does not depend on your physical circumstances. The psalmist knew that God would change his circumstances again, that the expectation which he had of God, would not disappoint.

If you belong to God this promise is also addressed to you. Even if you are really in a desperate situation at the moment, you may rely on God's presence and his love for you. Really believe that He will change your circumstances as well. And it will therefore not be hard for you to be radiant with joy despite your suffering!

❧ Lord, thank you for this suffering in my life. Thank you that I can still radiate joy in spite of my suffering because I know that You are near, that You love me, and that You will help me. Amen.

July 10

Praise God because He is with you.

READ: PSALM 46

Be still, and know that I am God; I will be exalted among the nations,
I will be exalted in the earth. The Lord Almighty is with us;
the God of Jacob is our fortress.
– PSALM 46:10–11

In Psalm 46 the psalmist praises the Lord for being a refuge to his people; for protecting them and helping them in times of trouble. For this reason he is not afraid, even if 'the mountains fall into the heart of the sea … and the mountains quake with their surging' (cf Ps 46:2–3). Everyone who serves the Lord may therefore let go of their fears – they do not even have to fear earthquakes. They may relax and acknowledge that the Lord is God. He can do anything: even make wars cease. He is the Almighty and He is with them.

Sometimes we are very worried when things go wrong in our lives. Dangerous situations are becoming everyday occurrences in our country. We dread having to drive at night; we no longer go for a walk in the evening. We live behind security gates and switch on the burglar alarms at night. Being careful is not wrong, but God's children do not have to live in fear. After all, God is still as omnipotent as at the time of the psalmists – and this great God is still with you. Think about all the times in the past when He helped and protected you. He will still protect when necessary.

✤ Lord, I praise You for the fact that I may leave my fears with You; that I can be still and acknowledge once again that You are God Almighty, and that You are with me. Thank you for your presence in my life. Amen.

July 11

Praise God because He guides you

READ: PSALM 48

Great is the Lord, and most worthy of praise, in the city of our God, his holy mountain ... Within your temple, O God, we meditate on your unfailing love ... For this God is our God for ever and ever; he will be our guide even to the end.
– PSALM 48:1, 9, 14

Psalm 48 is a psalm of praise about the city of Jerusalem and the God of Jerusalem. To the Israelites, Jerusalem was a very important city because the temple was there. To them the temple was the place where they met God, where God dwelt, therefore they went up to Jerusalem for the most important religious festivals. The psalmist praised the Lord for this 'city of our God' – because a close relationship between God and the city of Jerusalem existed for the Israelites. He also praised God because He had always led his people in the past and would also continue to do so in future.

God indeed led his people throughout history. He cut a road for them through the sea and led them through the desert. He was always with them: at night as a pillar of fire and during the day as a pillar of cloud.

Today buildings are no longer as important to us as in the days of the psalmist. We know that we cannot keep God in a building because He lives in us through his Holy Spirit. The God of Jerusalem is therefore with you, always and everywhere. He wants to go before you and lead you, every day. Praise Him for his presence and guidance!

❧ Lord, I praise You for living in me, for being with me and leading me every step of the way. Grant that I will always be willing to be led by You. Amen.

July 12

Praise God because He has forgiven your sin

READ: PSALM 51

Against you, you only, have I sinned and done what is evil in your sight ...
Cleanse me with hyssop, and I will be clean; wash me, and I shall
be whiter than snow. Let me hear joy and gladness ... O Lord,
open my lips, and my mouth will declare your praise.
– PSALM 51:4, 7, 8, 15

In this beautiful penitential psalm which David wrote after he had slept with Bathsheba, another man's wife and had her husband murdered, he pleaded with God to forgive his sin. He admitted his sin and asked God to restore to him the joy of his salvation and to give him the words to praise the Lord.

All sin is always levelled at God. If you do, say or think a wrong, you do what is wrong in the sight of the Lord, just like David. And because God is holy, He cannot ignore sin – He always demands the death penalty. God has therefore already sentenced you to death. Fortunately God loves you so much that He made a plan more than two thousand years ago to take away your sin. He let Jesus die on a cross to pay the penalty for your sin. His blood washed away your sin so that you can stand before God, cleansed from sin. If you believe in Jesus, your debt has been paid – and God is prepared to forgive your sin, time and again. Don't you think that, in gratitude for his great mercy, you should repent of your sin and let it go?

❧ Heavenly Father, I praise You for sacrificing your Son to die on the cross so that my sins could be forgiven. Thank you that his blood was shed for me, so that I can now stand before You, cleansed from sin. Amen.

July 13

Praise God because He knows when you are sad

READ: PSALM 56

Record my lament; list my tears on your scroll – are they not in your record? … By this I will know that God is for me. In God, whose word I praise … in God I trust.
– PSALM 56:8–11

When he wrote this psalm, the psalmist was surrounded by his enemies. 'My slanderers pursue me all day long; many are attacking me … They conspire, they lurk, they watch my steps, eager to take my life,' he complained to the Lord (Ps 56:2, 6). He pleaded that the Lord should help him. His enemies' destructive action was confronted with God's saving grace. The psalmist discovered that God already knew about his distress; God knew his grief and his tears. In fact, every tear had already been recorded by God. He therefore did not have to fear his enemies any longer.

Usually we go to God for help when people make us afraid or sad, or when people disappoint us. And God always knows the grief of his children – even the grief we hide from others, also when we think nobody knows about it. Like the psalmist you can rely on God in emergency situations. You do not have to fear enemies who want to kill you. You have the assurance that God lists your tears, that He has already recorded them. God is on your side, therefore no-one can really be against you. Present your thank-offerings to Him, like the psalmist.

❧ Lord, I praise You because You know when I am sad, and You are so concerned about my tears that You even record them. Thank you that I do not have to fear people, but that I only have to rely on You. Amen.

July 14

Praise God for hearing your prayers

READ: PSALM 65

Praise awaits you, O God, in Zion; to you our vows will be fulfilled.
O you who hear prayer, to you all men will come ... having
armed yourself with strength ... You crown the year with
your bounty, and your carts overflow with abundance.
– PSALM 65:1, 2, 6, 11

Psalm 65 is a song of joy in which the psalmist praises God as the One who hears our prayers, as the almighty God and as the Provider. He confesses that when he prays to God, God answers him with powerful deeds (v 6).

God gives in abundance – when we look at the wheatfields or the heavy-laden fruit-trees, we have to notice his abundance. Yet God's children do not always experience this in their daily life. Not all of us experience abundance. Perhaps you cannot see God's goodness in your own life at the moment. Perhaps you do not have abundance because you – unlike the psalmist in Psalm 65 – do not receive every-thing you ask of God. When you meditate on this again, you should realise that we actually received everything we really need at the cross. At the cross, Jesus earned God's abundance for you for the rest of your life. At the cross He made it possible for God to answer all your prayers, even if the answer is not the answer you would have wanted. When you look at the cross, you realise once and for all that God is omnipotent – that no-one can 'hurt' you because He protects you.

❧ Lord Jesus, thank you for having died for me so that God now hears my prayers, provides abundantly in all my needs, and answers me with powerful deeds. Amen.

July 15

Praise God even if you are no longer young

READ: PSALM 71

*From my birth I have relied on you ... I will ever praise
you ... Do not cast me away when I am old; do not forsake
me when my strength is gone ... Since my youth, O God, you
have taught me and to this day I declare your marvellous deeds.*
– PSALM 71:6, 9, 17

At the beginning of this psalm, the psalmist definitely did not feel like
praising God. He was old and weak, he felt forsaken by God. He
pleaded with God not to forsake him in his old age, and undertook to
tell the younger generations of the work and power of God. The
psalmist's supplication gradually turned into a psalm of praise: He
praised God because He was so great, because He had done such wonderful things for him.

As we grow older we sometimes feel God is far away. Old age
brings things like poor health and loneliness. You no longer feel like
praising God every day. However, when you start thinking about the
past, remembering the times when the Lord kept you and cared for
you – it becomes easier to praise Him, despite your age and despite
your circumstances. Follow the psalmist's example: Praise God and
tell your friends about his 'powerful deeds' in your own life.

❧ Heavenly Father, thank you for all the years that You carried me. Thank
you for the assurance that You are still with me, that You will never forsake
me, but that You will go with me through the valley of the shadow of death
until I am with You in heaven. Amen.

July 16

Praise God for your congregation

READ: PSALM 84

How lovely is your dwelling-place, O LORD Almighty! …
Blessed are those who dwell in your house; they are ever praising you …
Better is one day in your courts than a thousand elsewhere.
– PSALM 84:1, 4, 10

The temple played an extremely important role in the life of God's people. However, the psalmist not only yearned for the temple, but also for God whom he would meet in the temple. Those who remained close to God, who visited his temple and lived according to God's commands were blessed. They were blessed by Him: He opened up the springs for them when they had to pass through the desert and gave them rain in season.

We no longer meet God in a temple, but it is important for believers to assemble in a church building, to serve God as part of a congregation. Those who serve God in this way are so blessed by assembling together that they cannot stop praising God (v 4).

Unfortunately modern people no longer attend church services regularly. Some feel they are closer to God in nature than in a church-building. What does your attendance look like? Where do you find your strength? Do you really trust in the Lord, or do you rely on your own achievements and abilities to provide in your own needs? Meeting with fellow believers will strengthen your faith, and provide you with the opportunity to serve God in your congregation.

❦ Lord, I praise You for my church and congregation where I can meet with fellow-believers every Sunday. I also praise You for freedom of religion and for your blessing in my life. Amen.

Praise God for his protection

READ: PSALM 91

He will cover you with his feathers, and under his wings you will find refuge … A thousand may fall at your side, ten thousand at your right hand, but it will not come near you … For He will command his angels concerning you to guard you in all your ways.
– PSALM 91:4, 7, 11

The psalmist says here that you can only be safe if you belong to God and trust in Him. God is perfectly able to protect his children from danger, we therefore do not have to fear anything. And this protection, which actually points to God's presence, is not limited to certain times or places – it lasts for the rest of your life and is relevant wherever you go. God is always with you if you love Him and know his Name. He promises to hear your prayers, be with you in emergency situations, save you and give you a long life.

In the world in which we live we have become used to dangerous situations. Practically every South African has been personally involved in violent crime. Fortunately God's promises in Psalm 91 are still relevant to every child of God – also to you personally. You can rely on God's presence every moment of every day, wherever you go. Although God's children are not exempt from dangerous situations, He promises to be with you in the dangerous situation, to carry you through, even through death.

❧ Heavenly Father, I praise You for your promise of protecting me at all times and in all situations. I praise You for your presence, also when I have to go through the valley of the shadow of death. Thank you that I will even be safe there because You are with me. Amen.

July 18

Praise God who owns everything

READ: PSALM 95

Come let us sing for joy to the LORD … For the LORD is the great God,
the great King above all gods. In his hand are the depths of the earth, and
the mountain peaks belong to him. The sea is his, for he made it … for he
is our God and we are the people of his pasture, the flock under his care.
– PSALM 95:1, 3–5, 7

The psalmist calls readers to celebrate the kingship of God with songs of praise. God has made the world, and everything in it belongs to Him. However, the psalmist was worried that Israel would be disobedient and that they would try to cover up their sins with songs of praise. Should this happen, God would not pay any attention to their songs of praise.

God made you too, and therefore you, and everything you possess, also belong to Him. God's children have a special relationship with Him: He has not only made us, but we are his people and He is the Shepherd who leads us and cares for us. We should sing songs of praise to Him because He is not only the omnipotent Creator-King who owns everything, but also the Shepherd who cares for his children.

You should also kneel before Him and worship Him. However, it is useless to praise and glorify God unless you undertake to obey Him. If you do not intend to obey God, He might reject you like He did with the Israelites at Massah and Meribah (cf Exod 17:5–7).

❧ Lord, I praise You as the great Creator-King who created the world and everything in it. You are my God, and I also belong to You. Make me willing to obey You so that I will never be rejected by You. Amen.

July 19

Praise God for you were wonderfully made

READ: PSALM 100

Shout for joy to the Lord, all the earth. Worship the Lord with gladness;
come before him with joyful songs. Know that the Lord is God.
It is he who made us and we are his ... Enter his gates
with thanksgiving and his courts with praise.
– Psalm 100:1–4

In the first half of Psalm 100 the psalmist asks that everyone on earth should praise God and serve Him with gladness, that they should know that God has made them and that they belong to Him. In the second half, the congregation is called to praise God in the temple with songs of thanksgiving and songs of praise. God is good, his love is infinite and his faithfulness eternal.

God's children should take praising and glorifying Him seriously – they should praise Him every day of their lives and with all that is within them. God has made man in his own image. He has made you incredibly wonderfully – if you want to know how wonderful you are, do read a Biology text book. Every minutest part of your body has been planned with precision by a Master Brain. Your own brain carries out about five billion chemical processes every second. Each gram of brain tissue can contain up to 400 milliard synaptic connections. Consequently every cell in your body can communicate with another cell at the speed of light.[2] The more scientists discover about the human body, the more they are amazed by God's wonderful creative power. Don't you want to praise God with David because He has created you in such a marvellous way?

✤ Father, I want to praise You, because You wove me together even before my birth. You created me in a marvellous way. What You have done fills me with amazement. Amen (Ps 139:13-14).

July 20

Praise God because He heals the sick

READ: PSALM 103

Praise the LORD, O my soul; all my inmost being, praise his holy name.
Praise the LORD, O my soul, and forget not all his benefits – who
forgives all your sins and heals all your diseases; who redeems your
life from the pit and crowns you with love and compassion.
– PSALM 103:1–4

In this psalm the psalmist praises God for various reasons. One of these is that God had healed him. When King Hezekiah was seriously ill, he also knew only God could heal him. He prayed sincerely that God should heal him and the Lord heard his prayer and extended his life by fifteen years (Isa 38:1–8).

Although God can heal all diseases, He does not do so. Sometimes He uses illness to prove his omnipotence, as in the case of Lazarus' illness when Jesus told his disciples,' This sickness will not end in death. No, it is for God's glory …' (John 11:4).

Perhaps you can profess like Hezekiah that God has healed your disease – then you have to praise God for it. However, even if He did not heal you, you know that He can use your illness to glorify his Name. Through his power He will enable you to be a powerful witness for Him while you are ill. If you are seriously ill at the moment and are not getting better, you have the promise that, one day in heaven, there will be no disease or pain.

❧ Heavenly Father, thank you for healing the sick, for giving relief in pain. I pray that You will also heal my illness. However, if it is not your will, make me a radiant witness for You while I am sick. Amen.

Praise God for his great works

READ: PSALM 111

I will extol the LORD with all my heart in the council of the upright and in the assembly. Great are the works of the LORD; they are pondered by all who delight in them. Glorious and majestic are his deeds, and his righteousness endures for ever.
— PSALM 111:1–3

When we look at the dewdrops on a cobweb or admire the sunset over the sea, we just have to praise the great God who made everything. God reveals Himself in the things He does – and when we notice them and think about them, the great God who has created such a beautiful world for us fills us with joy and awe. The psalmist says that the fear of the Lord is the beginning of wisdom (cf v 10). Wisdom means that we will be able to distinguish between right and wrong.

God's deeds are like Him: great, majestic and magnificent. See the 'great works of the Lord' and praise Him when you are with other believers. And if you want to develop his true wisdom in your life, remember that both his law and deliverance are signs of his steadfast love and that you can only really be happy if you love and serve Him.

❧ Heavenly Father, I praise you for the great things You do: in nature and also in my own life. I want to meditate on these wonders and give You the glory. I also pray for your wisdom so that I will be able to distinguish between right and wrong. Amen.

July 22

Praise God for his Word

READ: PSALM 119:162–176

I rejoice in your promise like one who finds great spoil …
Great peace have they who love your law,
and nothing can make them stumble.
– PSALM 119:162, 165

The incredibly long Psalm 119 is a song of praise about God's words and law. David could not stop talking about what God's words and law meant to him – and David did not even have a complete Bible like we have today. Just listen to what he said about the words and the law of God: 'Your decrees are the theme of my song wherever I lodge … Your word is a lamp to my feet and a light for my path … The unfolding of your words gives light; it gives understanding to the simple' (v 54, 105, 130).

Is your Bible just as important and indispensable to you as God's words were to David? Your Bible contains enough wisdom to let you walk your path of life with confidence, your Bible contains hundreds of promises from God to his children. The better you know your Bible, the better you get to know God, and the clearer you will hear Him speak to you. When you have doubts about something, consult your Bible: it will also give you light and insight and wisdom. Set aside enough time to study your Bible in depth regularly.

❧ Heavenly Father, I praise You for your Word which is a light for my path every day, for your Word which teaches me how You want me to live, and which gives me insight and wisdom. Help me never to neglect your Word. Amen.

July 23

Praise God because He does not sleep

READ: PSALM 121

Indeed, He who watches over Israel will neither slumber nor sleep … The LORD will keep you from all harm – he will watch over your life; the LORD will watch over your coming and going both now and for evermore.
– PSALM 121:4, 7– 8

Psalm 121 is the song of a traveller who is on his way. He looks up at the mountains around him where many dangers are lurking and discovers that his help comes from the Lord only. He takes courage because He knows that God is the maker of heaven and earth, and that this Creator-God never slumbers nor sleeps. He is always available to his children. He knows exactly where we are at any given moment and He comes to our aid when we are in danger. Those who believe in Him have a Protector who is on the road with them, every step of the way. God has undertaken to protect his children against those who threaten their lives and also from dangers such as sunstroke and disease (cf v 6).

Every Christian is also on his road of life. Dozens of dangers lurk on our roads of life but, like the psalmist, you and I have a God who does not sleep – who is awake every moment of the day or night so that He can hear our prayers and protect us. You therefore do not have to lie awake at night worrying about your problems. God is awake, He will undertake for you. And if you do battle to sleep, use the extra time available to you to talk to Him.

❧ Heavenly Father, I praise You for being available to me day and night; for never being asleep. Thank you for always being there to listen to my prayers and to protect me. Amen.

July 24

A song of praise during the night

READ: PSALM 126

The Lord has done great things for us, and we are filled with joy …
Those who sow with tears will reap with songs of joy.
He who goes out weeping, carrying seed to sow,
will return with songs of joy, carrying sheaves with him.
– PSALM 126:3, 5–6

Although the Israelites had a long history of disobedience and un-faithfulness, they returned to God while they were in exile. And God listened to their prayers and took them back to Israel. Initially the exiles who had returned had a very hard time. Their country had been devastated, the temple was destroyed, their houses were ruins and the farmers battled. However, the heathen nations looking at the people of God had to admit that the Lord had delivered his people from captivity, and that He had done great things for them.

On their return, the Israelites were able to praise the God who had delivered them despite their difficult circumstances. The lessons from the past taught them that those who sow in tears would reap songs of joy. According to *Die Bybellenium*, 'Growth is usually accompanied by pain. In this way tears become the seed of the joy which is eventually experienced.'[3] When you are in the darkness of suffering again, may you sing a song of joy to God in the night because you know He will turn around your circumstances again: He will give you joy after suffering, jubilation after tears. Trust Him for this!

❧ Heavenly Father, I praise You for still doing great things for your children. Thank you that we can sing a song in the night, even when it is pitch dark around us, because we know that You will give us joy again. Amen.

July 25

Praise God for your children!

READ: PSALM 127

Sons are the heritage from the LORD, children a reward from him.
Like arrows in the hand of a warrior are sons born in one's
youth. Blessed is the man's whose quiver is full of them.
— PSALM 127:3–5

Of all the things you can praise God for, it is probably easiest to praise God for the children He has given you as a gift. (Not to mention your grandchildren!) Sometimes you take it for granted that you have children, but only until you are confronted with people who try for years to have children, but all in vain. Then you realise how grateful you should be for your children.

The psalmist declares plainly that children are gifts from God. It is He who gave you the children whom you love. They therefore do not belong to you – God lends them to you for a while so that you can raise them for Him. You therefore have a God-given responsibility to fulfil the promise you made at their baptism or dedication faithfully. Tell them from a tender age that God loves them very much and that He is with them every day. Teach them to love Him, to read from his Word and to pray. Then you will also one day be able to confess: 'Here am I, and the children the Lord has given me. We are signs and symbols … from the LORD Almighty … ' (Isa 8:18).

❧ Heavenly Father, today I want to praise and thank You for the children You entrusted to me and for all the joy they key into my life. Grant that I will always remember that they are gifts from your hand, and that they do not belong to me. Amen.

July 26

Praise God for his infinite love

READ: PSALM 136

Give thanks to the LORD for He is good. His love endures for ever ...
Give thanks to the Lord of lords: His love endures for ever ...
Give thanks to the God of heaven. His love endures for ever.
– PSALM 136:1, 3, 26

In this psalm the jubilation about God's love which endures for ever resounds 36 times! All the reasons for rejoicing are carefully recorded: God is omnipotent; He made the heavens and all the heavenly bodies with great understanding; He spread out the earth; He destroyed Israel's enemies; He delivered them time and again and looked after them. The psalmists enjoyed praising God for his love. 'The Lord is compassionate and gracious, slow to anger, abounding in love ... for as high as the heavens are above the earth, so great is his love for those who fear him ... But from everlasting to everlasting the LORD's love is with those who fear him,' the psalmist says in Psalm 103 (v 8, 11, 17).

God's infinite love for sinners still passes all understanding. Although He is the Creator and Preserver of the world, although He made millions of stars and planets in the heavens and our earth is only a very insignificant little planet, He sent his only Son into our world so that whoever believes in Him shall not perish but have eternal life (John 3:16). This is what his love for you looks like. Never fail to praise Him for this love.

❧ Heavenly Father, thank you for your infinite love for me. A love which I cannot comprehend or define, but which I experience every day of my life. Thank you that I know that love will never fade away and that nothing can ever separate me from it. Amen.

July 27

Praise God for his mighty deeds

One generation will commend your works to another;
they will tell of your mighty acts. They will speak of the glorious
splendour of your majesty … My mouth will speak in praise of
the Lord. Let every creature praise his holy name for ever and ever.
– Psalm 145:4–5, 21

Throughout history, God helped Israel and performed miracles on their behalf. He delivered them from slavery in Egypt and cared for them for forty years in the desert. 'During the forty years that I led you through the desert, your clothes did not wear out, nor did the sandals on your feet … so that you might know that I am the Lord your God,' Moses said in Deuteronomy 29:5–6.

God still performs mighty deeds: He saves and protects his children, He cares for them in difficult times and sees to it that they lack nothing. You should praise God for his care every day. God is the only One whom you can trust completely. All people are unreliable to a certain degree, but God is eternal and omnipotent and absolutely faithful. As in the days of Israel, He helps his children when they suffer, He sees to it that they lack nothing, He heals us when we are sick, encourages us when we are discouraged, and answers our prayers. He protects everybody who loves Him and glorifies his Name. And this is reason enough to praise and glorify Him for ever!

❧ Heavenly Father, I praise and glorify You for your mighty deeds in my own life. Thank you that I can rely on your help and faithful care every day of my life, and that I can know that You will rule for ever. Amen.

July 28

Praise the Lord for his omnipotence

READ: PSALM 147

How good it is to sing praises to our God, how pleasant and
fitting to praise him! ... He heals the broken-hearted and
binds up their wounds. He determines the number of
the stars and calls them each by name ...
he supplies the earth with rain ...
– PSALM 147:1, 3–4, 8

In this psalm the psalmist cannot stop talking about God's omnipotence. Although He is so great that He determines the number of the stars and even calls them by name; although He controls natural phenomena like rain, hail and snow from heaven, he loves insignificant man. He rebuilds Jerusalem again and gathers the exiles of Israel; He heals the broken-hearted and binds up their wounds. He helps everybody who needs help. He also provides for the animals and makes grass grow on the hills so that they have enough food.

When you look at nature and study phenomena like rain, hail and snow, you just have to realise the greatness and omnipotence of God and praise Him. It really passes our understanding that such an omnipotent God should still have time to care about us personally, to bless us and provide for us personally. However, the Bible assures you that this is true: Although God is great and powerful, He knows your name and He is near when you call Him. Praise Him for this!

❧ Father, I praise You because You are great and omnipotent. You determined the number of the stars and call them by name; You control the natural elements. I praise You for knowing my name as well and for undertaking to care for me. Amen.

July 29

Let everything praise the Lord!

READ: PSALM 148

*Praise the Lord from the heavens … Praise him, all his angels, praise him,
all his heavenly hosts. Praise him, sun and moon, praise him, all you
shining stars … Praise the LORD from the earth … small creatures
and flying birds … all nations … for his name alone is exalted …*
– PSALM 148:1–3, 7, 10–11, 13

We must never stop praising and glorifying God for all the things with
which He has so graciously blessed us. Everything created by God testifies to his creative power. In Psalm 148 the psalmist calls everything
and everybody to sing together in a symphony of praise: the heavenly
hosts, the sun, moon and stars, the elements, nature, the animals,
plants and people. And the people mentioned in this psalm cover the
full spectrum: kings, young people and the aged. Everybody should
praise God because He has given his children power and because his
majesty is above everything.

We can add another verse to this song of praise about an event of
which the psalmist was still ignorant. We know about the Child born
in Bethlehem 2 000 years ago, at whose birth the angelic choir sang
songs of praise. We also know about a cross on Golgotha 33 years
later which made it possible for you and me to become God's children. And we can also sing of the resurrection and ascension of Jesus
and of his second coming when He will fetch his children to be with
Him for ever.

❦ Heavenly Father, I want to add my own personal song of praise to the
songs of everybody the psalmist has called to glorify You. I praise your Name
because You are exalted and your majesty covers the whole earth. Amen.

July 30

Everything that has breath, praise the Lord!

READ: PSALM 150

Praise the LORD! Praise God in his sanctuary ... Praise him with the
sounding of the trumpet, praise him with the harp and lyre, praise
him with tambourine and dancing, praise him with the strings
and flute ... Let everything that has breath praise the LORD!
– PSALM 150:1, 3–4, 6

Psalm 150 is the only psalm which gives no reason for praising the
Lord. 'It is as if the overwhelming joy of Psalm 150 arises from all the
'becauses' in the other psalms. Psalm 150 invites the whole creation
and heavens to praise God. Since God is being praised, no reason has
to be given. It is enough to say: "Let everything that has breath praise
the Lord,"' the writers of *Die Wonder van Gebed* say.[4]

We often struggle to find the right words or the right reasons why
God should be praised. This month we pointed out thirty reasons
why God's children should praise Him. But you do not need reasons
to praise God. And you can use the words of the psalms when you
lack words of your own. This praise to God should be part of your life.
When you start talking to God and you think about how great and
wonderful He is, you have to praise the Lord with everything that has
breath. Not for any particular reason, merely because He is God. If
you can play an instrument, praise Him with you flute, your harp,
your guitar or your piano.

🌺 Father, with everything that has breath - with instruments and with my
whole being - I want to praise and glorify You. How great you are! To You
be the glory and honour for ever! Amen.

July 31

Lord my God,

how great and wonderful You are!
I praise You for being my refuge,
for listening when I pray,
for healing my diseases.
I praise You for the wonderful world which You created,
for the sea and the mountains, the sun, moon and stars,
for the wind and the rain, the hail and the snow,
for the animals and fish and birds.
I praise You for making me so wonderful
that, although You are great and omnipotent,
and I am small and sinful,
You still love me with your infinite love,
that You know all about my suffering,
that You know my name
and meet all my needs.
I praise You for the wonder of your Word,
I praise You for being a Helper in need.
I praise You for sending your Son into the world
so that my sin could also be forgiven
and so that I can stand before You, cleansed from sin.
I praise You for the people I love:
for my marriage partner, my children and
my grandchildren, family and friends;
I praise You for my congregation, my church,
and for other believers with whom I can praise You.
Thank you that You never sleep, that You are there for me,
every moment of my life.
With everything that has breath,
I want to praise You just because You are God –
to You be the praise and the honour and the glory
for ever and ever.

Amen

The purpose of suffering

The Lebanese philosopher, Kahlil Gibran, wrote that joy and sorrow are inseparable: 'Your joy is your sorrow unmasked … The deeper that sorrow carves into your being, the more joy you can contain … When you are joyous, look deep into your heart and you shall find it is only that which has given you sorrow that is giving you joy,' he said.[1]

Pain indeed teaches us to be joyous, to appreciate life anew. After his serious heart attack at the age of 34, my husband and I saw life in a different way. We realised for the first time how precious life was; and that we had to change our priorities, simply because there was no time to do things which were not worthwhile.

Both of us discovered that, even in the pain and suffering in life, Psalm 16:11 is spot-on: 'You have made known to me the path of life; you will fill me with joy in your presence, with eternal pleasures at your right hand'.

August

I am the Lord!

READ: ISAIAH 42:3–9

A bruised reed he will not break, and a smouldering wick he will
not snuff out … 'I, the LORD, have called you in righteousness;
I will take hold of your hand, I will keep you and make you … '
– ISAIAH 42:3, 6

Through the prophet Isaiah, God assured Israel, who had been taken captive, that only He would be able to bring them back to their country. Although God is sovereign and omnipotent, He is very patient with sinners. None of us would keep useless things like a broken reed or a smoking wick, but God promised that He would not snuff out broken people who had been crippled by suffering. He is after all the Lord, nothing is impossible for Him. He has undertaken to support and hold his children in the hollow of his hand in difficult times; He Himself protects us.

When your own distress and suffering at times become too much for you, hold on to this promise. If you love God, you also know that nothing can happen to you which is beyond his control. When his disciples were desperately afraid one stormy night on the lake because they thought a ghost was walking on the water, Jesus gave them the same message as Isaiah: 'It is I. Don't be afraid' (Matt 14:27). If you are experiencing a dark period in your life at the moment, look carefully to see whether you can perhaps recognise God in your problems. He is still with you, and He is always in control.

❧ Heavenly Father, I worship You as the omnipotent Lord of my life. I praise You for being with me in my suffering, for being so patient with me and for holding me in the hollow of your hand. Amen.

August 1

All things work together for good!

READ: ROMANS 8:28–31

And we know that in all things God works for the good of those who love him, who have been called according to his purpose ... What, then, shall we say in response to this? If God is for us, who can be against us?
– ROMANS 8:28, 31

Paul promised the church in Rome that God works all things for the good of those who love Him, for those who are called according to his purpose. And since God's children have the assurance that He is on their side, nothing in the world can really be against them.

None of us can go through this life without hurt and suffering. Yet God's children can take this promise personally. God is on your side therefore you can have a tremendous sense of security: God makes all things in your life work together for your good – He can use anything to achieve his purpose in your life: even your deepest pain, your greatest sorrow, that disillusionment and disappointment which nearly cost you your faith.

In fact, He uses suffering in your life to make you more like Jesus, so that you can be 'conformed to the likeness of his Son' (cf Rom 8:29).

Children love licking mixing-bowls. Yet cake mixtures as such are rather unpleasant – no-one eats bicarb and flour or raw egg separately, but once mixed and baked, once the cake is literally oven-fresh, it's very tempting. Likewise God will make all the negative circumstances in your life work together so that, ultimately, everything will work together for your good.

❧ Heavenly Father, thank you that You let all things in my life, even suffering, work together for my good. Thank you that You called me and predestined me to be like Jesus. Amen.

August 2

Three wishes

READ: PHILIPPIANS 3:7–14

I want to know Christ and the power of his resurrection and the fellowship of sharing in his sufferings, becoming like him in his death, and so, somehow, to attain to the resurrection from the dead.
– *PHILIPPIANS 3:10–11*

Paul confessed to the church in Phillipi that he had three wishes in his heart. He wanted to know Jesus, experience the power of his resurrection in his own life and he wanted to share Jesus' suffering.

I agree with Paul that I would like to know Jesus better and experience the power of his resurrection. However, my problem is Paul's third wish: I would not like to share Jesus' suffering and death. Surely no-one would choose to suffer and die like Jesus. After all, Jesus' whole life on earth was characterised by suffering: He was born in a stable, He did not have a house or any conveniences, He died a terrible death on a cross. Few Christians would be willing to experience the above, yet Jesus said that to follow Him we would have to take up our 'crosses' like He did. The cross would probably not be a literal cross, but as the German theologian, Dietrich Bonhoeffer, said quite rightly: When someone carried a cross in Jesus' day, it meant one thing only – he was going to die on it. Christianity therefore demands self-sacrifice and self-denial. And this could be very hard …

Do you want to follow Jesus? Then you would have to be prepared to bear your share of suffering on earth. He will give you the strength to do so.

Lord Jesus, I want to know You better and experience your power in my life. Please make me willing to deny myself with the same attitude You had, knowing that I will share in your resurrection one day. Amen.

August 3

Through suffering you reflect God's glory

READ: 2 CORINTHIANS 3:12–18

And we, who with unveiled faces all reflect the Lord's glory,
are being transformed into his likeness with ever-increasing glory,
which comes from the Lord, who is the Spirit.
– 2 CORINTHIANS 3:18

When Isaiah wrote about the servant of the Lord in chapter 53, he said that this servant was a 'man of sorrows' who was 'familiar with suffering'. He took the suffering of others on himself and bore their diseases. He was pierced for the transgressions of others and crushed for their sins. The punishment that would bring them peace was on him, and they were healed by his wounds (cf Isa 53:3–5).

This prophecy was fulfilled while Jesus was on earth. The 'they' became 'we'. He was willing to bear practically unbearable suffering on the cross for you and me, therefore He became the source of eternal salvation for those who believe in Him. Our sins are forgiven! God is now prepared to forgive our sin because He paid the penalty for our sin by dying on the cross.

Jesus' suffering was therefore to your advantage. And this is also true of your own suffering. The more you suffer, the closer you are drawn to Him. Your negative circumstances on earth may remain unchanged when you believe in Jesus, but you will change. During your difficult times God makes you a mirror of his glory, and you say, with the psalmist, that: 'It was good for me to be afflicted so that I might learn your decrees' (Ps 119:71).

❧ Lord, thank you that I learn your instructions through my suffering, so that I can gradually change and radiate more of your glory. Amen.

August 4

An angel's message

READ: DANIEL 10:12–19

Then he [the angel] continued, 'Do not be afraid, Daniel.
Since the first day that you set your mind to gain understanding
and to humble yourself before your God, your words were heard,
and I have come in response to them … Do not be afraid,
O man highly esteemed. Peace! Be strong now; be strong.'
– Daniel 10:12, 19

A few years ago an opthalmic surgeon recommended that our granddaughter undergo a brain scan. This was one of the longest weeks in my life. I once again discovered how much I loved my little namesake and it was unthinkable that she could have a brain tumour. I returned to the above verses in Daniel 10 time and again. These verses also gave us peace of mind so many years ago when my husband had to have a heart bypass operation. We held on to the promise: 'Do not be afraid. All will be well … ' The results of the scan were negative – nothing was wrong with our little love. We were incredibly grateful and happy.

A year later the daughter of a friend was in fact diagnosed with a brain tumour. The tumour was furthermore malignant and after several operations, merely continued to grow. This time all was not well, yet God revealed Himself in a wonderful way to my friend and her family. They remained calm and believing though it must have been extremely difficult for them. God therefore does not heal all diseases – but He gives you the strength to live with your suffering. He wants to do this for you, too.

🐾 Heavenly Father, thank you for the angel's message that your children do not have to fear; that all will be well, even if we are not healed. Amen.

August 5

God plans to prosper you

READ: 1 CORINTHIANS 10:10–14

*No temptation has seized you except what is common to man.
And God is faithful; he will not let you be tempted beyond
what you can bear. But when you are tempted, he will
also provide a way out so that you can stand up under it.*
— *1 Corinthians 10:13*

Whenever you yield to temptation, you always feel awful. This usually happens because you forget how dependent you are on God and you then rely on your own strength. All temptation comes from the devil. God cannot tempt anyone. However, He can and will support you while you are being tempted. When Jesus was being tempted by the devil in the desert, God gave Him the power to resist, and He wants to do the same for you. He therefore promises that you will not be tempted beyond what you can bear, but that He will also provide a way out when you are tempted by the Evil One.

Temptation is unavoidable, but with God's help you can overcome it. God only wants to give you the best. He will never leave his children in the lurch, because He plans prosperity for us: 'For I know the plans I have for you … plans to prosper you and not to harm you, plans to give you hope and a future. Then you will call upon me and come and pray to me, and I will listen to you,' He promised through the prophet Jeremiah (Jer 29:11–12).

God is still faithful. If you are faced with a difficult situation again, He Himself will provide the way out.

❧ Heavenly Father, thank you for your faithfulness, for not permitting me to be tempted beyond what I can bear, but that you are planning my prosperity and a way out. Amen.

August 6

When problems become friends

READ: JAMES 1:2–7

Consider it pure joy, my brothers, whenever you face trials of many kinds,
because you know that the testing of your faith develops perseverance.
Perseverance must finish its work so that you may be
mature and complete, not lacking anything.
– JAMES 1:2–4

Nobody can pass through this life without problems. All of us have to face problems at some time or other. However, problems could become friends! According to James you can rejoice about problems and suffering, because problems strengthen your faith, and they teach you that you cannot survive without God. The stronger your faith in God, the easier it becomes to persevere. When, with God's help, you persevere to the end, you will grow spiritually until, according to James, you will be 'mature and complete, not lacking anything'.

You will definitely experience problems, but with God on your side, you never have to be overwhelmed by them. By his power you are perfectly able to overcome those problems. Only you can decide how you will handle your own problems. Tackle them the way James suggests. Regard problems positively, as challenges. Believe that God will help you to overcome them; persevere in faith, and use your problems to become stronger spiritually, until you will eventually be 'mature, attaining to the whole measure of the fulness of Christ' as promised in Ephesians 4:13.

🌺 Lord, my problems have never been my friends. Thank you that I could learn that problems provide an opportunity to grow; to strengthen my faith and make me persevere so that I can become perfect like You. Amen.

August 7

Acknowledge your dependence

READ: MATTHEW 5:3–12

Blessed are the poor in spirit, for theirs is the kingdom of heaven.
– MATTHEW 5:3

While my Bible study group studied Jesus' Sermon on the Mountain, we agreed that this verse was the crux of the Beatitudes. All the other instructions of Jesus in his Sermon on the Mountain only make sense once we grasp the importance of our absolute dependence on God. In fact, we cannot keep the law without God's help, we could not have been reconciled to Him or our neighbour if Jesus had not made it possible, we cannot be pure or love our enemies, help the poor and forgive those who hurt us or be free from worrying if God does not give us the strength. Yet we still resist dependence – all of us would rather be independent – be in control of our own boat of life.

Do you realise that, without God, you are absolutely useless? Do you also find that you cannot face anything unless He is with you; that you are in mortal danger unless He protects you; that you cannot take any decisions without Him? Only when you reach the stage where you are prepared to leave everything in God's hands, only when you discover that you cannot do anything about your situation, will you have reached the place where God wants you to be. Only then does He promise you that the kingdom of heaven will one day be yours.

❧ Heavenly Father, I find it difficult to acknowledge my total dependence on You, but I realise now that I cannot do anything without You. Make me dependent so that your kingdom will one day be mine. Amen.

August 8

Promise of abundance

READ: PSALM 66:5–12

For you, O Lord, tested us; you refined us like silver.
You brought us into prison and laid burdens on our backs.
You let men ride over our heads; we went through fire and water,
but you brought us to a place of abundance.
– PSALM 66:10–12

Life is never easy. Not even for God's children. The psalmist makes this very clear in Psalm 66: God tests his children, He refines them like silver; He lays a heavy burden on them and even allows others to step on them. However, for the children of God the end is always positive. Even when God permits us to go through fire and water, He ultimately leads us to abundance because heaven awaits us after our suffering on earth. He furthermore promises to be with us when we have to go through the waters, that when we have to pass through the river, the river will not sweep over us; that fire will not scorch and flames will not burn us (cf Isa 43:2).

Although you have to expect your own hurt and suffering, you may look forward to the glorious end which God is preparing for you in heaven even now. Your end will always involve a victory, heavenly abundance and Divine blessing. And this beautiful promise of heavenly glory eventually cancels all suffering on earth, as promised in 2 Corinthians 4:17: 'For our light and momentary troubles are achieving for us an eternal glory that far outweighs them all.'

Lord, You are so merciful! I praise You because my suffering on earth will one day culminate in an all-embracing glory which You are preparing for me in heaven even now. Amen.

August 9

Forsaken by God

READ: PSALM 22

My God, my God, why have you forsaken me? Why are you so far
from saving me, so far from the words of my groaning? O my God,
I cry out by day, but you do not answer, by night, and am not silent …
Do not be far from me, for trouble is near and there is no-one to help.
— PSALM 22:1–2, 11

The psalmist's suffering was so severe that he felt as if God had forsaken him. He pleaded with God to listen to him, because he was in
distress and no-one else could help him. However, in verses 22–23 he
discovered that God had never left him. 'I will declare your name to
my brothers; in the congregation I will praise you. You who fear the
LORD, praise Him!' he rejoiced.

Sometimes when your suffering continues for a long time, it feels
as if God is far from you, as if He no longer hears your prayers or
wants to respond to them. However, Jesus was the only One who was
really forsaken by God. On the cross God punished Him for the sin of
the whole world. Jesus suffered without God's presence or support, so
that you can never be forsaken by God.

'The LORD … is at my right hand, I shall not be shaken,' the psalmist says (Ps 16:8). Because He forsook his Son on the cross, He is always with you – even in your worst trouble, even when you are not
aware of his love and presence. Trust Him.

❧ Heavenly Father, thank you that I know You will never forsake me; that
You will hold me in the hollow of your hand and that You will help me, even
when You feel far away from me. Amen.

August 10

If you are desperate

READ: PSALM 18:6–19

In my distress I called to the Lord; I called to my God for help ...
He reached down from on high and took hold of me; he drew
me out of deep waters ... He brought me out into a spacious
place, he rescued me because he delighted in me.
– PSALM 18:6, 16, 19

When David wrote this psalm, he was extremely distressed. It felt as if he was drowning in 'deep waters'. He pleaded with God to help him. And his cries were not in vain. God heard his cries and responded so that David could testify that God had reached down and drawn him out of the waters. In Psalm 40 he writes about a similar situation: 'I waited patiently for the LORD; he turned to me and heard my cry. He lifted me out of the slimy pit ... and gave me a firm place to stand' (Ps 40:1–2).

All of us experience emergency situations from time to time when we land at the bottom of the pit and cry out to God to help us. When you are in a desperate situation, you can, like David, cry out to God with confidence, knowing that He will listen to you, that He will stretch out his hand to help you. You can trust Him to turn to you and change your circumstances, to set your feet on a rock. However, it is wrong to approach God only when you are desperate. God loves you so much that He wants you to communicate with Him every day, even when all is well.

❧ Father, thank you for listening when I am desperate, thank you for turning to me and saving me. Thank you that I can always rely on You to help me. Amen.

August 11

God is with you in the darkness

READ: EXODUS 20:18–26

Moses said to the people, 'Do not be afraid. God has come to test you,
so that the fear of God will be with you to keep you from sinning.'
The people remained at a distance, while Moses approached
the thick darkness where God was.
– EXODUS 20:20–21

When God gave Moses the Ten Commandments on Mount Sinai, this event was accompanied by the sound of a trumpet, thunder, lightning and smoke. The Israelites were terrified by this revelation of God, and pleaded that Moses should speak to them and not God, because they were sure that they would die should God speak to them personally. However, Moses reassured them, saying that God had come to test them because He wanted them to fear Him. They still feared the dark cloud on the mountain, but Moses went closer because he knew God was in the dark cloud.

Sometimes God allows darkness in your life because He wants to test you. And in this dark cloud you discover that God is with you in the darkness. He furthermore promises to be with you when it turns dark around you. 'You are my lamp, O LORD; the LORD turns my darkness into light,' David said in 2 Samuel 22:29. Job also said to his three friends, 'He reveals the deep things of darkness and brings deep shadows into the light' (Job 12:22).

❧ Heavenly Father, it is good to know that I do not have to fear dark periods in my life because, not only are You with me in the dark cloud, but You will also give me light in the darkness. Amen.

August 12

A song in the night

READ: JOB 35:9–16

Men cry out under a load of oppression;
they plead for relief from the arm of the powerful.
But no-one says, 'Where is God my Maker, who gives songs in the night.'
– JOB 35:9–10

Job's friend Elihu did not have much patience with Job's sob-stories. He should stop complaining and rather ask God's help, because God could give his children songs even during the night, he said. The nightingale's song is usually heard at night and therefore it is so special. In fact, only the children of God manage to 'sing' at all when darkness settles around them. But in our darkest hours, God wants to teach us precious lessons for life. 'I will give you the treasures of darkness,' God promised through Isaiah (Isa 45:3).

William Taylor said, 'We have to understand that, if God wants to teach us to sing a song in the night, He first has to let night 'fall' on us!' He also explained that just as a ship can only be tested in a storm, the power of the gospel can only be fully proved when a Christian experiences the fiery trial.[2] If, with God's help, you can sing a song to Him in a time of darkness, others will be able to see that you are different, that you are prepared to believe in God and trust Him, even in negative circumstances.

❧ Father, it is very dark around me at the moment. It is so dark that I cannot even see a glimmer of light. Please help me to sing a song to You in this darkness. Amen.

August 13

One day at a time

READ: MATTHEW 6:25–34

Therefore do not worry about tomorrow, for tomorrow will worry about itself. Each day has enough trouble of its own … your heavenly Father knows that you need them. But seek first his kingdom and his righteousness, and all these things will be given to you as well.
– Matthew 6:34, 33

In his Sermon on the Mountain, Jesus reassured his disciples that they did not have to worry about all kinds of things. Worry cannot even add another hour to our lives. Furthermore, God is there: He undertakes to care for his children, He knows exactly what we need, and He will also give us what we need at the right time.

One of my friends who is in a wheelchair, bought a flat in a complex for herself and her mom. The complex was selected because it had a sickbay. A few years later, however, the sickbay was moved to another place! When her mom fell ill she had to call a taxi every day to visit her. To my question as to how she managed to cope, she answered, 'I take it one day at a time.'

Don't try to look into the future and then worry about it. It is far better to learn to trust God anew every day, one day at a time. The secret of true peace of mind is actually not to want to see too far into the future. In a hopeless situation you can learn to trust God for today, and leave tomorrow and the day after tomorrow in his hands.

❧ Lord, You know how often I worry about tomorrow. Teach me to leave my future in your hands and to trust You to provide for me. Amen.

August 14

In the fiery furnace of suffering

READ: DANIEL 3:13–29

Then King Nebuchadnezzar leaped to his feet in amazement and asked …
'Weren't there three men that we tied up and threw into the fire? …
I see four men walking around in the fire, unbound and
unharmed and the fourth looks like a son of the gods.'
– DANIEL 3:24–25

When King Nebuchadnezzar had Daniel's three friends bound and thrown into the fiery furnace because they had refused to worship him, a strange thing happened: Instead of burning to death immediately as everyone had expected, the spectators saw them walking around in the fire unbound and unharmed. What was more, a fourth person who looked 'like a son of the gods' was with them in the furnace. King Nebuchadnezzar realised that the God whom Daniel and his three friends worshipped so faithfully had sent his angel to save them, and to prevent them from dying in the fire. He thereupon called to them to come out and commanded that only their God was to be worshipped in future (Dan 3:29).

This incident from our Bible history teaches us an important lesson which we should remember when we face dangerous situations in our personal lives: Suffering cannot destroy you. The Lord does not always deliver you from the 'furnace' of suffering, but He does something even better: He is with you in that furnace, the way the angelic being was with Daniel's friends. You can also hold on to the promise in Isaiah 43:2–3: 'When you walk through the fire, you will not be burned; the flames will not set you ablaze. For I am the LORD, your God … '

❧ Heavenly Father, I praise You because You are able to assist and preserve me in the furnace of suffering, although You do not always protect me against it. Amen.

August 15

Suffering develops obedience

READ: 1 PETER 4:1–13

*Therefore, since Christ suffered in his body, arm yourselves also with
the same attitude, because he who has suffered in his body is done
with sin. As a result, he does not live the rest of his earthly life
for evil human desires, but rather for the will of God.*
– 1 PETER 4:1–2

Suffering in the lives of God's children could make them more obedient so that, after the suffering, their lives will no longer be controlled by sin, but they will now obey the will of God. The translation in *The Message* defines this beautifully: 'Since Jesus went through everything you're going through and more, learn to think like Him. Think of your suffering as a weaning from that old sinful habit of always expecting to get your own way. Then you'll be able to live out your days free to pursue what God wants instead of being tyrannized by what you want.'

Jesus' suffering on earth was indescribable and He obeyed the command of his Father to the letter. '… [He] became obedient to death – even death on a cross!' Paul wrote to the church at Philippi (Phil 2:8).

That suffering makes us more obedient is a Biblical fact. In Psalm 119:67 David confessed, 'Before I was afflicted I went astray, but now I obey your word.' If you therefore have to suffer you will gradually discover that the suffering is making you a more obedient child of God. For that reason you can praise God for your suffering.

❧ Father, thank you for the lesson I could learn: that suffering makes me more obedient to You. I want to do the things which please You for the rest of my life. Please show me your will. Amen.

August 16

And if you do not suffer?

I have told you these things,
so that in me you may have peace.
In this world you will have trouble.
But take heart! I have overcome the world.
– JOHN 16:33

Joni Eareckson-Tada, the American author who was paralysed as a result of a diving accident as a teenager, wrote a remarkable book about the positive effect of suffering in one's life. Since she herself has had to suffer severely, she has excellent advice for those who are struggling at the moment. One day she was confronted by one of her friends who wanted to know what happens to those people who do not suffer. Do they miss the lessons in which suffering teaches God's children to make them stronger?

I must admit that I have also wondered at times why I am so blessed personally. I am happy and healthy, all is well with those I love, I have a work which I love and which I find fulfilling. Life, for me, is indeed a feast! Sometimes all this prosperity makes me anxious and makes me wonder whether my suffering is still waiting somewhere in the future.

When you are really blessed, never forget that everything you have comes from God. Know that your happiness and prosperity are also gifts which you receive from Him. Never become so self-confident in times of prosperity that you forget that you are totally dependent on God.

❧ Lord, I want to thank You for all the blessings I receive from You, that I have never experienced serious catastrophes or distress. Grant that I will always be filled with gratitude and be aware of my dependence on You. Amen.

August 17

An infusion of strength

READ: PHILIPPIANS 4:10–20

I can do everything through him who gives me strength ...
To our God and Father be glory for ever and ever. Amen.
– PHILIPPIANS 4:13, 20

As soon as something crops up in my life which I know I cannot handle on my own, I read Philippians 4:13 – in all the Bible translations I can lay my hands on! 'I have strength for all things in Christ who empowers me. I am ready for anything and equal to anything through Him who infuses inner strength into me. (That is, I am self-sufficient in Christ's suffiency),' reads *The Amplified Bible.*[3]

It always gives me tremendous peace of mind knowing that, although I can't, God is omnipotent, that He can and will. All I have to do is to ask his help, trust Him and leave the problem in his hands. By his power, the problems have always been solved.

When you come to the end of your strength again, go to God to be infused with his strength. He promises that you can do all things through Him who gives you the strength. Whether it is a handicapped child, an unbelieving husband, an unhappy marriage, sickness, pain, an ungrateful family or serious financial problems – whatever is sapping your strength, you can overcome all things when God makes his infinite power available to you. Pray with Paul, 'Now to him who is able to do immeasurably more than all we ask or imagine, according to his power that is at work within us, to him be glory in the church and in Christ Jesus throughout all generations, for ever and ever! Amen' (Eph 3:20).

❧ Lord, I desperately need another infusion of your strength. I praise You for being able to do much more than I can pray or imagine, and I want to give You all the glory. Amen.

August 18

Beyond tears

READ: 1 SAMUEL 30:1–6

So David and his men wept aloud until they had no strength left to weep …
each one was bitter in spirit because of his sons and daughters.
But David found strength in the LORD his God.
– 1 SAMUEL 30:4, 6

At this stage of his life David had already been persecuted by his enemies for ten years. He had a number of followers with him … not quite the cream of his army, only those who were prepared to throw in their lot with him. One day when they returned from a raid, they discovered that the Amalekites had raided their camp and had taken their wives and children captive. They wept until they had no strength left to weep, reads our passage of Scripture. Then, to crown it all, David's men turned against him and threatened to stone him. Although David could not understand the Lord's purpose with these events, he nevertheless sought the Lord. In the end David and his men pursued the Amalekites and defeated them. All the women and children who had been taken captive were rescued unharmed and they also brought back the herds and flocks of the Amalekites (1 Sam 30).

If something happens to you which is so terrible that you feel as if you are in the same situation as David, that you have no more tears left, that you have no strength left to weep, ask the Lord's help. He will help you like He helped David. When you reach the end of your strength, you will find his strength when you turn to Him. If He is with you, the end is always positive, regardless of how bad the situation appears to be.

❧ Lord, at the moment I also feel beyond all tears. Please intervene in my situation and help me like you helped David. Amen.

August 19

Pain is vital!

READ: JEREMIAH 10:17–22

Woe to me because of my injury! My wound is incurable!
Yet I said to myself, 'This is my sickness, and I must endure it.'
— *JEREMIAH 10:19*

Jeremiah was a prophet who suffered terribly and therefore the one person, apart from Job, from whom we can learn the most about pain. Jeremiah found it difficult to come to terms with his pain: 'My splendour is gone and all that I had hoped from the LORD,' he complained in Lamentations 3:18. But then he discovered time and again that God's compassions never fail, that they were new every morning (Lam 3:22–23).

Dr Paul Brand, the brilliant doctor who worked among lepers for many years, said that pain (about which all of us complain) is vital for our continued existence. Lepers become blind and lose their limbs not as a result of their illness, but because they cannot feel pain. 'Most people regard pain as an enemy,' Dr Brand wrote, 'but, as proved by my leprous patients, pain compels us to pay attention to those things which threaten the body. Without pain coronaries, strokes, ruptured appendixes and stomach ulcers would occur without warning. Who would visit a doctor if it weren't for the warnings of pain?'[4]

God's children have one consolation in the midst of painful situations: God knows when we are suffering, and He is with us in the midst of our worst pain and distress. If your own pain becomes too much, trust that God's grace will also be enough for you and hold on to the promise that all your suffering will one day be over for ever.

❧ Heavenly Father, I am battling to bear my own burden of suffering at the moment. Thank you that your grace is sufficient for me, and thank you that this suffering will not continue for ever. Amen.

August 20

Followers and cross-bearers

READ: 2 TIMOTHY 3:10–17

Everyone who wants to live a godly life in Christ Jesus will be
persecuted, while evil men and impostors will go from bad to
worse, deceiving and being deceived. But as for you, continue
in what you have learned and have become convinced of …
– 2 TIMOTHY 3:12–14

Paul warned Timothy that those who were really committed Christians would be persecuted by others, while those who rejected God would go from bad to worse. Jesus Himself admitted that his followers would not be immune from suffering on earth, but at the same time He promised that He would be with them in their suffering, that they could come to Him when the burdens of the world became too much for them, because his burden was light and his yoke easy (cf Matt 11:28–29). Sometimes it is difficult to understand why God's children have to suffer while people who openly reject Him are successful.

If you are a follower of Jesus, you will obviously also be a cross-bearer like your Master. 'Since you have kept my command to endure patiently, I will also keep you from the hour of trial that is going to come upon the whole world to test those who live on the earth,' reads God's message to the church in Philadelphia (Rev 3:10). Although you probably won't escape persecution either, God promises to keep you and support you when life becomes difficult. For that reason you can trust Him fully in times of trouble.

❧ Heavenly Father, make me willing to be a cross-bearer for You in the world. Thank you for the promise that You will hold me when I am battling. Amen.

August 21

From trial to joy

READ: 1 PETER 4:12–19

Dear friends, do not be surprised at the painful trial you are
suffering, as though something strange were happening to you.
But rejoice that you participate in the sufferings of Christ,
so that you may be overjoyed when his glory is revealed.
– 1 PETER 4:12–13

Suffering is often called a painful trial in the Bible. Peter said we should not be surprised at the painful trials. We should actually expect them, since they are not something strange. No-one will miss this painful trial. It does, however, have a positive side. Just as fire is used to refine metals such as gold and silver to remove the impurities, God uses suffering to refine us, to remove sin from our lives, so that we will return to Him.

Through the prophet Zechariah God announced that He would refine Jerusalem: two-thirds of the disobedient people would be killed so that only one-third would remain. 'This third I will bring into the fire; I will refine them like silver and test them like gold. They will call on my name and I will answer them; I will say, "They are my people," and they will say, "The LORD is our God"' (Zech 13:9).

When you suffer a fiery trial again, know that God is permitting it because He wants to refine you so that you will call to Him and He will answer your prayers; so that your relationship with Him will be renewed and He will turn your fiery trial into joy.

❧ Lord, You sometimes use suffering to refine me, to lead me back to You. Thank you that I know that You will always turn my fiery trial into joy. Amen.

August 22

Suffering is good for you

READ: ROMANS 5:1–11

We also rejoice in our sufferings, because we know that suffering produces
perseverance; perseverance, character; and character, hope. And hope
does not disappoint us, because God has poured out his love into
our hearts by the Holy Spirit, whom he has given us.
– ROMANS 5:3–5

Suffering is good for God's children, Paul wrote to the church in Rome. He also listed the virtues which suffering would key into our lives: perseverance, character and hope.

The frangipani tree in our garden used to bear only a few flowers every year. We watered and fertilised this tree more and more in the hope that it would produce an abundance of flowers, but in vain. I would look at the frangipanis along the tarred road – they were covered in flowers – and I wondered why our tree refused to flower. However, after the water restrictions in 2004 something very odd happened: For the very first time our tree was also covered in hundreds of blooms. Only when I read in a book on gardening that shrubs like hibiscus and frangipani flowered best when they were starved of water and nutrition did I understand. They bear more flowers when they struggle so that the plant can be propagated.

The frangipani tree reminded me of our core verse. The more you suffer, the more 'flowers' you will bear for Jesus because your problems force you to spend more time with Him, to pray more, and to do more in-depth Bible study. And the better you know Him, the more He will pour his love into your heart.

✤ Lord, thank you that suffering in my life makes my relationship with You more intimate so that perseverance, character and hope can flower in my life. I now see that the suffering was to my advantage. Amen.

August 23

Suffering is a training camp

READ: ISAIAH 30:19–29

Although the Lord gives you the bread of adversity and
the water of affliction, your teachers will be hidden
no more; with your own eyes you will see them.
– ISAIAH 30:20

Throughout history God's people often found that He allowed them to suffer because He wanted to teach them. He also pointed out the right way whenever they got lost. 'Whether you turn to the right or to the left, your ears will hear a voice behind you, saying, "This is the way; walk in it"' (Isa 30:21). The Lord therefore let his people suffer because He wanted them to return to Him. When they obeyed God, turned away from their sinful ways, and returned to Him, they were always blessed again.

'God still teaches his children by allowing them to suffer. God does not train his soldiers in comfortable tents, but by sending them on long marches and exhausting boot camps. He lets them cross strong currents, swim through rivers, climb mountains and march many exhausting kilometres with heavy backpacks,' Spurgeon wrote.[5]

The suffering which God therefore permits in your life is his training camp where He teaches you to be fit, to turn back from the wrong way you are going. If you are willing to listen to Him, and make a U-turn, back to Him, you will also experience his blessing in your life.

❧ Lord, I don't like being trained! Make me willing to listen to You and to turn back when You expect me to so that You can bless me again. Amen.

August 24

Does suffering serve a purpose?

READ: 2 CORINTHIANS 1:3–11

We were under great pressure, far beyond our ability to endure,
so that we despaired even of life. Indeed, in our hearts we felt
the sentence of death. But this happened that we might not
rely on ourselves but on God, who raises the dead.
– 2 CORINTHIANS 1:8–9

At times the suffering of Paul and his company was so severe that they 'despaired even of life'. But these disasters occurred so that they would not rely on themselves but on God, he wrote to the church in Corinth.

In the year 2000 the world was shattered by a tragedy in Colorado when 15 pupils and a teacher of a local high school were shot and killed by two racist teenagers. Can any good result from such a terrible tragedy, people asked themselves. Yes, Philip Yancy maintains.[6]

The membership of youth groups in the city grew after this tragedy, the father of one of the victims became an evangelist, while the father of another led a campaign to improve weapon-control. God can create something good even from a very evil deed. For this reason He can also let all things work together for good in your own life, even those things which left you shocked and perhaps embittered. Trust God to let all things work together for your good – after all, He promises to do this in his Word (Rom 8:28).

❧ Lord, I really cannot see how You will eventually be able to use the disaster in my own life to my advantage. However, I know that You have shown me that I cannot live without You. Amen.

August 25

To see God

READ: JOB 42:1–6

My ears had heard of you, but now my eyes have seen you.
Therefore I despise myself and repent in dust and ashes.
– JOB 42:5–6

Job was a God-fearing man; so much so that even God was proud of him. However, Job only 'saw' God once everything had been taken away from him. Until his suffering his knowledge of God was mainly hearsay knowledge. However, after his suffering he knew God in a totally different way. God had become a reality to him. He could communicate with God directly, with confidence; he was even able to pray for his friends who had actually left him in the lurch. And when this happened, God turned Job's circumstances around and blessed him even more than before. The incomprehensible disasters in his life eventually brought him more blessings than Job could have imagined.

One of my friends, who has a severely handicapped child, told me that she could never have faced the responsibility if she had known in advance what was awaiting her. Yet she confesses that God provides her with the necessary strength day after day. In her difficult circumstances she has come to know and love God in a completely new way. Through your own suffering you will also see God in a new way, because your pain opens your eyes so that you can see God face to face.

Lord, thank you that my suffering has enabled me to see You face to face for the first time and has let me get to know You in a new way. Amen.

August 26

Life is unfair!

READ: PSALM 58

Do you rulers indeed speak justly?
Do you judge uprightly among men?
No, in your heart you devise injustice,
and your hands mete out violence on the earth.
– PSALM 58:1–2

You don't have to be very old before you discover that life is actually very unfair! At school the bright ones achieve high marks effortlessly, while those who are not as well-endowed with grey cells have to work very hard. Our current system also makes it hard for us to swallow the injustice sometimes committed in the name of affirmative action in certain workplaces. Like Job and David before you, you cannot understand the apparent injustice of people prospering although they pay no attention to God, while 'good Christians' battle to survive.

'If it is absolutely vital that you know the answers to all the questions in life, forget the journey,' Madame Jean de Guyon wrote, 'you will never make it, because it is a journey of the unfathomable – of unanswered questions, enigmas, things which defy understanding, and above all, injustice.'[7]

Therefore, do not expect to be treated justly; to be rewarded for your input. Here on earth things will unfortunately remain unfair and you will definitely not receive answers to all your Whys. If you have a problem with this 'injustice', it is best to come to terms with the fact that life is not fair. One day, after your death, you will reap the fruit of your good life.

❧ Heavenly Father, You know that I have often wondered about the injustice in life. Thank you that You are absolutely just. Amen.

August 27

Hold on to God!

READ: PSALM 116

*The cords of death entangled me, the anguish of the grave
came upon me; I was overcome by trouble and sorrow.
Then I called on the name of the LORD: 'O LORD, save me!'
… I believed, therefore I said, 'I am greatly afflicted.'*
– PSALM 116:3–4, 10

In a previous century a Scottish minister who had lost his wife very suddenly, preached an exceptionally emotional sermon in which he confessed before his congregation that he could not understand how people who experience a terrible disaster or loss could reject their faith. 'Those of you who are in the sunlight may believe in faith, but we who are in the shade simply must believe it. We have nothing else,' he said.[8]

Many people have to experience the shock of a tragedy, illness or death in their lives before they realise what their faith means to them. When nothing else can help, we always reach out to God, just to discover that He is already waiting impatiently to have mercy upon us. 'I believed; therefore I said, "I am greatly afflicted." And in my dismay I said, "All men are liars",' the psalmist said in Psalm 116:10–11. Follow the psalmist's example when you experience a crisis again. Hold on to God. Believe in Him. There is actually nothing else you can do. And God has never failed any of his children who trusted in Him. He has always been with you in every crisis, and his everlasting arms were always underneath you.

❧ Lord my God, I praise You that I can continue to believe in You in crisis situations, because I have found that You always help me. Amen.

August 28

Jesus experienced suffering

READ: JOHN 18:1–11

*Then Simon Peter, who had a sword, drew it and struck the high
priest's servant, cutting off his right ear ... Jesus commanded Peter,
'Put your sword away! Shall I not drink the cup the Father has given me?'*
– JOHN 18:10–11

After Jesus had pleaded urgently in the Garden of Gethsemane that
his Father should take away from Him the cup of suffering, He was
nevertheless taken away by a company of soldiers. The impulsive
Peter drew his sword and cut off the ear of the high priest's servant,
Malchus. Thereupon Jesus said, 'Put your sword away! Shall I not
drink the cup the Father has given me?'

If you have thought that your faith would protect you against suffering, look at Jesus' life. God did not protect his Son against suffering while He was on earth, not even against death on a cross.
However, Jesus' suffered for a reason: He died in your place so that
God will not hold you responsible for your sin; God also permits
suffering in your own life for a reason: to make you stronger spiritually; to let you realise that you cannot live without God; to draw you
closer to God.

Jesus was prepared to drink his cup of suffering so that God's will
could be done in his life. What about you? Would you be able, at this
stage, to bear the suffering in your life to become spiritually stronger?

❧ Lord Jesus, How great You are - You were willing to drink your cup of
suffering so that God could forgive my sin. Please make me willing to allow
my suffering to draw me closer to You. Amen.

August 29

God's comfort

READ: ISAIAH 40:1–11

Comfort, comfort my people, says your God.
– ISAIAH 40:1

The prophet Isaiah assured the people of God who were in exile at that stage, that He would give them an escape. 'Comfort, comfort my people, says your God. Speak tenderly to Jerusalem and proclaim to her that her hard service has been completed, that her sin has been paid for, that she has received from the LORD's hand double for all her sins.' God still offers his comfort to his children who are suffering. However, He asks that we will pass on his comfort to others who may need it.

Henri Jowett believes that you have to be trained to comfort others: 'Such training makes heavy demands because if you really want to go all out, you have to undergo the same sufferings which cost blood and tears for countless hearts. Your own life then becomes the hospital ward where you will be taught the holy art of comforting. You will be wounded so that you can learn how to apply first aid to the wounded while your own wounds are treated by the Great Healer. God does not comfort us so that we can be comforted, but so that we can comfort others,' he wrote.[9]

Should you ever need comfort, ask God to comfort you. He is always available in emergency situations to offer you his comfort and give you an escape.

❧ Father, I now see that I can only learn to comfort others once I have also suffered. Thank you that You are using this hurt in my life to turn me into a comforter. Amen.

August 30

Be of good courage!

READ: EPHESIANS 3:7–13

In him and through faith in him we may approach God with freedom
and confidence. I ask you, therefore, not to be discouraged because
of my sufferings for you, which are your glory.
— *EPHESIANS 3:12–13*

Paul requested the church in Ephesus not to become discouraged because he was suffering for their sake – they should rather regard it as an honour. Paul wrote his letter to the Ephesians while he was in jail – his circumstances were critical, but he was still able to encourage the church and refused to become discouraged. In 2 Corinthians 7:4 he confessed, 'In all our troubles my joy knows no bounds.'

Sometimes we become discouraged about the suffering of other Christians, sometimes about our own. Dozens of things make us discouraged: problems at work; illness, marital problems, disobedient children, financial problems … If you belong to God, you can, like Paul, refuse to become discouraged. Usually the devil whispers in your ear that you are in the slough of Despond. Confront him: you know, don't you, that Jesus conquered him on the cross, and that you can also conquer him in the power of God. God is still on your side, and his promise in Jeremiah 31:25 still applies to you personally: 'I will refresh the weary and satisfy the faint.' Ask Him to do this for you, too!

❧ Lord Jesus, I praise You for having conquered the devil, and that I therefore do not have to yield to the temptation of discouragement. Thank you that I may rely on You to fill me with fresh courage. Amen.

August 31

Lord God,

I praise You for discovering that joy
and sorrow are two sides of the same coin.
Thank you for being with me in difficult times;
that my suffering takes me closer to You
and once again makes me realise how
utterly dependent I am on You.
Thank you that, ultimately, You let all things
work to my advantage because I am being changed
in such a way that I can radiate more of your glory.
I know that my suffering on earth
makes me more obedient
and that it will one day lead
to the all-encompassing glory
which You are preparing for me in heaven.
How good You are!
You are with me in times of darkness,
You promise to help me sing a song to You
even in darkness.
Help me to live one day at a time,
to tackle my crises in your power.
I now know that I need pain in my life,
that suffering strengthens my relationship with You;
and that You will eventually turn my fiery trial into joy.
I realise that my suffering has enabled me to see You.
Thank you that I may hold on to You in the midst of suffering,
so that I can experience your comforting
and can pass it on to others.
Thank you for promising me new strength and power
time and again.

Amen

Wealth

Wealth and possessions are regarded as very important in the world in which we live. In 500 AD, a certain Jacob of Sarug said that worshipping Mammon, or Money, was the most important form of idolatry the devil was using at a time in which the ancient gods had lost their appeal for the christianised population!

Nevertheless, most Christians do not like to discuss their finances – is it perhaps because we feel guilty about the way we think about our money? Jesus saw money in a totally different light. He advised the rich young man to give away all his possessions and follow Him; He praised Mary when she poured expensive perfume on his feet; He compared Israel's wealthiest king to wildflowers!

How important are your money and possessions to you? Stop your furious chasing after securities and, this month, discover what true wealth means and learn how to use your money in the best possible way – in serving God's kingdom.

September

The rich young man

READ: LUKE 18:18–25

*Indeed, it is easier for a camel to go through the eye of a needle
than for a rich man to enter the kingdom of God.*
– LUKE 18:25

When a wealthy young ruler came to Jesus and asked Him how he
could inherit eternal life, his answer shocked the young man: 'Sell
everything you have and give it to the poor ... Then come, follow
me.' (Luke 18:22). This answer disappointed the young man because he was so wealthy that he couldn't face the idea of parting
with his possessions.

The story of the rich young man scares us: What would you do
if Jesus expected you to sell all your possessions and give the money
to the poor? The practical implications of such a step are incomprehensible. However, this is not what Jesus expects of us literally. His
response to the rich young man seems rather unfair to us, but Jesus
was merely testing whether his wealth was more important to him
than his love for Jesus. The rich young man did not pass the test. To
him money was an idol which he had to get rid of before he could
follow Jesus – and he was not prepared to do this. God does not
expect you to part with every cent you possess – but He wants to
know whether your possessions are more important to you than
your love for God.

✤ Lord Jesus, please forgive me when my money and possessions are also
at times more important to me than You. Help me not to idolise my money,
but always to put You first. Amen.

September 1

Zacchaeus

READ: LUKE 19:1–10

But Zacchaeus stood up and said to the Lord, 'Look, Lord.
Here and now I give half of my possessions to the poor, and if I have
cheated anybody out of anything, I will pay back four times the amount.'
– LUKE 19:8

Unlike the rich young ruler, Zacchaeus offered to make his money available to Jesus. When he met Jesus, his whole life and attitude towards money changed. He undertook to give half his possessions to the poor and pay back four times the amount to anyone he had cheated. At the time tax collectors were notorious for their avarice. In fact, they were prepared to betray their own people by collecting taxes for the Romans and in the process they filled their own coffers.

However, Zacchaeus' love for Jesus was much greater than his love for money. He set Jesus above his money without even being asked to do so. Jesus saw that Zacchaeus' heart was right: 'Today salvation has come to this house,' He said.

Although Zacchaeus was also wealthy, his wealth did not come between him and Jesus. To him his relationship with Jesus was more important than his money. Jesus did not judge the rich young man because he was wealthy, but because he was not prepared to use his wealth the way God wanted him to use it.

What about you? Are you prepared to use your money for the extension of God's Kingdom?

❧ Lord, forgive me for being so slow in using my money to further your Kingdom in the world. Please make me more generous and willing to help others. Amen.

September 2

God and Money

READ: MATTHEW 6:24

No-one can serve two masters. Either he will hate the one and
love the other, or he will be devoted to the one and despise
the other. You cannot serve both God and Money.
– MATTHEW 6:24

In his Sermon on the Mountain Jesus named money after an idol –
Mammon. He personified wealth to emphasise its power. Money is
never merely a neutral asset, but something which could claim your
whole being, get its claws into you, and stir a love for it in you. Money
could play such an important role in your life because you could develop a love for it so that it eventually becomes more important to
you than God.

Christians should always be on the alert regarding the power of
money. Guard against the avarice which money could stir in you. The
more money you have, the more careful you should be that your
money does not eventually have you in its power so that you bow the
knee before Mammon. The life of every person has room for one God
only, and the God you worship is a God who demands undivided
devotion (Exod 20:5). He will not surrender his place in your life to
the god of money. It is furthermore impossible to make room for
both God and the god of money in your life. You will have to choose
the one who is the most important to you.

However, all of us need money. When you use your money to proclaim the gospel and to help others who have less than you have, you
use your money the way God wants you to.

❧ Father, please show me how to use my money in your service so that
your Kingdom can be extended. Amen.

September 3

Wealth and the kingdom

READ: MATTHEW 6:24–34

But seek first his kingdom and his righteousness,
and all these things will be given to you as well.
– MATTHEW 6:33

It has now become time to ask yourself whether you are really seeking the Kingdom of God or whether your material assets are still more important to you. Are you serving God or the god of money? Remember, you cannot serve both simultaneously or equally. Although worldly treasures are unimportant and temporary, they are still more important to most Christians than the Kingdom. 'Now you know why the rich do not really long for heaven. The problem is not that they cannot enter the gate of the new Jerusalem because they are carrying too many possessions on their backs. The problem is that they do not want to go in. They are not looking forward to heaven, because they feel they already have heaven on earth. They are not interested in the place the Lord Jesus has gone ahead to prepare for us. They are perfectly happy where they are,' Piet Naude writes.[1]

However, Jesus promised that if you put his Kingdom first, He would give you all the material securities you need. Here it concerns the giving of yourself totally. Seek first the Kingdom of God, give yourself to Him first, and then He will give you everything you need. If you are willing to give everything, you also receive everything. God does not demand anything, but He offers his love.

❧ Lord, I want to accept your offer of love. Please make me willing to give myself to You knowing that You will then give me everything I need. Amen.

September 4

Enough is as good as a feast!

READ: PROVERBS 30:5–9

Give me neither poverty nor riches, but give me only my daily bread.
Otherwise I may have too much and disown you and say,
'Who is the LORD?' Or I may become poor and steal,
and so dishonour the name of my God.
– PROVERBS 30:8–9

A well-known proverb says: Enough is as good as a feast!

Unfortunately very few people are content with 'enough'. It is human to strive to have more and better things, to try to 'keep up with the Joneses'. The harder we work and the more securities we have, the harder we struggle to get even more and the stronger the hold our money has on us.

God's children must always remember that our money is only a loan which God gives us and which we should invest in his Kingdom voluntarily. You and I do not own our investments, shares and bank balances, we are merely the stewards of God's possessions. Rather than asking how much of the money I have earned I am willing to give God, I should ask how much of God's money which He makes available to me am I prepared to plough back into his kingdom?

When your investments and money increase, you should see red lights flickering. Pay attention to the warning in Psalm 62:10b: 'Though your riches increase, do not set your heart on them'.

❧ Lord, I confess that I am not satisfied merely with enough. Please forbid that my possessions will become too important to me. Amen.

September 5

Learn to be generous

READ: MATTHEW 5:38–42

*Give to the one who asks you, and do not turn
away from the one who wants to borrow from you.*
— MATTHEW 5:42

People with begging letters or homeless people begging for food, are
forever approaching homes without security fencing and security
gates. It is practically impossible to give food to everybody who
knocks. But what are we to do about Jesus' command that we should
be willing to give to those who ask? I'm afraid that, where possible,
Christians are expected to give if people are in need.

One of the best things to do with our money is to give it away,
Richard Foster says in his book, *Money, Sex and Power*.[2] Giving is
also one of our best weapons against the power of the god of money.
And, according to Jesus Himself, if we see people who are hungry
and we give them something to eat; if we see people without clothes
and give them clothes; if we provide for the needs of those who have
less than we have, it indirectly means we are doing these good deeds
for Him personally. 'I tell you the truth, whatever you did for one of
the least of these brothers of mine, you did for me,' reads Matthew
25:40. If someone knocks on your door again, decide to give to those
who ask you for something.

Heavenly Father, thank you that I am in a position to help others. Grant
that I will always know that what I am doing for them, I am actually doing
for You. Amen.

September 6

Give with the right attitude

READ: MATTHEW 6:1–4

When you give to the needy, do not let your left hand know what
your right hand is doing, so that your giving may be in secret.
Then your Father, who sees what is done in secret, will reward you.
– MATTHEW 6:3–4

Some people like giving – but at the same time they want everybody to see what they are doing for others. In this way they want others to admire them. However, in his Sermon on the Mountain, Jesus says explicitly that you are not to give with a view to being seen by others. If you give to others your attitude must be right. Give because you care, not to be seen. We cannot do good to others if we do not have a heart for their needs. Before we can meet the needs of others, we have to be aware of those needs.

At the moment so many people in our country have nothing to eat, or they sleep cold. Much of the violence is caused by these needs: People break in and steal because they cannot afford the most basic foodstuff. We become discouraged and angry and criminals indeed get away with murder at present, but perhaps we could do something about crime by being more generous.

Poor people are not the only ones who need your help. Some people have financial means, but need your physical and emotional help and involvement. If you cannot give money, perhaps you can offer to help and get involved with the lonely.

❧ Lord, please give me compassion for those around me and show me where You need me and my money the most at the moment. Amen.

September 7

Treasures in heaven

READ: MATTHEW 6:19–21

Do not store up for yourselves treasures on earth, where moth and rust destroy, and where thieves break in and steal. But store up for yourselves treasures in heaven … where your treasure is, there your heart will be also.
– MATTHEW 6:19–21

People become so attached to their worldly 'treasures'! We live in a very affluent community. According to statistics, Somerset West has the most millionaires per square metre in the country. On Sundays my husband and I feast our eyes on the luxury cars parked at our church – yet the budget of our congregation often does not balance. The reason for this imbalance is that many members of the congregation are so busy increasing their treasures on earth, that they forget about their treasures in heaven.

Treasures on earth are never a very good investment – particularly not in our current society. Burglaries and thefts, despite alarm systems and security gates, can easily 'relieve' you of your treasures. It is far better to invest in heavenly treasures – ultimately such investments are much more precious.

In his book *Money, Sex and Power*, Richard Foster writes that if we want treasures in heaven one day, we should invest in the lives of people here on earth because although we cannot take our money with us, there will be people in heaven.[3] Therefore, look for people who need your help – in this way you will collect treasures which you can take to heaven with you. And remember – your heart will be where your treasure is!

❧ Heavenly Father, I'm afraid most of my 'treasures' are still on earth. Help me to invest in people so that I will one day have a treasure in heaven. Amen.

September 8

Depend on God

READ: JAMES 4:13–17

Now listen, you who say, 'Today or tomorrow we will go to this or
that city, spend a year there, carry on business and make money.'
Why, you do not even know what will happen tomorrow … Instead,
you ought to say, 'If it is the Lord's will, we will live and do this or that.'
— JAMES 4:13–15

Nobody likes being told what they should do with their money and possessions. And the wealthier we are, the more independent we become. We want to decide how we will accumulate our money (sometimes in dishonest ways!), and most people leave God out of the equation completely. We even think we could easily get along without Him. The Lord nevertheless holds our finances in his hand. It is his will that you should submit to Him when you take decisions regarding your business transactions, on the way you run your business, or on what you are going to spend your money.

It is quite ironic that most people who are prepared to give to others are usually those who do not have much themselves. Everybody who has participated in street collections knows that usually those who do not have much, put money in the money boxes while the wealthy walk past, pretending not to notice the collector.

You are 'blessed' if you realise how dependent you are on God, Jesus said in his Sermon on the Mountain. He promised that He Himself would care for those who were dependent. Do consult God about your financial decisions and plans in future: pray first and then invest!

❧ Father, forgive me for being so independent. Help me to discuss my financial decisions with You in future, and grant that I will rely on You totally. Amen.

September 9

Do not despise the poor

READ: JAMES 2:1–9

Listen, my dear brothers: Has not God chosen those who are poor
in the eyes of the world to be rich in faith and to inherit the kingdom
he promised those who love him? But you have insulted the poor …
– JAMES 2:5–6

People and organisations are inclined to discriminate against people if they are poor. In our society banks treat the rich much better than the poor – we therefore discriminate on the basis of money and possessions. However, God sees people and money in a different way. He does not write off people if they do not have much money. In fact, He actually chooses people who are poor in the eyes of the world to be rich in faith. These are the people He has promised would inherit the Kingdom, James wrote.

What do you look at when you assess people? Do you look at who they are or at what they have? Never look down upon those who have less than you have – rather try to help them in the way God helped you to live the way you are living. If you are wealthy, be careful not to miss your purpose in life, do not let your money take God's place in your life. You should also bear the extra responsibility which wealth places on your shoulders. God blesses you to be a blessing to others: 'From the one who has been entrusted with much, much more will be asked,' Jesus said in Luke 12:48.

❧ Heavenly Father, please forgive me for also having discriminated against people who have less than I. Help me to meet my financial responsibilites. Amen.

September 10

Put your money where your heart is!

READ: JAMES 2:14–17

What good is it, my brothers, if a man claims to have faith but has no deeds? Can such faith save him? Suppose a brother or sister is without clothes and daily food. If one of you says to him, 'Go, I wish you well; keep warm and well fed,' but does nothing about his physical needs, what good is it?
– JAMES 2:14–16

It's useless to confess God but ignore brothers or sisters who need food and clothes. Such a faith is dead, James says. In 1 John 3:18, John warns that our faith should not merely be words and lip service, but that we should follow up our confession with sincere deeds.

Your budget is a theological document. It indicates the things you idolise, says an anonymous quotation. The things on which you spend your money indeed reflect the condition of your heart. And the hearts of God's children must be right – also with regard to their financial affairs.

Three things need conversion, Martin Luther said: your heart, your mind and your wallet. Consider your personal spending patterns. What do you spend the most money on? Stop accumulating for the future, rather invest in God's kingdom. Remember, the more money you have, the more difficult it will be to choose for God. 'Though your riches increase, do not set your heart on them,' reads Psalm 62:10.

❧ Heavenly Father, I realise that my purse needs conversion urgently. Make me aware of the need around me and make me willing to do something about it. Amen.

September 11

The poor and the rich

READ: JAMES 1:9–11

The brother in humble circumstances ought to take pride in his high position.
But the one who is rich should take pride in his low position,
because he will pass away like a wild flower.
– JAMES 1:9–10

The rich and the poor will always be with us. Having few possessions is actually good for one's faith – when you know you cannot meet your own needs, it teaches you to trust God for your tomorrows. Wealth, on the other hand, can be dangerous, because it makes you self-sufficient – the more money you have, the less you need God. That's what you think. Those who are rich in earthly possessions must always remember that their wealth is transitory.

Jesus taught his disciples to pray for their daily bread, but few people who hold this book in their hands are not assured of their daily bread. Apart from bread we also have lots of food in our pantries, fridges and freezers. In gratitude for all this, you should be prepared to reach out to others who have less than you and help them.

If you have less money than you would like at the moment and if you cannot afford everything you need, remind God of his promise to care for you. 'My God will meet all your needs according to his glorious riches in Christ Jesus,' Paul promised the church in Philippi (Phil 4:19).

❧ Lord, thank you for your promise that You will provide in all my needs - when I prosper as well as when I need material things. Amen.

September 12

Rich in good deeds

READ: 1 TIMOTHY 6:17–19

*Command those who are rich in this present world ... not to put their
hope in wealth, which is so uncertain, but to put their hope in God, who
richly provides us with everything for our enjoyment. Command them to
do good, to be rich in good deeds, and to be generous and willing to share.*
– 1 Timothy 6:17–18

The retirement centre where my mom lives has an annual 'open day'
when the children of all the residents join in the celebrations – an in-
formal bazaar where biscuits and rusks, jams and canned fruit as well
as beautiful handicrafts are sold. Most of the items are made by the
residents themselves. This year, before the sales started, I saw a little
old lady sitting at her own table on the verandah. I immediately spot-
ted the delicious salt-rising bread and ripe guavas (which my husband
loves but which are practically unobtainable these days). When I
asked the little lady why she was sitting all alone with her products instead of selling inside with the others, she told me that half her profit
was earmarked for the Sudan because she helped to support two mis-
sionaries there. She was obviously not well-to-do, yet, like the widow
at the temple treasury, she was prepared to give the money she herself
needed to extend the kingdom of God.

When your own bank account grows and your purse is stuffed
with notes, remember not to put your hope on your money or possessions but on God, and be 'rich in good deeds'.

🌿 Father, make me willing to be rich in good deeds, without calculating in
advance whether I can afford it or not. Amen.

September 13

How much do you love your money?

READ: 1 TIMOTHY 6:6–10

People who want to get rich fall into temptation and a trap and into many foolish and harmful desires that plunge men into ruin and destruction. For the love of money is a root of all kinds of evil.
– 1 TIMOTHY 6:9–10

Money has become a symbol of status, influence and power to modern man. At heart, people are avaricious – and the more money they have, the more they want. Most crimes are committed because people want money – people commit fraud and perjury because they want to make even more money; others rob and steal because they do not have enough to eat. 'But if it's only money these leaders are after, they'll self-destruct in no time. Lust for money brings trouble and nothing but trouble. Going down that path, some lose their footing in the faith completely, and live to regret it bitterly ever after,' 1 Timothy 6:9 reads in *The Message*. 'A spiritual power does indeed lie behind money – power which could demand an all-encompassing devotion from us,' Richard Foster writes.[4] Yes, lovers of money will do absolutely anything to get their hands on more money.

Consider what you are prepared to do for money; what criteria apply to you personally when you assess people – and what you withhold from the tax collector … If you answer these questions honestly, you will soon discover how important your money is to you.

Perhaps it has become time for you to change your own attitude towards money.

❧ Heavenly Father, please forbid that my money become a root of all kinds of evil in my life, and keep me from avarice. Amen.

September 14

The rich fool

READ: LUKE 12:13–21

*But God said to him, 'You fool! This very night your life will
be demanded from you. Then who will get what you have
prepared for yourself?' This is how it will be with anyone who
stores up things for himself but is not rich towards God.*
– LUKE 12:20–21

Jesus told the parable of the rich man who thought he had accumulated enough money to live in luxury for the rest of his life. He not only
thought he had accumulated enough money, but also that he himself
was in control of his life – and that he could retire with confidence.

Today it is a very real problem to know when you have accumulated enough money to retire with confidence. A few years ago a million rand was regarded as a fortune, while today the interest on it is
hardly enough to live on. The rich fool also thought he had arrived
– that he had enough money to sit back for the rest of his life and
enjoy his money. That was not to be. The Lord did not approve of his
attitude and took his life away. The rich man had to discover that
money and possessions are only important while you are still on
earth. In God's kingdom money and possessions have no value at all.

What do your calculations for retirement look like? Before you
think you have arrived, read Jesus' judgment in Luke 12:15 again:
'Take care! Protect yourself against the least bit of greed. Life is not
defined by what you have, even if you have a lot' (The Message).

❧ Lord, I now see that I often think like the rich fool. Teach me again that
my life is in your hand and make me rich in You. Amen.

September 15

Bring your gifts

READ: PHILIPPIANS 4:12–20

Not that I am looking for a gift, but I am looking for what
may be credited to your account … They [the gifts you sent]
are a fragrant offering, an acceptable sacrifice, pleasing to God.
– PHILIPPIANS 4:17–18

The only way to assure that you will be 'rich in God' is to give your money and possessions so that others can be blessed. In his letter to the Philippians, Paul said that he knew what poverty was and that he had also experienced abundance. However, it was very important to him that those who had shared their gifts with him would also become spiritually richer as a result of their gifts.

When you help others, the gifts you give them will be like a fragrant offering to God. Bring your gifts; God promises to care for you and to 'meet all your needs according to his glorious riches' (v 19). God does not expect you to give what you do not have (cf 2 Cor 8:12). All He asks is that you contribute to his work according to your abilities; that those of us who have an abundance will help those who are in need. God will receive that gift as a fragrant offering to Himself.

Throughout the world thousands of people live in luxury while millions live in dire poverty. God expects his children to notice the material need of others and meet those needs. If you are prepared to do this, you yourself will experience rich spiritual blessing.

❧ Father, please make me willing to use my gifts in your service. Thank you for the bonus that not only will it make me spiritually rich, but it also assures me of your provision. Amen.

September 16

Stewards

READ: PSALM 39

Man is a mere phantom as he goes to and fro: He bustles about,
but only in vain; he heaps up wealth, not knowing who will get it.
But now, Lord, what do I look for? My hope is in you.
— PSALM 39:6–7

In Psalm 39 David says people work as if in a dream and they work themselves to death for nothing. They accumulate possessions without knowing who will inherit their money when they die. God, not our possessions, should be our only hope.

As Christians, our money is merely a loan from God so that we can invest it in his kingdom again, Philip Yancy writes.[5] You should always realise that your money does not really belong to you – that you do not have to accumulate so much money and so many possessions, because you do not know who will get it. Don't pin your hope on your bank balance or your securities. Rather confess like the psalmist, 'My hope is in You.'

You are God's steward on earth – not an accumulator for your own needs. It is your job to manage the money He has entrusted to you to the best of your ability. God gives you good gifts because He loves you, and you should return your money and possessions to Him because you love Him – and your neighbour. Stewardship is correct only if it has been tested by the law of love, Calvin writes. Never forget from Whom you received your material blessing – or to Whom your money really belongs.

❧ Lord, forgive me for hoarding. I now realise that my possessions actually belong to You. Please make me a responsible steward for You. Amen.

September 17

Give yourself first to God

READ: 2 CORINTHIANS 8:1–8

*For I testify that they gave as much as they were able, and even beyond
their ability. Entirely on their own, they urgently pleaded with us for
the privilege of sharing in this service ... they gave themselves
first to the Lord and then to us in keeping with God's will.*
– 2 CORINTHIANS 8:3–5

In 2 Corinthians 8 we read the beautiful testimony of the Macedonians who did not have much, yet voluntarily offered to contribute to caring for the Christians in Jerusalem. It was easy for them to give, since they had already given themselves to God. And that is the way God wants it.

It always strikes me when my domestic tells me how their whole community helps when one of them needs help. The wealthy among us still have much to learn about generosity and loving one's neighbour. If you still find it difficult to share your money and possessions, do what the Macedonians did – first give yourself to the Lord before you decide to give part of your money to Him.

It's no use giving your money to God if you still do not belong to Him. Only once your relationship with God is right will your money matters and your attitude about your money also be sorted out.

The Macedonians' positive response to Paul's fund-raising effort bore testimony to their love for God. Because they contributed voluntarily and above their ability, they proved that their love for God was sincere and not mere lip-service.

What about your contributions to the church and your willingness to give to others?

❧ Lord, thank you that I have already given myself to You. Please set my heart right before I open my purse. Amen.

September 18

God loves a cheerful giver

READ: 2 CORINTHIANS 9:6–10

Each man should give what he has decided in his heart to give,
not reluctantly or under compulsion, for God loves a cheerful giver.
And God is able to make all grace abound to you, so that in all things
at all times, having all that you need, you will abound in every good work.
– 2 CORINTHIANS 9:7–8

Giving is a joy! This is a secret which all givers have already discovered. It is not for nothing that there is a saying that it is more blessed to give than to receive.

However, the Bible warns the tight-fisted among us: 'Whoever sows sparingly will also reap sparingly, and whoever sows generously will also reap generously' (2 Cor 9:6). We know from experience that a farmer who sows sparingly cannot expect a big harvest. The same is true of the financial 'seed' which you sow in the kingdom of God. If you are willing to use your money as 'seed', God Himself will see to it that this seed will yield a big harvest for his kingdom – but if you sow sparingly, your harvest will also be small.

One of the best things you can do with your money is to share it with others. God loves people who share their money with joy. Giving sets us free to care for others, says Richard Foster.[6] Giving also teaches you to provide for others the way God provides for you. Only when you have learned to give can you possess money without being possessed by your money.

❧ Lord, teach me to give to others freely and cheerfully, because I have received so much from You. Amen.

September 19

Blessed to bless!

READ: 2 CORINTHIANS 9:11–15

*You will be made rich in every way so that you can be
generous on every occasion, and through us your
generosity will result in thanksgiving to God.*
— 2 CORINTHIANS 9:11

God gives you material prosperity with a specific purpose: so that you can, in turn, meet the needs of others. He blesses you so that you can bless others. In the Bible generosity is regarded as a service to God. After all, it is God who provides you with enough money and possessions. He therefore expects you to be generous to Christians who have less than you have. Never be stingy – giving starts a positive chain reaction, as set out in 2 Corinthians 9:13. People who receive gifts say thank you by praying for the givers: 'Because of the service by which you have proved yourselves, men will praise God for the obedience that accompanies your confession of the gospel of Christ, and for your generosity …'

'You show your gratitude through your generous offerings to your needy brothers and sisters …' reads a translation of this verse in *The Message*. Directly after Paul told us that it is God who makes us generous, he thanks God for his gift, 'Thanks be to God for his indescribable gift!' (2 Cor 9:15). Jesus is the greatest gift God has ever given mankind. Your own generosity should always be a response to God's indescribable gift to you.

Ask Him to show you where your gifts are needed most, and pray that He will make you even more generous.

❧ Lord, thank you for blessing me so that I can, in turn, bless others. Please show me where You need this blessing most at the moment. Amen.

September 20

Don't rely on your wealth

READ: PROVERBS 11:28–30

Whoever trusts in his riches will fall,
but the righteous will thrive like a green leaf …
The fruit of the righteous is a tree of life,
and he who wins souls is wise.
– PROVERBS 11:28, 30

By now you should realise that you cannot rely on your wealth and that it should not prevent you from depending on God. Wealth can vanish, regardless of how much you possess: the stock exchange can crash, your house can burn down, you can lose all your possessions. The Bible warns repeatedly that doing the will of the Lord is far better than accumulating wealth. 'Do not wear yourself out to get rich; have the wisdom to show restraint. Cast but a glance at riches, and they are gone, for they will surely sprout wings and fly off to the sky like an eagle,' the wise writer of Proverbs warned (Prov 23:4–5).

Shortly after retirement we personally experienced the truth of this verse. Our financial plans for our retirement were already in place when we nearly lost practically all our savings overnight because we trusted a swindler. Fortunately we also experienced in the meantime the incredible way in which the Lord had protected us. The lesson that we can trust Him because He can and will provide is a lesson we will never again forget!

Make Proverbs 15:16 your motto: 'Better a little with the fear of the LORD than great wealth with turmoil.'

❧ Lord, thank you for the precious lessons that your children do not have to accumulate wealth and that we are foolish to rely on wealth. I want to live in total dependence on You from today. Amen.

September 21

The widow at the temple

READ: MARK 12:41–44

Calling his disciples to him, Jesus said,
'I tell you the truth, this poor widow has
put more into the treasury than all the others.'
– MARK 12:43

In this story it almost seems as if Jesus had deliberately sat down in front of the temple to look at the people who were putting money into the treasury. However, Jesus does not merely look at people. He can also distinguish the attitude with which they give their gifts. Apart from the many rich people who put in much money, a poor widow also came to the temple and put in two mites. Thereupon Jesus told the surprised disciples that the poor widow had made the biggest contribution: 'They all gave out of their wealth; but she, out of her poverty, put in everything – all she had to live on' (Mark 12:44).

To God the size of your offering is less important than what it costs you to give the offering. The widow was willing to make all she had to live on available to God. God therefore regarded this widow's 'poverty' as 'wealth'.

Those who love God never calculate the cost of their gifts to Him. Mary poured half a litre of precious, very expensive nard on Jesus' feet to demonstrate her love for Him (cf John 12:3). Your love for God can also often be gauged by the money you are prepared to spend on his affairs and in the interest of his kingdom.

❧ Lord Jesus, forgive me for still calculating the cost of my offerings down to the last cent. Make me willing to surrender everything to You. Amen.

September 22

Tithes

READ: MALACHI 3:6–12

*'Bring the whole tithe into the storehouse, that there may be food
in my house. Test me in this,' says the LORD Almighty, 'and see if
I will not throw open the floodgates of heaven and pour out so
much blessing that you will not have room enough for it.'*
– MALACHI 3:10

Tithing remains an issue among Christians. What exactly is a tenth?
Is it a tenth of our net or gross income? Does tithing still apply today?
You no longer have to puzzle over the exact size of your 'tenth'. Tithing
is no longer a legalistic command as in Old Testament times. However,
if your attitude towards money and your relationship with God are in
line, giving a 'literal' tenth will no longer be an insurmountable problem to you.

Tithing also proves your gratitude to God for caring for you. You
may leave the unknown future in his hands (without worrying about
the fact that you cannot accumulate huge financial reserves to fend
off every disaster which might overtake you). Therefore, give Him
his share of your money. We have experienced this time and again in
the past: If you are willing to do this, you may sit back and see how
the Lord 'opens the windows of heaven' for you, figuratively! He will
look after you just as He looked after the people in Malachi's day and
gave them rain.

❧ Lord, please teach me once again that I can trust You completely with
my finances and that I do not have to hesitate to give You your rightful share
of my money. Amen.

September 23

The generous widow

READ: ACTS 9:36–43

In Joppa there was a disciple named Tabitha ...
who was always doing good and helping the poor.
– ACTS 9:36

Widows were usually very poor in Tabitha's day. They were usually totally dependent on others for support. Tabitha was the exception. Apparently she not only had enough money for her own needs, but also enough funds to help other widows. However, Tabitha not only gave her money, she was also prepared to give of herself – after her death her grieving widowed friends showed Peter the clothes she had made for them herself. This remarkable woman was always doing good. With her generosity and willingness to serve, Tabitha indeed earned the love and loyalty of her friends. They therefore rejoiced when Peter raised Tabitha from the dead and returned her to her friends.

Generous people are always popular because they demonstrate their caring for others by the things they are willing to do and give. They are the people who really fulfil Jesus' command that we should get involved with others and help them the way He did while He walked the earth. How generous are you? Perhaps it is time to consider again what you are prepared to do and give. Not only to those who need food and clothes but also to those close to you who need your love, time and care more than your money.

❧ Lord, I tend to give my money to others easily, but I'm stingy with my time and physical involvement. Make me willing to give of myself to others. Amen.

September 24

Do not worry about money!

READ: MATTHEW 6:25–31

So do not worry, saying,'What shall we eat?' or 'What shall we drink?'
or 'What shall we wear?' For the pagans run after all these things,
and your heavenly Father knows that you need them.
– MATTHEW 6:31–32

Christians do not have to be worrywarts. Look at the birds and the lilies, Jesus said in his Sermon on the Mountain. They do not sow or reap and they do not store away in barns, yet your heavenly Father feeds them and He also undertakes to look after you. For this reason you no longer have to worry about money. The birds sing while they look for food. Learn from them!

Unbelievers are still very concerned about their money and possessions. They think they are in control of their lives if their bank balances are big enough. If God enables the birds to live without worries, He will also do it for you. Do your work from today without worrying about where the bread and money for tomorrow and the day after tomorrow will come from. Leave the finer details to God without worrying. He knows exactly what you need, and He will also give it to you in abundance. Stop being such an incurable worrier and decide to trust Him! If you still worry, ask God to deliver you from your financial worries and follow Peter's advice: 'Cast all your anxiety on him because he cares for you' (1 Pet 5:7).

❧ Lord, I want to cast my anxieties on You for the last time and leave them with You. Thank you for your promise that You will care for me. Amen.

September 25

Give generously and with joy

READ: 1 CHRONICLES 29:6–9

The people rejoiced at the willing response of their leaders,
for they had given freely and wholeheartedly to the LORD.
– 1 CHRONICLES 29:9

In 1 Chronicles 9 David reminded the people how it had been possible for him to find the building material for the temple. The whole nation had contributed voluntarily and wholeheartedly. The joy of the nation and the king is emphasised here as well as in David's prayer of thanksgiving which follows. David acknowledged that everything they were able to give belonged to the Lord in the first place: 'Everything comes from you, and we have given you only what comes from your hand,' 1 Chronicles 29:14 reads.

Some people find it extremely difficult to put their hands into their pockets to give for the extension of God's kingdom. Before they give something to someone, they first calculate and recalculate to make quite sure that they will not perhaps need the object concerned somewhere in the future. However, this is not what God wants. It is his will that his children should give freely and with joy and that they will realise that everything belongs to Him anyway.

If you are a cheerful giver, the amount you give is less important than your attitude when you give. After all, God does not need your money – everything on earth already belongs to Him: 'The silver is mine and the gold is mine,' declares the Lord Almighty, according to the prophet Haggai (Hag 2:8). Once you discover this, it will be much easier for you to use your money in God's kingdom.

❧ Lord, I now know that everything I have actually belongs to You. Please make me willing to give my money back to You freely and cheerfully. Amen.

September 26

Give God the glory

READ: DEUTERONOMY 8:10–20

You may say to yourself, 'My power and the strength
of my hands have produced this wealth for me.
But remember the LORD your God for it is he
who gave you the ability to produce wealth …
– DEUTERONOMY 8:17–18

In Deuteronomy 8 God once again told Israel that their prosperity was not a result of their competence, but of his grace. Throughout their history – from the exodus from Egypt, during their journey through the desert until they reached the promised land – the people experienced firsthand how the Lord had delivered them and cared for them. God requested them never to forget that He cared and provided for them, and asked them to thank Him by obeying Him.

Intelligent, competent businessmen who make money to burn, often forget that it's not their business acumen which enables them to be so prosperous, but God's grace. If you are a wealthy woman and you perhaps feel your intelligence has made this success possible, think again. Never minimize God's input in your success. Give God the glory for your success. After all, He has enabled you to be prosperous. You should, like Israel of old, decide to obey God in future, and never lose sight of his care for and mercy on you. You can also show your gratitude by being even more generous towards others.

❧ Lord, I want to give You the glory for my success and praise You for everything You did for me in the past. I promise to be generous and obedient in gratitude for what You have done. Amen.

September 27

God will provide

READ: PHILIPPIANS 4:10–20

And my God will meet all your needs
according to his glorious riches in Christ Jesus.
– PHILIPPIANS 4:19

People who have a childlike faith that God will answer their prayers and meet all their needs, have a completely different attitude towards their money and possessions. If you acknowledge God's ownership of your possessions, you will no longer cling to them so fanatically either. I see John Wesley, the well-known minister, as an excellent example in this regard: When his house burnt down, he was not in sackcloth and ashes about what he had lost, he merely said: 'The Lord's house has burnt down – one less responsibility for me!'

In our core verse Paul thanked the church at Philippi for their financial contribution to his work. He was willing to accept it (unlike the contribution made by the Corinthians), because they were giving their contribution with the right attitude and this was proof that God was providing for his needs. He confessed that he had learnt to be content whatever his circumstances – whether in need or in plenty (cf Phil 4:11–12). As the Philippians had provided for his need, he had everything he needed. Likewise God would, in turn, meet their needs so that they would have everything they needed, he promised. This promise still applies to you and me even today. God still undertakes to meet the needs of those who believe in Him and trust Him.

❧ Heavenly Father, thank you for the assurance that I never have to be anxious about money, because You are able to meet all my needs according to your riches. Amen.

September 28

Everything belongs to God

READ: PSALM 24

The earth is the LORD's, and everything in it,
the world, and all who live in it.
— PSALM 24:1

Three things have become clear to us this past month: Your money actually belongs to God; you should therefore be willing to use it in his service and to extend his kingdom, and you must always be on your guard so that your money and possessions do not become more important to you than God.

Friends of ours have a beautiful house in the Port Alfred Marina and we were privileged to spend a holiday there. All the beautiful things in the house reminded us of our friends and we thoroughly enjoyed the unfamiliar luxury. However, we were very conscious of the fact that it did not belong to us. This is how you should view God's money and possessions which He 'lends' you temporarily. Instead of asking how much you will give the Lord in future, you should rather ask how much of the Lord's money you are prepared to return to Him.

Once you acknowledge that everything you have actually belongs to God, your attitude towards your money will change completely. The fact that you are prepared to surrender your selfish hold over your money is also a confirmation of your trusting God to care for you. Remember that money can do one of two things: It can either take you closer to God, or it can take God's rightful place in your life.

❧ Heavenly Father, help me to remember that everything I have actually belongs to You. Help me to spend my money in such a way that it takes me closer to You. Amen.,

September 29

True wealth

READ: 2 CORINTHIANS 8:9–15

For you know the grace of our Lord Jesus Christ,
that though he was rich, yet for your sakes he became poor,
so that you through his poverty might become rich.
– 2 CORINTHIANS 8:9

This is proof of his incredible love for us: Jesus, the King of the heavens, was willing to come into the world and be poor so that we could be rich. 'You are familiar with the generosity of our Master, Jesus Christ. Rich as He was, He gave it all away for us – in one stroke He became poor and we became rich ... The best thing you can do right now is to finish what you started ...' the translation of 2 Corinthians 8:9 reads in *The Message.*

Before Jesus came into the world, He was rich. For our sake He became poor so that we could share in his spiritual wealth. And this is the kind of wealth no-one can take away from you – this is the only kind of wealth which you can take to heaven and which will last for ever. This is indeed the 'treasure' Jesus spoke of in his Sermon on the Mountain – the treasure which moth and rust cannot destroy. If you belong to God, you are very wealthy. In fact, the heavenly treasures already belong to you. The Bible also tells you how to thank God for the riches Jesus has transferred to you: by sharing your money and possessions with other believers. Are you willing to do so?

❧ Lord Jesus, thank you for having been willing to become poor so that I can be spiritually rich for the rest of my life. Amen.

September 30

Lord Jesus,

during the past month I was shocked to discover

that my money and possessions

have indeed become my god,

without my even being aware of it.

Forgive me, Lord, that my wealth has been so close to my heart;

that I have been so tight-fisted in giving to You;

that I always wanted to accumulate even more for myself

and that I was so worried that I

would not have enough money.

Thank you for the new freedom which You have given me:

I now know that my money actually belongs to You,

because everything comes from You –

that it is your will that I should give freely and

cheerfully to others –

that you have blessed me financially

so that I can bless others.

Make me content with just having enough

and teach me once again

that You will meet all my needs abundantly.

Grant that I will give my contributions for your kingdom

with the right attitude –

and that I will always remember that I am merely a steward.

Thank you for having been willing to become poor

so that I can be rich for ever,

so that my riches and my heart will be in the right place.

I now want to surrender myself to You, Lord,

not only my money, but also my life,

so that everything I have will always be available to You.

Amen

Surrender

'Surrendering to God is the heart of worship. It is the natural response to God's wonderful love and mercy.' This is what Rick Warren writes in his bestseller, *The Purpose-Driven Life.*[1] However, most people are not comfortable with the expression 'surrender' – it sounds somewhat dangerous to surrender absolutely everything to God. After all, surrendering means that I have to be willing to give up myself and my desires, my possessions and my dreams for God's dream for my life.

Obedience to God's will, even if it differs completely from mine, means being available when God needs me … But God asks this of you – because He was prepared to give his Son to be crucified so that you could have eternal life. In the month which lies ahead, we will discover together what it means to be truly surrendered to God and his will.

October

Offer yourself to God

READ: ROMANS 12:1–8

Therefore, I urge you, brothers, in view of God's mercy, to offer
your bodies as living sacrifices, holy and pleasing to God –
this is your spiritual act of worship.
– ROMANS 12:1

When I was still at primary school I loved going with my parents to the prayer meetings during the Pentecost week. What I enjoyed most was the singing before the prayer meeting started. My favourite hymn was, 'I surrender all'. Whenever I read Romans 12:1, I am reminded of the words of this hymn. This was exactly what Paul asked the church in Rome: that they should be willing to surrender their lives to God totally, to become living sacrifices to Him; to live in total commitment to Him for the rest of their lives. And, Paul said, the motivation for this decision would be 'God's mercy'. God loved them so much that He had sacrificed his Son to die on the cross so that their sin could be forgiven. They therefore should be willing to live for Him.

Surrendering yourself to God means to be in a new relationship with God; to make a decision to live according to God's will, out of love and gratitude because Jesus gave his life for you on the cross. God's 'mercy' is revealed in his love for you. If you want to offer yourself to Him, you will prove your love for Him with your life.

❧ Lord Jesus, You were the Lamb sacrificed for me. I now want to offer myself to You and surrender myself to You for the rest of my life. Amen.

October 1

Say no to the world!

READ: ROMANS 12:1–8

Do not conform any longer to the pattern of this world, but be transformed by the renewing of your mind. Then you will be able to test and approve what God's will is – his good, pleasing and perfect will.
– ROMANS 12:2

Surrendering to God means to renounce the world. If you want to say yes to God, you simultaneously have to say no to the world and the things of the world. If we were quite honest we would have to admit that the world is a very pleasant place, and that we can live in and with it very comfortably and conveniently.

However, surrendering to God is very different. It does not come by itself. Surrendering means that we should be willing to sacrifice ourselves, to take second place so that God can take the first place in our life. By nature we are sinners – the Bible is quite clear about this. 'There is no one righteous, not even one; there is no one who understands, no one who seeks God,' Paul writes in Romans 3:10–11. And he then continues, 'All have turned away, they have together become worthless; there is no-one who does good, not even one' (Rom 3:12).

Are you prepared to turn your back on certain things of the world and, from today, live the way God wants you to? If so, Jesus' promise in John 12:25 is specially for you: 'The man who hates his life in this world will keep it for eternal life.'

❧ Heavenly Father, You know that the world still has a very strong appeal for me. Please help me to say no to the world; to love You above all else. Thank you that I will one day have eternal life. Amen.

October 2

Surrender your thoughts

READ: 2 CORINTHIANS 10:4–8

We take captive every thought to make it obedient to Christ.
– 2 CORINTHIANS 10:5

If you want to live a life of surrender to God, you have to begin with your thought life. One of the most important things which you have to surrender to God is your thought life. No-one does anything wrong until we have thought about it. Sin therefore always strikes root in our thoughts before it is manifested by our deeds.

To the Jews it was very important to eat the right food. They would not dream of eating anything which was regarded as unclean by their laws. However, Jesus told them that one cannot become unclean by eating the wrong foods, but by thinking the wrong thoughts: 'Nothing outside a man can make him "unclean" by going into him. Rather, it is what comes out of a man that makes him "unclean" … For from within, out of men's hearts, come evil thoughts, sexual immorality, theft, murder, adultery, greed, malice, deceit, lewdness, envy, slander, arrogance and folly. All these evils come from inside and make a man "unclean"', He said (cf Mark 7:15, 21–23).

Think carefully whether you would be comfortable if your friends were able to read your thoughts. And remember, God can read them! Decide right now to surrender your thought life to God, and to focus your thoughts on the things which are true, noble, right, pure and worthy of praise in future (cf Phil 4:8).

🌿 Lord Jesus, I commit my thoughts to You - I often forget that You know every detail of what I am thinking. Please forgive the sinful thoughts which come from my heart, and help me to commit every thought to You to be made obedient to You. Amen.

October 3

Serve God with your whole life

READ: ROMANS 6:1–13

Do not offer the parts of your body to sin, as instruments of wickedness,
but rather offer yourselves to God, as those who have been
brought from death to life; and offer the parts of your
body to him as instruments of righteousness.
– ROMANS 6:13

Every human being is dead as a result of sin, but God makes us alive – He delivers us from our 'body of death', as Paul calls it in Romans 7:24. And He does this by the intervention of Jesus.

If you believe in Jesus, you have already been redeemed from sin and should now live for Jesus. 'For we know that our old self was crucified with him so that the body of sin might be done away with, that we should no longer be slaves to sin … In the same way, count yourselves dead to sin, but alive to God in Christ Jesus,' Paul wrote in Romans 6:6 and 11.

There is only one reason why you are dead to sin: Jesus has died for you and He cancelled the penalty for your sin on the cross once and for all. From now on you are a new person, and you should live every day to the full for God, and make yourself fully available to serve God who has redeemed you. If you are willing to do this, God will be able to use you fully in his kingdom and you will be able to testify to his great mercy in your life every day.

❧ Lord Jesus, how great You are! You were willing to pay the penalty for my sin on the cross. Please help me to serve You fully for the rest of my life. Amen.

October 4

Freedom and surrender

READ: ROMANS 6:15–23

But thanks be to God that,
though you used to be slaves to sin,
you wholeheartedly obeyed the form
of teaching to which you were entrusted.
– ROMANS 6:17

Only God can set you free from the prison of sin. And when He has set you free, you are free indeed. 'But thank God You've started listening to a new master, one whose commands set you free to live openly in his freedom!' This is the translation of the core verse in *The Message*.

Once God has delivered you from sin, your whole life changes. You are now under the grace of God and no longer a slave to sin. You can therefore (always with God's help) live as a redeemed person.

Bill Bright, the founder of the Campus Crusade movement says that he entered into a contract with God as a young man. He wrote on a slip of paper: 'From today I am a slave of God' and signed it. Bill was willing to surrender his life totally to God, and through the work of Campus Crusade more than 150 million people have already given their hearts to the Lord. For example, through the staff of Campus Crusade, the tract Four Spiritual Laws has been distributed to thousands of people and the Jesus film has been screened to more than four million people.

If you are willing to let God do with your life whatever He wants to, He might also use you in an incredible way as He used Bill Bright.

❧ Heavenly Father, I praise You for delivering me from the slavery of sin. Please help me to live only for You in future. Amen.

October 5

Slaves of God

READ: ROMANS 6:14–22

For sin shall not be your master, because you are not under law,
but under grace ... You have been set free from sin and
have become slaves to righteousness.
– ROMANS 6:14, 18

You used to be a slave to sin. Because you believe in God, you have been delivered from the power of sin, but you are still a slave – you are now a slave of God! In Old Testament times slaves belonged to their owners in every respect. He had bought them and they had no say over themselves – they had to do whatever their owner desired of them. That is exactly what God did with you. He redeemed you from sin. To do this, the blood of his only Son had to be shed on the cross. Jesus' blood set you free from sin, but now you no longer belong to yourself but to God – and you no longer have any say over your own life. Even if you should sin again, God would forgive you because you have been redeemed by his Son. However, God now expects you to live a holy life and to do his will.

In verse 22 Paul lists the gifts God gives everyone who has been set free from sin and become his slaves: the benefit you reap is an ever-increasing holiness, and the end is eternal life. Don't wait any longer before you accept God's wonderful gifts!

❧ Heavenly Father, thank you for having delivered me from sin and that I may now serve You full-time. Please help me to do your will for the rest of my life. Amen.

October 6

Surrender brings peace

READ: JOB 22:21–30

Submit to God and be at peace with him;
in this way prosperity will come to you.
Accept instruction from his mouth and
lay up his words in your heart.
– Job 22:21–22

Job's friend Eliphaz tried his best to encourage his friend to make peace with God again. He asked Job to 'submit' himself to God again, surrender his life to God. Only once Job's relationship with God was restored would he be able to live in peace and enjoy prosperity again. Job listened to Eliphaz, and this promise was fulfilled. Job discovered the greatness of God when he looked at creation, he stopped questioning God and worshipped Him. He confessed his sin and prayed for his friends. And the Lord blessed the latter part of Job's life even more than the first.

This good advice[?] of Eliphaz the Temanite still applies to you even today. When you are prepared to submit yourself to God, you experience God's peace in your life. When you experience problems in your own life, renew your relationship with God and recommit yourself to Him. If you are willing to follow the advice of Eliphaz, his promise applies to you as well: 'Then you will find delight in the Almighty and will lift up your face to God. You will pray to him, and he will hear you, and you will fulfil your vows. What you decide on will be done, and light will shine on your ways' (Job 22:26–28).

❧ Lord, please forgive me for being so slow to surrender my whole life to You. Help me to submit myself to You so that I can enjoy your peace and prosperity in my life again. Amen.

October 7

Implicit obedience

READ: 1 JOHN 3:18–24

And [we] receive from him anything we ask,
because we obey his commands and do what pleases him …
Those who obey his commands, live in him, and he in them.
– 1 JOHN 3:22, 24

God expects implicit obedience from his children: 'God does not owe you any explanation or reason for anything He asks you to do. Understanding can wait, but not obedience. Instant obedience will teach you more about God than a lifetime of studying the Bible. In fact, you will fail to understand some of God's commands until you have obeyed them. Obedience unlocks understanding,' Rick Warren says.[2]

When Abraham was prepared to obey God's 'impossible' command, God promised him: 'Through your offspring all nations on earth will be blessed, because you have obeyed me' (Gen 22:18). Peter knew very well that it was impossible to walk on water, yet when Jesus invited him to come to Him, he was willing to listen and to obey Him. And then he did the impossible – he walked towards Jesus on the water.

Surrender always assumes obedience; it asks you to do what God wants, not what you want, to set aside your own plans for the sake of God's plans for your life. If you are willing to obey God unconditionally, you will also experience miracles in your own life. Things which seem impossible, will become possible for you, because nothing is impossible for God. You can obey His commands without the slightest hesitation.

❧ Father, I find it hard to be obedient. Please help me to obey You implicitly in future, and to experience your miracles in my own life. Amen.

October 8

Noah did what God requested

READ: GENESIS 6:9–22

So God said to Noah … 'Make yourself an ark of cypress wood …
You are to bring into the ark two of all living creatures,
male and female, to keep them alive with you.'
Noah did everything just as God commanded him.
– GENESIS 6:13–14, 19, 22

God gave Noah a task which seemed practically impossible: Not only did he have to build a gigantic vessel inland without a dry dock, he also had to bring two of each kind of animal (and bird) into the ark. Noah did not argue with God – he tackled the job exactly as God had instructed him.

Only someone whose life is truly committed to God would be willing to obey such an impossible instruction. The people in Noah's day must have ridiculed him – this man who was building a boat so far from the sea! Building the ark was probably still possible, but how on earth would he manage to get all the animals into the ark? Yet Noah did not hesitate – and the ark was ready at exactly the right time, and God Himself did the impossible and brought the animals to the ark (Gen 7:8–9).

Those who are prepared to say yes to God discover time and again that God works miracles in their lives. If you are willing to obey God unconditionally and surrender your whole life to Him, you will also experience that God will realise the things He asks of you in his own time and in his own way.

✤ Lord, I know that You will do miracles in my life as well. Help me to trust You to make the impossible possible in my life. Amen.

October 9

Abraham obeys God's command

READ: GENESIS 22:2–18

*Then God said, 'Take your son, your only son, Isaac, whom you love,
and go to the region of Moriah. Sacrifice him there as a burnt
offering on one of the mountains I will tell you about.'*
— GENESIS 22:2

God asked two practically superhuman things of Abraham: First he
had to leave his country without knowing where he was going (cf Gen
12:1), and then he had to take the son he and Sarah had waited for so
many years and sacrifice him to God. And Abraham did not hesitate:
He was willing immediately because his life was committed to God.
He left the very next morning and told the slaves that he and Isaac
would go on to worship God. At the place God pointed out, Abraham
built an altar, bound his son and placed him on the altar. Only when
he reached out his hand to take the knife to slay his son did God intervene. 'Do not lay a hand on the boy,' He said. 'Do not do anything
to him. Now I know that you fear God, because you have not withheld
from me your own son, your only son' (Gen 22:12).

Because Abraham was obedient, God promised to bless him and
make his descendants as numerous as the stars in the sky and the
sand on the seashore. As in Abraham's case, God still blesses those
who obey his commands. If you really want to be surrendered to God,
you will have to be willing to set aside your own interests so that
God's will can be fulfilled in your life. If you do this, He promises to
bless you abundantly.

❧ Father, make me willing to be so close to You that I will obey instructions
like Abraham, even if they seem impossible to me. Amen.

October 10

Joseph resisted temptation

READ: GENESIS 39:7–23

Joseph was well-built and handsome,
and after a while his master's wife
took notice of Joseph and said,
'Come to bed with me!' But he refused …
– GENESIS 39:6–8

The attractive wife of Potiphar must have been a tremendous tempta-tion to the young Joseph but, with God's power, he resisted the temp-tation. He succeeded only because his life was committed to God. At first it seemed as if Joseph's irreproachable conduct had been in vain. Mrs Potiphar was furious because he had scorned her and she told her husband that Joseph had tried to rape her. Thereupon the innocent Joseph was thown into prison.

The story sounds very unfair. Why didn't the Lord do something to help Joseph, who served Him? But God had a greater plan with Joseph's life. 'But while Joseph was there in the prison, the LORD was with him; he showed him kindness … the LORD was with Joseph and gave him success in whatever he did' (Gen 39:20–23).

Perhaps you have also had unfair experiences when you could not understand the Lord's action. God is always with his children who are surrendered to Him, even when you feel He is not paying any atten-tion to you. If you are willing to remain faithful to Him, He will make his plan with your own life known to you at the right time.

❧ Lord, I don't understand everything You allow to happen to me either. Please help me to hold on to You despite my doubt because I know that You are with me in your faithful love. Amen.

October 11

Mary makes herself available to God

READ: LUKE 1:26–38

'How will this be,' Mary asked the angel, 'since I am a virgin?'
The angel answered, 'The Holy Spirit will come upon you, and the power of the
Most High will overshadow you.' 'I am the Lord's servant,' Mary answered …
– LUKE 1:34–35, 38

It must have been very hard for Mary to say 'yes' to God by obeying the angel's command. She knew very well that no-one in her village would believe the angel's far-fetched story about God having come upon her and an immaculate conception! She was probably also very concerned about how Joseph, the man to whom she was betrothed, would react when he discovered that she was pregnant. However, Mary did not hesitate even for an instant; she made no excuses as to why she would not be willing … She obeyed God's command immediately – to be the mother of his Son. She made herself available to be used by God immediately.

Madeleine L'Engle wrote a poem about Mary's implicit obedience:

This is the irrational season
when love blooms bright and wild.
Had Mary been filled with reason
there'd have been no room for the Child.[3]

Who knows what miracles God can do in your life if you were willing, like Mary, to make yourself fully available to Him?

❧ Lord, I want to make myself available to You. Please show me your will with my life and make me willing to carry out that will. Amen.

October 12

Paul turns around

READ: ACTS 9:1–18

Meanwhile, Saul was still breathing out murderous threats against the Lord's
disciples. . . . As he neared Damascus on his journey, suddenly a light
from heaven flashed around him. He fell to the ground and heard
a voice say to him, 'Saul, Saul, why do you persecute me?'
– Acts 9:1, 3–4

On the road to Damascus Saul was confronted by this Jesus Whom he was persecuting so zealously. When he decided to listen to the voice of God, his life was turned inside out. Things which used to be very important to him became totally irrelevant. The same Saul who used to persecute the Christians with such zeal now became Paul who dedicated his life to making disciples for Jesus. He himself testified, 'But whatever was to my profit I now consider loss … I consider everything a loss compared to the surpassing greatness of knowing Christ Jesus my Lord, for whose sake I have lost all things. I consider them rubbish, that I may gain Christ and be found in him' (Phil 3:7–9).

When people meet God face to face their lives change for ever – they no longer live for themselves but for God. If you have already surrendered your life to God, your life should have changed radically. You are now a new creation and from now on you will obey God's guidelines in his Word and live the way He asks you to. Is this true about you yet?

❧ Lord, thank you for having turned my life around. And that I can discover day after day that I no longer live, but that You live in me. Grant that knowing You will also make everything else of less importance to me. Amen.

October 13

God's will must come first

READ: 2 CORINTHIANS 5:1–10

So we make it our goal to please him,
whether we are at home in the body or away from it.
– 2 CORINTHIANS 5:9

When Paul wrote this letter to the Christians in Corinth, death was already staring him in the face, but he testified that God was strengthening him spiritually day after day. He was looking forward to his true home in heaven but as long as he was still on earth it was extremely important to him to obey God's will.

Those who want to live fully surrendered to God, are serious about living in accordance with the will of God. By yourself you can never succeed in living according to God's will. Only God can make this possible for you by his Holy Spirit. In Paul's prayer for the church at Colossae he summarised this beautifully: 'We have not stopped praying for you and asking God to fill you with the knowledge of his will through all spiritual wisdom and understanding' (Col 1:9).

Obeying God's will is not easy. It will cost concentration and perseverance! You will have to try again and again when you fail. 'You need to persevere so that when you have done the will of God, you will receive what he has promised,' the writer of the letter to the Hebrews wrote (Heb 10:36). As Paul says in our core verse, you should also strive to please God by living according to his will.

❧ Heavenly Father, please reveal your will to me and enable me, by your Holy Spirit, to obey your will. Amen.

October 14

Surrendering to the will of God

READ: MARK 14:32–42

Going a little farther, he fell to the ground and
prayed that if possible the hour might pass from him.
'Abba, Father,' he said, 'everything is possible for you.
Take this cup from me. Yet not what I will, but what you will.'
– MARK 14:35–36

As usual Jesus set the very best example for us here. He set his Father's will first in everything He did. Even in Gethsemane when He earnestly pleaded that God should remove the cup of suffering from Him, He pleaded so intensely that his perspiration was like drops of blood – but his prayer was still that God's will should be done.

Before we are really willing to pray that God's will should be done, we must be willing to surrender our own will. Alan Redpath says, 'Before we pray: "Father, let you kingdom come", we first have to be willing to say: "Let my kingdom go."'[4]

Should you, like Jesus, ask that God's will be done in your own life, you might also, like Jesus, experience God's no in your life. God's will and our will are often poles apart. The way He answers our prayers is always best for us, but definitely not always the answer we want. Make a decision of the will to live surrendered to God's will in future even if it should mean that your own will has to 'go'.

Lord Jesus, teach me to be willing to surrender my own will, like You, so that the will of the Father can be done in my life. Amen.

October 15

Surrender your purse

READ: LUKE 14:25–33

In the same way, any of you who does not give
up everything he has cannot be my disciple.
– LUKE 14:33

Surrendering to God involves every area of life. And the area which we probably find the most difficult to give up is our finances. What Jesus asks of his disciples in the core verse for today, sounds rather impossible to us. He also made it very clear in his Sermon on the Mountain that no-one could be his disciple unless he or she was prepared to give up everything they possessed. Most of us are willing to give a tenth of our possessions to God, but we back away when God asks us to give everything.

Two people were prepared to surrender their finances to God: Zacchaeus and Matthew. And both were tax collectors, people who were notorious for their avarice – they were prepared to betray their own people and act as tax collectors for the Romans. However, when these two tax collectors surrendered their lives to Jesus, their attitude towards money changed completely – it was no longer the most important thing in their lives. Zacchaeus undertook to give half his money to the poor and to compensate fourfold those he had cheated. Matthew left his bag of money right there and followed Jesus.

What about you? Are you also willing to surrender your purse and your securities to Jesus, or do your money and possessions still take priority in your life?

✤ Lord, You know I still battle to surrender all my possessions to You. Please make me willing to do so. Amen.

October 16

Surrender your fears

READ: 1 JOHN 4:13–18

There is no fear in love. But perfect love drives out fear,
because fear has to do with punishment. The one
who fears is not made perfect in love.
– 1 JOHN 4:18

We never have to doubt God's love for sinners – it is underlined in the Bible far too often. Every Christmas and Easter we are once again reminded of that love. And the fact that God loves us so much, relieves us of the fear for judgment day and the possible punishment. As soon as you realise the extent of God's love for you, you no longer fear death. You also discover that this perfect love of God for you has the power to deliver you from all other fears. If God proved his love for you by sacrificing his Son for you, He really wants only the best for you. You can therefore have peace of mind for the rest of your life and leave every fear in your life in his hands, knowing that He cares for you.

Do you still fear certain things? God's perfect love can allay all your fears. God will convince you of his love for you through his Holy Spirit. And because He loves you so much, you can surrender all your fears to Him. He is omnipotent; nothing is impossible for Him. He is with you and promises to help you therefore you do not have to fear anything – because there is no fear in love.

❧ Heavenly Father, I praise You for your perfect love for me and that perfect love drives our all fear. Thank you that your Son has already borne your penalty for my sin. Amen.

October 17

Surrender your worries

READ: PSALM 55

Cast your cares on the Lord and he will sustain you;
he will never let the righteous fall.
— PSALM 55:23

Psalm 55 is a desperate cry of someone who is beset by fear and stress. He prays that God should help him because people have joined forces against him – even his friends are against him. Yet, at the end of the psalm he discovers once again that he does not have to live in fear. All he had to do was to tell the Lord about his anxieties and surrender them to Him. Those who trust in God can rely on his protection every day.

In the world in which we live, many things make us anxious and stressed. However, the psalmist's advice still applies to every pessimist. God's children do not have to worry unnecessarily. We know that God will take care of us, that He never forsakes his children.

If you are weighed down by your personal burden of worries at the moment, listen to the good news: you can program yourself so that you will not go through life worrying. Follow David's advice in Psalm 131:1–2: 'I do not concern myself with great matters or things too wonderful for me. But I have stilled and quietened my soul; like a weaned child with its mother, like a weaned child is my soul within me.' Do not hesitate any longer to exchange your anxieties for God's care and peace.

❧ Lord, I know that You will never forsake me. I therefore want to give You my heavy burden of worries - please give me your peace instead. Amen.

October 18

Surrender your stress

READ: MATTHEW 11:25–30

Come to me, all you who are weary and burdened,
and I will give you rest. Take my yoke upon you
and learn from me, for I am gentle and humble
in heart, and you will find rest for your souls.
– MATTHEW 11:28–29

Total surrender to God means that you will be willing to give God your whole life as well as those things which make your life difficult. Thousands of people in the world are unhappy and stressed. The reason for this stress (which is totally unnecessary for Christians) is that they try to run everything in their lives themselves and fail time and again. The more this happens, the more stressed they become until their health is eventually ruined. Jesus invites you to come to Him when you are tired and burdened. When you reach the end of your tether, He wants to make his miracle-working power available to you. He offers you his peace and rest in your frenetic, stressed life.

If you are particularly stressed at the moment, you can also do a few practical things to reduce your stress levels. Develop healthier eating habits – lots of fruit and vegetables and less meat. Breathe deeply when you feel stressed and stretch your muscles. Listen to soothing music and tidy your home – chaos and mess aggravate stress.

❧ Lord Jesus, I accept your invitation and give you everything which keeps my stress levels high. Please give me your peace in my agitated life. Amen.

October 19

Don't look back

READ: LUKE 9:57–62

*Jesus replied, 'No-one who puts his hand to the plough
and looks back is fit for service in the kingdom of God.'*
– LUKE 9:62

Don't look back when you have decided to surrender your life to God.
Lot's wife looked back towards Sodom and turned into a pillar of salt,
and this is a warning for everyone who wonders whether they are
doing the right thing. Looking back once you have decided to follow
Jesus is always wrong. In Luke 14:26–27 Jesus used another image: 'If
anyone comes to me and does not hate his father and mother, his wife
and children, his brothers and sisters – yes, even his own life – he cannot be my disciple. And anyone who does not carry his cross and
follow me cannot be my disciple,' He said. This sounds drastic, but
Jesus merely wanted to stress that you have to choose to belong to
Him with your whole life. If you are not willing to follow Him in
every respect, you are not suitable for his kingdom.

However, if you do in fact decide to surrender your life to God,
you should live according to God's will.

If you are willing to do this, a beautiful promise has been given in
Matthew 19:29: 'And everyone who has left houses or brothers or
sisters or father or mother or children or fields for my sake will receive
a hundred times as much and will inherit eternal life.'

❧ Lord Jesus, forgive me for sometimes having cold feet when I want to
surrender my life to You. Please help me not to look back but to live fully
surrendered to You in future. Amen.

October 20

Surrender is self-denial

READ: LUKE 9:23–27

Then he said to them all: 'If anyone would come after me,
he must deny himself and take up his cross daily and
follow me. For whoever wants to save his life will lose it,
but whoever loses his life for me will save it.'
– LUKE 9:23–24

Those who want to follow Him must be willing to do three things: deny themselves, take up their cross and follow Him, He told his disciples. Being his disciples could mean that they would lose their lives, but He promised those who listened to his message that day: 'Some who are standing here will not taste death before they see the kingdom of God' (Luke 9:27). Those of us who comply with his requirements will also see something of his kingdom in our time.

Surrendering to God is never easy, because we love ourselves far too much. Being surrendered to God assumes that you will renounce your natural disposition and live according to God's will. You will have to follow God from now on: do the things God asks; surrender your own little kingdom so that God's kingdom can come into the world; be willing to deny yourself, take up your cross every day and even be prepared to lose your life for the sake of God's kingdom. Are you prepared to do this at all? If your answer to this question is: 'Yes, Lord, I want to do this by the power of your Holy Spirit,' God will envelop you in his love for the rest of your life, protect and lead you, and meet all your needs.

❧ Lord Jesus, I want to follow You. Please make me willing to surrender myself, to take up my cross daily and to follow in your footsteps. Thank you that something of your kingdom is already visible on earth, and that heaven is awaiting us. Amen.

October 21

Surrender your dreams

READ: LUKE 12:13–21

'And I'll say to myself, "You have plenty of good things laid up for many years. Take life easy; eat, drink and be merry."' But God said to him, 'You fool! This very night your life will be demanded from you. Then who will get what you have prepared for yourself?' This is how it will be with any-one who stores up things for himself but is not rich towards God.
— LUKE 12:19–21

The rich man in our parable thought he had arrived. He had fulfilled all his dreams and was dreaming of a wonderful life of leisure. However, this man had concentrated only on himself and had left God out of the picture altogether. God was not satisfied with his way of life, and demanded his life from him.

In realising our own selfish dreams we often leave God's dream for us out of the picture. Like the rich man in our parable we are also so full of ourselves that we lose sight of God completely.

Have you given all your dreams to God yet, or are you still Number One in your life and are you still slaving to accumulate enough treasures for 'some day'? Jesus offers you a much better retirement policy: 'Do not store up for yourselves treasures on earth, where moth and rust destroy … Store up for yourselves treasures in heaven, where moth and rust do not destroy … where your treasure is, there your heart will be also,' He warned (Matt 6:19–21).

Only when your dreams have been committed to God will your treasure and your heart be in the right place. Is this true about you?

❧ Lord, my dreams are very precious to me, but I want to hand them to You today so that my treasure and my heart will both be in the right place. Amen.

October 22

Total surrender

READ: JAMES 4:1–10

Submit yourselves, then, to God. Resist the devil,
and he will flee from you … Humble yourselves
before the Lord, and he will lift you up.
– JAMES 4:7, 10

The cause of strife among people is usually their selfish desires, James wrote. When they ask God to fulfil their desires, their prayers are not answered, because they do not pray correctly. God wants his children to belong only to Him and to renounce their love for the world; He wants them to surrender their lives to Him and to submit to Him.

The translation of our core verse in *The Message* gives a clear picture of total surrender: 'So let God work his will in you. Yell a loud no to the Devil and watch him scamper…. Get down on your knees before the Master; it's the only way you'll get on your feet.'

Surrender and commitment mean basically the same thing: If you are willing to surrender yourself to God, it goes without saying that you will also be willing to commit yourself to Him, to spend more time with Him, to live only for God from today. Then He will give you the power to resist the temptations of the devil. 'Come near to God and he will come near to you,' James promised (Jas 4:8). If you come nearer to God, you will always discover that He also comes closer to you.

🌺 Heavenly Father, help me to be implicitly obedient to You, to live totally surrendered to You and to resist the devil. Amen.

October 23

Be fully committed to the Lord

READ: 1 KINGS 8:54–61

But your hearts must be fully committed to the LORD our God,
to live by his decrees and obey his commands, as at this time.
– 1 KINGS 8: 61

After Solomon had completed the temple, he prayed a beautiful prayer to God, thanking and praising Him and asking Him to forgive the sin of the people (1 Kgs 8:22–53). Thereupon he blessed the people and prayed that God would make them willing to live according to his will and to obey his commands. Unfortunately Solomon himself was not fully committed to God, and his relationship with God crumbled towards the end of his life.

To remain committed to God you have to live according to God's instructions in his Word and obey his commands. You have been created to worship God and to obey Him, and this is the only way you can really be happy in this imperfect world.

If you want to live totally surrendered, you will have to be willing to surrender yourself and your own desires, and live according to God's will. God's instructions are found in his Word – if you want to know how you should live, you will have to study his Word so that you can know what his commandments involve. And God Himself will enable you to obey Him by his Holy Spirit who dwells in you.

❧ Heavenly Father, I want to live fully surrendered to your will and law for the rest of my life. Please help me to do so by the power of your Holy Spirit who dwells in me. Amen.

October 24

Surrender is trust

READ: PSALM 37

Commit your way to the LORD;
trust in him and he will do this.
— PSALM 37:5

Surrender and trust are closely related: If you are willing to trust God fully, you have probably already surrendered your life to Him and you trust Him to care for you.

In Romans 12:1 Paul writes that we should offer ourselves to God as living sacrifices. Surrendering to God can happen in an instant, but really living this surrender will take the rest of your life. This surrender is never static nor does it happen as a matter of course – it has to be renewed from day to day. Like Paul you will most probably often discover that you do the things you had vowed not to do; that as soon as you think you have crucified yourself, you commit exactly the same sin which you have just confessed. 'The problem with a living sacrifice is that it can crawl down from the altar,'[5] Rick Warren says. The sacrifices which you offer God are still subject to your own will; the self is far from dead. You will therefore have to recommit your life to God repeatedly – on a daily basis. Have you noticed that Jesus says in Luke 9:23 that whoever wants to follow Him would have to take up his cross daily and follow Him? Surrender is never a once-only event but something which has to be done all over again daily.

✥ Lord, I have offered myself to You so often, and then disappointed You and myself time and again by sinning again. I want to surrender myself to You once again and trust You to finish the work You began in me. Amen.

October 25

False surrender

READ: JEREMIAH 3:6–13

'Because Israel's immorality mattered so little to her,
she defiled the land and committed adultery with stone and wood.
In spite of all this, her unfaithful sister Judah did not return to me
with all her heart, but only in pretence,' declares the LORD.
– JEREMIAH 3:9–10

Israel promised time and again to keep their side of the covenant, but they did not really take their promises seriously. As soon as the Lord had helped them and all was well again, they exchanged the Lord for heathen gods. The people promised Joshua to serve the Lord faithfully in future – but they broke these promises time and again. Their intention to remain faithful to God never lasted very long. However, they knew the Lord very well when they were in trouble. God was not satisfied with such false surrender.

We often resemble ancient Israel. Like Israel we also frequently feign surrender to the Lord. However, as soon as everything goes well again, we easily forget the promises we have made to God when we were desperate. We only know the Lord when we need Him.

Perhaps it is time to look at your own surrender under a magnifying glass; did you really mean it when you committed your life, your purse, your dreams to God? If not, it's not too late to turn round – and really commit your life to God.

❧ Lord, forgive me for not always meaning my surrender. I want to turn around now and surrender to You once again. Help me to live fully committed to You. Amen.

October 26

Committed to worldly pleasures

READ: ECCLESIASTES 2:1–11

I thought in my heart, 'Come now, I will test you with pleasure
to find out what is good.' But that also proved to be meaningless.
'Laughter,' I said, 'is foolish. And what does pleasure accomplish?'
— ECCLESIASTES 2:1–2

The Preacher put everything on earth to the test. He pursued pleasure, built houses and planted vineyards, accumulated silver and gold.
He was wealthier and more powerful than everybody before him. He
furthermore possessed extraordinary wisdom. All these things he was
involved in pleased him, but ultimately he realised that worldly pleasures never lasted. 'Yet when I surveyed all that my hands had done
and what I had toiled to achieve, everything was meaningless, a chasing after the wind; nothing was gained under the sun,' he said in
Ecclesiastes 2:11.

Like the Preacher, many people today enjoy pursuing worldly
pleasures and accumulating securities. Eventually they discover that
these things do not sastify them or make them happy. The empty
pleasures which the world offers you form a contrast to the lasting joy
which only God can key into the lives of his children. The Preacher
writes about this, 'So I commend the enjoyment of life, because nothing is better for a man under the sun than to eat and drink and be
glad. Then joy will accompany him in his work all the days of the life
God has given him under the sun' (Eccles 8:15). And the best way to
experience God's joy in your life is to be surrendered to Him.

❧ Lord, I have also discovered that the things of the world cannot give me
lasting joy. I therefore pray for your lasting joy in my life. Amen.

Failed surrender

READ: 1 KINGS 9:1–9

As for you, if you walk before me in integrity of heart and uprightness,
as David your father did, and do all I command and observe my
decrees and laws, I will establish your royal throne over Israel
for ever, as I promised David your father when I said, 'You
shall never fail to have a man on the throne of Israel.'
– 1 KINGS 9:4–5

God gave the young King Solomon a beautiful promise: If he were prepared to be fully committed to God, to do everything He commanded him and observe his decrees and laws, God Himself would confirm his throne over Israel and one of his descendants would always be on the throne of Israel.

Initially all went well with the young king; the whole world was aware of his incredible wealth and wisdom. Unfortunately Solomon's story did not have a happy ending. He was not really commited to God. Solomon deliberately chose to stray from God, whereupon his own desires and the gods of his heathen wives replaced God in his life. The warning in verse 7 was fulfilled literally: The Israelites were taken captive and their temple was destroyed.

Today God's warning is addressed to you personally: If you are not willing to be fully committed to Him, you will discover what it means to be without God's blessing in your life, just like Solomon did to his own cost. Get right with God and guard against other things which become more important to you than God.

❧ Heavenly Father, forgive me for still having so many other things in my life which are important to me. Help me to live uprightly and fully surrendered to You and to obey your decrees. Amen.

October 28

To surrender means you no longer live

READ: GALATIANS 2:15–21

For through the law I died to the law so that I might live for God.
I have been crucified with Christ and I no longer live,
but Christ lives in me. The life I live in the body,
I live by faith in the Son of God, who loved me
and gave himself for me.
– GALATIANS 2:19–20

Surrender to God means that you no longer live, but that God now lives in you. After Paul had surrendered his life to the Lord, the things which used to mean so much to Him were no longer important. He regarded those things as worthless because to know Jesus Christ as Lord surpassed everything else. Compared to the privilege of knowing Jesus Christ as Lord, everything he once thought important had become insignificant. He regarded only Christ as important in his life (cf Phil 3:7).

Surrender assumes that you no longer have to try to earn your deliverance: God gives it to you because Jesus paid the penalty for your sin by his death on the cross. By his Holy Spirit in you, God changes you from day to day so that your sinful self will gradually be changed so that you will become more like Jesus. But you will have to prove this surrender in your life: by living in such a way that others will be able to see that God is the most important Person in your life, so that they will be able to look at the things you do and give God the glory.

❧ Lord, make me willing to surrender myself to You so that nothing of my sinful self will be left, but that the Spirit will take full control of my life. Amen.

October 29

God is faithful

READ: 1 KINGS 8:22–30

O Lord, God of Israel, there is no God like you in heaven above
or on earth below – you who keep your covenant of love with
your servants who continue wholeheartedly in your way.
– 1 KINGS 8:23

In Solomon's prayer at the inauguration of the Temple, he stressed the fact that God remains faithful to those who serve Him wholeheartedly.

God is still absolutely faithful; He keeps every promise in his Word and you will also experience this if you are prepared to live fully surrendered to Him. Once, when Hezekiah of Judah fell ill, the prophet Isaiah brought him the message of doom from God saying, 'This is what the Lord says: "Put your house in order, because you are going to die; you will not recover."' Hezekiah was shattered by this message, but he reminded God that he had been fully committed to Him, 'Remember, O Lord, how I have walked before you faithfully and with wholehearted devotion and have done what is good in your eyes' (2 Kgs 20:1–3). And God listened to the plea of this child of his who had been prepared to commit his life to Him: He promised to extend Hezekiah's life by another fifteen years and also said that He would deliver him and his city from the hand of the king of Assyria (2 Kgs 20:6).

If you are willing to commit your life to God, He will fulfil his promises in your life too. And then you may remind Him like Hezekiah did that you have been fully committed to Him.

🌿 Heavenly Father, I praise You for being absolutely faithful, that You will fulfil all your promises in my life if I surrender myself to You. Amen.

October 30

Daily surrender

READ: ROMANS 7:15–25

I do not understand what I do. For what I want to do I do not do,
but what I hate I do … As it is, it is no longer I myself
who do it, but it is sin living in me.
– ROMANS 7:15, 17

We cannot think of anybody who was more committed to God than Paul. However, in his letter to the church in Rome this same Paul confessed that he was still doing the wrong things which he had already committed to God. That he fell into sin time and again, although he had been redeemed by God. Fortunately he knew exactly what to do when this happened – and he shared it with us: 'What a wretched man I am! Who will rescue me from this body of death?' he asked in desperation in Romans 7:24. And then he answers what he himself already knows 'Thanks be to God – through Jesus Christ our Lord!' (v 25). The vast majority of Christians have the same problem as Paul. As soon as we have committed our sin to God and tried to let it go, we trip over the same sin. Surrender is therefore a life-long story. You will have to commit your life to God all over every day. 'If anyone would come after me, he must deny himself and take up his cross daily and follow me. For whoever wants to save his life will lose it, but whoever loses his life for me will save it,' Jesus said in the well-known passage in Luke (Luke 9:23–24). Are you prepared to do this?

❧ Lord Jesus, I want to declare myself ready to commit my life to You anew every day. Forgive my sins and help me to live the way You want me to live. Amen.

October 31

Heavenly Father,

thank you that, this past month, I could once
again learn what surrendering to You
and your will really means.
I now want to offer myself as a living sacrifice to You:
I undertake to say no to the world in future
so that I can serve You and love You above all else in future.
I also want to take captive every thought
to make it obedient to You;
teach me to think in a new way.
From now on I want to be fully
in your service all the time.
Make me absolutely obedient to You
so that I will do exactly what You ask
without hesitation.
Reveal your will to me and make me willing
to surrender my own will,
so that your will can be done in my life.
I give You my money and possessions, Lord,
my fears, worries and dreams –
I bring everything to You and surrender them to You.
I also undertake to surrender myself,
to take up my cross and follow in your footsteps
for the rest of my life.
I want to rely only on You in future
so that I will no longer live
but You will live in me and
your Spirit will take full control of my life.
I praise You for your promise
that You are faithful and
that You will fulfil all your promises
to those who are fully committed to You.
Make me willing to recommit myself to You every day.

Amen

The peace which God gives _____

Reinhold Niebuhr wrote a prayer which could be of tremendous value to everybody at the end of the year:

> God, grant me the serenity
> to accept the things I cannot change,
> the courage to change the things I can,
> and the wisdom to know the difference.
> To live one day at a time,
> to enjoy one moment at a time,
> and to accept suffering as the way to peace,
> to take the sinful world as it is
> and not as I would have it,
> believing that God will make all things work together
> for good if I live surrendered to his will –
> so that I will be reasonably happy
> in this life and experience
> the greatest joy with Him for ever.[1]

During the very full month of November, when we have nearly forgotten what it means to experience God's peace in our lives, we will make this prayer part of our lives every day and, with God's help, have his perfect peace in our lives.

November

God's consolation

READ: PSALM 94

Blessed is the man you discipline, O LORD,
the man you teach from your law; you grant him
relief from days of trouble ... When anxiety was great
within me, your consolation brought joy to my soul.
– PSALM 94:12–13, 19

While he was writing this psalm, the psalmist was greatly distressed. Outwardly he was in a desperate situation – certain people were trying to kill him and they were gloating over his misfortune. Now he was longing for the peace God had promised him. This is also true of most of us towards the end of the year. By this time we are usually stressed and overworked. We can hardly face the remaining two months of the year. We don't sleep well, wake up early or struggle to wake up. We are worried and depressed and we yearn for the peace and quiet in our lives which only God can give.

The anxiety in the psalmist's innermost being was allayed because God consoled him. Anyone who needs a moment of peace and quiet, would really benefit from this advice. True peace can only come from God. Now is the time to decide once again to accept Jesus' invitation in Matthew 11:28–30, 'Come to me, all you who are weary and burdened, and I will give you rest. Take my yoke upon you and learn from me, for I am gentle and humble in heart, and you will find rest for your souls. For my yoke is easy and my burden is light.'

Lord Jesus, I am so stressed at the moment and I know only You can give me lasting peace. I come to You right now so that I can receive your peace. Amen.

November 1

Peace comes from God

READ: JOHN 14:23–31

Peace I leave with you; my peace I give you.
I do not give to you as the world gives. Do not
let your hearts be troubled and do not be afraid.
– JOHN 14:27

Jesus promised his disciples that He would leave them an inheritance consisting of peace when He went back to his Father. This peace and the peace of the world which they knew would be poles apart. His peace would not be determined by their physical circumstances and would also remove their fear and dismay. The Hebrew meaning of the word translated as peace actually means 'to be whole', or 'to be fulfilled'. Before we can experience Jesus' peace in our own lives we first have to realise that only God can give us real inner peace and tranquility. 'Tranquility, or peace, is a gift of God. We cannot produce it. We will never find a real, sincere and developing relationship with God outside in the world,' Trevor Hudson writes in his book, *The Serenity Prayer.*[2]

If you lack tranquility in your own life at the moment, pray that God will give you his peace; that He will replace the restlessness and stress in your heart with his tranquility and peace. He wants to do this for you, but you then have to undertake to turn back to Him. Once you do this, He Himself will give you his heavenly peace in exchange.

❧ Lord Jesus, I desire the peace which You give. Thank you for your promise that I can be rid of all my fears once and for all when your peace enters my life. Amen.

November 2

Acceptance is essential

READ: JOB 2:1–10

He replied, 'You are talking like a foolish woman.
Shall we accept good from God, and not trouble?'
– JOB 2:10

When a series of unexplained disasters hit poor Job, his wife encouraged him to curse God. However, Job refused. We have to accept good as well as trouble from God, he told her.

The first step on the road to peace is to learn to accept the things in your own life which you cannot change. In the long term you will not benefit from kicking against the pricks when disaster overtakes you, when you suffer from a chronic disease, or when you stress about big mistakes made in the past. If you cannot do anything to reverse these situations, the very best advice is to decide, like Job, to accept the things which come your way even if you would have preferred different circumstances. Discuss with God the things which you find hard to understand, ask Him to help you to accept them and learn to commit everything to Him. He already has the whole world in his hands, according to a well-known Negro spiritual. He can handle your major problems with his eyes shut. You can entrust each one of your problems to Him and safely leave them with Him.

❧ Lord, please help me to accept the negative things which have come my way because I know I will be able to handle everything with your help. Please help me to trust You completely. Amen.

November 3

Be still with God

READ: DEUTERONOMY 32:1–12

Let my teaching fall like rain and my words descend like dew,
like showers on new grass, like abundant rain on tender plants.
– DEUTERONOMY 32:2

In the beautiful song of praise which Moses recited to Israel, he described to them how Israel's God of the Covenant had made his people and had kept them, how He had cherished and led them. He also told them that the words of God would refresh his people like dew; that his teaching would be like rain, like rain showers on wheat.

All of us who have experienced drought in nature, know exactly how essential rain is for the soil; how wonderful a rain shower can be on the wilted plants, or how refreshing morning dew can be. God's children desperately need this refreshing which He gives – we cannot survive without it, just as the vegetation in nature cannot survive without water. For this reason every Christian should have daily devotions at a set time to study the Word of God and to talk to Him.

Make time to be still with God. The busier your daily programme, the more you need his refreshing. As soon as you become anxious, as soon as problems threaten to swamp you, commit them to the Lord immediately. Stop trying to handle them yourself. Ask Him every day to give you his peace and wisdom so that his refreshing teaching can be part of your life every day.

Father, thank you for daily quiet times with You when your Word can refresh me like dew and I can talk to You and listen to You. I now want to bring each of my problems to You - please give me the solutions. Amen.

November 4

Proviso for peace

READ: ISAIAH 32:9–20

The fruit of righteousness will be peace; the effect of
righteousness will be quietness and confidence for ever.
– ISAIAH 32:17

Modern man yearns for peace – in our country where violence continues its upward spiral and also in our lives where we have practically forgotten to be at peace with ourselves and others. However, true peace seems to evade us. Isaiah's prophesy over Israel does not seem to apply to us at all, because we no longer expect confidence and peace as a reward for 'righteousness'.

If you really want to experience God's peace 'which passes all understanding' in your own life and circumstances, you will have to to turn away from things which could jeopardise your own peace or the peace of others. Peace-seekers and peacemakers should know how to get the best from each situation. They should 'turn away from evil and do good; seek peace and pursue it' as the psalmist says in Psalm 34:14.

There is another requirement – you cannot pass on God's peace to others unless you already have that peace in your own heart and life. Ask God to make you a peacemaker where you live. If you are willing to do this, you may claim the promise in Matthew 5:9 for yourself: 'Blessed are the peacemakers, for they will be called sons [daughters] of God.'

❧ Father, I pray that You will make me a peacemaker, that You will place your peace in my heart and life, and that I will pursue this peace for the rest of my life. Amen.

November 5

Courage to change

READ: PSALM 31:14–24

But I trust in you, O LORD; I say, 'You are my God.'
My times are in your hands ... Be strong and
take heart, all you who hope in the LORD.
– PSALM 31:14–15, 24

We do not like admitting our mistakes, nor are we willing to change the wrong things in our lives. It always takes courage to recognise and admit our mistakes.

Think carefully about the things in your own life which have a negative effect on yourself and others: Perhaps your quick temper, your tendency to speak before thinking, your lovelessness towards others, the racism you just cannot get rid of. We know exactly what our shortcomings are. Identify your own characteristics which require change and also ask the Lord to point out characteristics which need to be changed. True change should come from the heart. Trust God to change you. If you ask Him, God will enable you by the power of his Holy Spirit to overcome your weaknesses. Just remember not to try to do this in your own strength, because it would then fail right at the start. However, with God's help you will succeed so that you will be able to say with the prophet Isaiah, 'Say to those with fearful hearts, "Be strong, do not fear, your God will come ..."' (Isa 35:4).

❦ Lord, I am so aware of all the negative things in my own life which need to be changed. Please give me the courage to confess these things before You and help me to get rid of them with your help. Amen.

November 6

You need wisdom

READ: PROVERBS 9:1–12

The fear of the LORD is the beginning of wisdom,
and knowledge of the Holy One is understanding.
– PROVERBS 9:10

When God has given you the courage to change the things in your life which you can change, you still need the wisdom to distinguish between accepting the inevitable and changing what can be changed. True wisdom is something only God can give you. It begins with serving the Lord, and only those who really know Him have understanding, the wise writer of Proverbs says in the core verse for today. The wisdom of God will enable you to know the difference between right and wrong in your own life; it will help you to make the right choices and be a happier person in future.

If you are trapped in a loveless marriage or a soul-killing job at the moment; if you really don't know whether you should simply slog on or risk making a change – ask God to give you the right answer. Pray about your problem. Discuss it with other Christians. Read your Bible and use the insight you find there. Listen attentively to God's voice in your life for a change. 'The wisdom we so desperately need cannot be bought or earned or discovered. It is given by God and has to be asked,' Trevor Hudson writes.[3]

Ask God right now to give you his Divine wisdom.

❧ Lord, please give me the wisdom which only You can give. Give me the ability to distinguish between right and wrong, between good and evil, so that I will be able to solve my problems with your understanding. Amen.

November 7

God will give you wisdom

READ: JAMES 1:2–8

If any of you lacks wisdom, he should ask God, who gives generously
to all without finding fault, and it will be given to him. But when
he asks, he must believe and not doubt, because he who doubts
is like a wave of the sea, blown and tossed by the wind.
– JAMES 1:5–6

The Bible has good news for you about the wisdom which you so desperately need. God wants to give it to you. Everything you should know about God's will in your life can be found in his Word. To obtain wisdom you must therefore know and study your Bible. When God's Word is unfolded, it gives light; it gives insight to those who are still inexperienced, writes the psalmist (cf Ps 119:130).

If you still have doubts about certain things, if you don't always know what to do, look in God's Word for answers to your worrying questions. He Himself will give you the necessary wisdom if you ask Him. Remember one condition though: You have to pray believing and not doubting that God is able to help you. Prayer should always be linked to faith, and it should also be manifested by your deeds. Therefore, if you ask God for wisdom, you must believe that He will give it to you – otherwise you are, in James' words, like a wave of the sea, blown and tossed by the wind (Jas 1:6).

❧ Heavenly Father, thank you for wanting to give me your wisdom. Help me to believe, without doubting, that You will answer my prayer. Amen.

November 8

When God whispers

READ: 1 KINGS 19:3–12

After the earthquake came a fire,
but the LORD was not in the fire.
And after the fire came a gentle whisper.
– 1 KINGS 19:12

Asking God for wisdom and believing that He will give it to you, is all very well – but sometimes it is difficult to decipher God's anwer. He does not always speak clearly, so that we sometimes have to listen very carefully to hear his whisper. Elijah thought he would hear God's voice in the earthquake or the fire, but after the fire there was a lull – and God spoke to Elijah in a gentle whisper.

God's personal message to you will easily be lost if you do not make time for Him in your busy daily programme. We are approaching the end of the year. Most of us are tired and discouraged, and our resistance is low. We have an overwhelming desire for peace and tranquility, for that serenity which only God can give you. If everything becomes too much, if God speaks so softly that you cannot hear Him, tell Him. Ask Him to give you his wisdom and peace. He promised to do this – in his own time and in his own way. However, remember that James says we have to pray without doubting (cf Jas 1:5–6).

❧ Lord, today I need You more than ever, but I can't seem to hear your voice clearly. Please show me what I should do - attune my ear to hear your whisper so that I will hear your message clearly. Amen.

November 9

One day at a time

READ: PSALM 68:19–29

Praise be to the Lord, to God our Saviour,
who daily bears our burdens.
– PSALM 68:19

God promises to carry us day after day; not week after week, or year after year. If you want to experience God's peace in your life, you will have to stop stressing about the future and merely pray for enough grace to get through today, to accept the challenges of today, to defuse the crises of today and to receive answers to the problems of today. For this reason Niebuhr's prayer reads: 'Grant me the serenity … to live one day at a time.'[4]

Those who have learnt this lesson for life can remain calm in the midst of the greatest crises because they have learnt to leave every-thing in God's hands. Decide right now to trust God one day at a time. He has more than enough knowledge to help you and to solve your specific problems. If you cannot handle them yourself any longer, leave them with Him and trust Him to undertake for you and to give you peace and prosperity.

Nothing is impossible with God. You can leave the unknown fu-ture in his hands with absolute peace of mind, because He is there, and He already knows what the future holds for you. He sees your ways and counts all your steps (Job 31:4). He promises to carry you until you are old and to be responsible for you.

❧ Father, thank you that I know that You will carry me day after day - until the end of my life; that You will meet all my needs and give me everything I need. Help me to trust you without wavering. Amen.

November 10

The gift of this day

READ: PSALM 118

This is the day the LORD has made;
let us rejoice and be glad in it.
– PSALM 118:24

Psalm 118 is a song of thanksgiving in which the psalmist praises God because He is good. He also calls everybody to praise God. Everybody, Israel, the house of Aaron, and everybody who serves the Lord, should praise God for his goodness.

Today, this day which you are experiencing at the moment, has been made by the Lord, and we must be glad about it, writes the psalmist. Most people plan far ahead – only to find that their plans are not fulfilled, because no-one knows what the future holds. The 'to-morrow' about which so many people are stressed, is still in the future – perhaps it will never dawn for you; yesterday is already past – unfortunately you cannot do anything about the mistakes and blunders of the past. Fortunately God gives you today to live to the full, to enjoy to the full.

Make today the happiest day in your life. Live with joy, notice the beautiful things around you, share your love lavishly with everyone you meet, notice the people who need your help and help them, be cheerful and kind and grateful. Laugh at yourself, make today a happy day for others, too. Today is a gift from the hand of God – according to an old saying, this day is called 'the present' because God gives it to you today, as a present – use it and enjoy it!

❧ Father, thank you for this day which You have made so that I can rejoice and be glad. Help me to live every day to the full with joy and gratitude. Amen.

November 11

Enjoy your life

READ: ECCLESIASTES 3:9–17

*I know that there is nothing better for men than to be happy and
do good while they live. That everyone may eat and drink, and
find satisfaction in all his toil – this is the gift of God.*
– ECCLESIASTES 3:12–13

According to the Preacher in Ecclesiastes, we enjoy nothing more than
being happy and doing good while we live. The ability to eat and
drink and to surround ourselves with things which make us happy is
after all a gift of God. God gives us so many things about which we
should rejoice – unfortunately many people take the ordinary little
joys for granted and completely forget to be happy about them.

You have to make a habit of enjoying the beautiful and enjoyable
things in your own life consciously, not to take anything for granted,
but to be aware of God's love and mercy in your life every day. Appreciate the things which He gives you. Make a list of the things you
enjoy; and allow enough time to be able to enjoy them. Perhaps today
is already later than you think, perhaps you do not have too many
tomorrows left. Do the things which you enjoy and find satisfying
today, and don't postpone them until you have enough time or
money. Tomorrow might be too late for you for ever.

❧ Lord, thank you for this day in which I can enjoy the good and pleasant
things in my life to the full. I praise You because I know that all these joys
come from your hand. Amen.

November 12

Learn to be grateful

READ: HEBREWS 12:25–29

Therefore, since we are receiving a kingdom
that cannot be shaken, let us be thankful and
so worship God acceptably with reverence and awe.
– HEBREWS 12:28

It is God's will that his children should be grateful people. And there are so many things to be grateful for. Things which God gives us by his grace: people we can love, health, food, clothes, possessions, beauty, music, books – all these things can light the flame of joy in our hearts. We should live in such a way that those who look at us will notice this gratitude and be more grateful for having known us.

Grateful people are people who have learnt to count their blessings every day and to praise God for them. Grateful people not only offer their gratitude to God but also to those around them. When last have you thanked someone who has helped you by making a telephone call or giving a small gift? Decide right now to make a list of all the things for which you are grateful and of all the people whom you owe a 'thank you'. Thank God every day for the blessings you receive from his hand and thank others lavishly – but see to it that you never expect a thank you when you have been kind to someone. And should you at times realise that you are feeling ungrateful and discontented, look around you and notice those who have far less reason to be grateful than you.

❧ Lord, please forgive me for so often being ungrateful, for so often taking your blessings for granted and forgetting to thank You. Help me to be more grateful in future. Amen.

November 13

Giving thanks for everything

READ: EPHESIANS 5:4B, 15–20

*… Thanksgiving … always giving thanks to God the Father
for everything, in the name of our Lord Jesus Christ.*
— EPHESIANS 5:4, 20

Christians should always be grateful. In due course you often discover that those things which had been the hardest to bear were actually the things which taught you the most about gratitude. An anonymous quotation says, 'Those who enjoy each ray of sunshine with gratitude, will also survive in the shade'.

As we grow older, we should realise more and more that gratitude is a way of life; that one can learn to be grateful in every circumstance, particularly about things which you would rather have changed. I have already mentioned one of my friends in a wheelchair and the other friend who has a handicapped child. Both of them have repeatedly said that these very situations have made them grateful people and have brought them into an intimate relationship with God. If everything in your life runs smoothly, you do not need God as much as when there is a reason to cling to Him. The Preacher therefore says the following for a reason: 'However many years a man may live, let him enjoy them all' (Eccles 11:8).

Think carefully about that one thing in your own life which you battle to accept with gratitude, and ask the Lord to make you grateful about it. He will show you why you should come to terms with it, because those things which we find the most difficult to accept are actually the things which teach us the most precious lessons for life.

❧ Lord, teach me to be grateful in everything - particularly that specific thorn in the flesh which I find so hard to come to terms with. Amen.

November 14

You will have trouble!

READ: JOHN 16:25–33

A time is coming … when you will be scattered,
each to his own home … I have told you these things,
so that in me you may have peace. In this world you will
have trouble. But take heart! I have overcome the world.
– JOHN 16:32–33

Shortly before his crucifixion, Jesus warned his disciples that a difficult time would come: a time when they would be scattered, a time when He would not be with them to help and to guide them. Although all of them would leave Him, He would not be alone because his Father would be with Him. He also told them plainly that they would have trouble in this world – yet this trouble which they would experience should never discourage them – they knew that Jesus had already conquered the world. For this reason those who believe in Him can have peace in their hearts in the midst of suffering.

We should accept the hard times in our lives as the way to peace, reads Reinhold Niebuhr's prayer. And this is not so easy, because suffering actually removes peace from our lives. However, if you are expecting suffering, it is eventually easier to come to terms with it. No-one can escape trouble on this earth – all we can do is to come to terms with it and hold on to Jesus' promises – after all, we know that trouble on earth moves us closer to the Father.

❧ Lord Jesus, I'm sorry that my problems sometimes make me doubt You; that they make me disgruntled so that I lose your peace. Thank you for the promise that You have already conquered the world. Amen.

November 15

Suffering is a reason for rejoicing

READ: JAMES1:1–8

Consider it pure joy, my brothers, whenever you face trials of many kinds,
because you know that the testing of your faith develops perseverance.
Perseverance must finish its work so that you may be mature
and complete, not lacking anything.
– JAMES 1:2–4

If we are struggling, we have to rejoice because trouble leads God's children to spiritual maturity, writes James. He also tells us what we can do to apply these lessons of trouble to our own lives: We have to be willing to endure and to persevere; we must pray for God's support and grace, and these prayers of ours must be rooted in faith. When we struggle we have the assurance that God shares our trouble and that He weeps with us.

'God shares our suffering,' Trevor Hudson writes. 'He is very deeply involved in all aspects of our lives – no fear, loss, grief, loneliness, despair, addiction or suffering can overtake us without God knowing about it and sharing it.'[5]

Joni Eareckson Tada who was paralysed in a diving accident as a teenager, wrote about her personal suffering in a book entitled *When God Weeps*. She wanted to stress the fact that God weeps with his children when they are suffering. For that reason we can rely on his love and mercy for us even when our world is shaken and when we have doubts, fears and questions. Do this when your own troubles try to jerk the rug from under your feet again.

❧ Heavenly Father, I struggle to rejoice about my own suffering. Please help me to persevere in faith and never to doubt You. Amen.

November 16

Joy in suffering

READ: PSALM 34:1–9

Those who look to him are radiant;
their faces are never covered with shame ...
Taste and see that the LORD is good.
– PSALM 34:5, 8

David had probably been in peril of his life shortly before he wrote this psalm. He said that the Lord had heard his cry and had saved him from the dangerous situation. For this reason he praised the Lord saying that it was possible to be cheerful even in difficult times.

Usually you do not feel radiant when you are struggling. Only children of the Lord can be cheerful in times of suffering because they know the Lord is with them; that He will carry them through the time of trouble. Because we know that God will never forsake us, we are able to smile through our tears. David also invites us in Psalm 34 to confirm this fact ourselves: We must taste and see that the Lord is good, he writes in verse 8.

When you are in trouble again, do what the psalmist recommends: Look up to God, remember how He has helped you in the past, time and again, and be glad! In the end you will discover that the trouble of the moment actually brought you closer to God, because it made you realise that you were totally dependent on Him, and God used your suffering to round off your maturity of faith and to strengthen you as his child.

🦋 Heavenly Father, please enable me to be radiant in times of trouble because I know You are with me and You will answer my prayers. Amen.

November 17

The world is a vale of tears

READ: ACTS 14:21–28

We must go through many hardships
to enter the kingdom of God.
– ACTS 14:22

When Paul and Barnabas addressed the believers in Lystra, Iconium and Antioch, they told them quite frankly that God's children would go through many hardships before they would enter the kingdom of God. This fact is still true in our day and it is furthermore stressed daily in our modern news media: You merely have to switch on the television news or page through a newspaper to hear and read about the negative things which happen in the world daily – in our country, and in the towns and cities where we live.

Sometimes we become discouraged when conditions seem to become worse and the future seems so negative. However, it is never necessary to become discouraged. God is still in control, even when it seems as if sin is running riot, as if Christians are battling more and more. According to Trevor Hudson,[6] God wants to meet you and bless you in these very situations. He is present in each one of your crises. Ask Him to solve your problems for you. He is perfectly capable of doing this.

As his child you have a task in this vale of tears on earth. God asks you to be salt and light; to spread his good news and to make a positive difference to the world around you. Are you doing this yet?

❧ Lord, the conditions in the world sometimes make me depressed and then I even doubt whether You are still in control. Please forgive me for this lack of faith and teach me once again that You hold the future in your hand. Amen.

November 18

Aliens and strangers

READ: 1 PETER 2:11–17

Dear friends, I urge you, as aliens and strangers in the world,
to abstain from sinful desires, which war against your soul.
– 1 PETER 2:11

Yesterday it was confirmed that this world in which we live is at best a vale of tears. According to Peter, God's children should not be citizens of this vale of tears, merely aliens and strangers. My grandmother often said that the Lord's children are 'in the world but not of the world'. 'Friends, this world is not your home, so don't make yourselves cosy in it,' the translation in *The Message* reads. 'Do not love the world or anything in it,' agrees John. 'If anyone loves the world, the love of the Father is not in him' (1 John 2:15).

Here on earth you are merely a visitor, merely passing through, and your visit lasts only a short time while you are preparing yourself for your real home in heaven. If you enjoy the world too much – so much that you actually do not look forward to heaven – you should see red lights flickering. See to it that your treasure is not on earth but in heaven because, as Jesus said in his Sermon on the Mountain, 'Where your treasure is, there your heart will be also' (Matt 6:21).

❧ Lord, I admit that I enjoy being on earth - that many things are precious to me and I wouldn't like to give them up. Please remind me that I am merely a visitor, and that my real home is with You in heaven. Amen.

November 19

God lets all things work together for good

READ: ROMANS 8:26–30

In all things God works for the good of those who love him,
who have been called according to his purpose.
– ROMANS 8:28

Paul writes to the church in Rome that God knows exactly what things you find hard and what circumstances you find discouraging. God knows you intimately and personally. If you have problems in your life at the moment which make you doubt God's love for you, He already knows about them. The work of the Holy Spirit is actually to submit these things to God's throne of grace so that God can provide for you. God is familiar with your difficult situation of the moment, and He is also able to reverse that situation, to work it into something good for you.

Lasting inner peace in your life is possible only if you believe that God will eventually make all things work together for your good; that He can also use the negative things in your life to your advantage. And this is not too difficult to accept – the Bible assures you in our core verse for today that God uses every event in your life to achieve his purpose with you. In the end all is well for God's children. The psalmist agrees with this in Psalm 138:8, 'The Lord will fulfil his purpose for me; your love, O Lord, endures for ever.'

Remember this promise if everything goes wrong in your life, and take God at his Word.

Lord, at the moment everything seems to be going wrong in my life, but I want to take You at your Word right now. Please let all things work together for my good eventually. I trust You for this. Amen.

November 20

Trust in the Lord

READ: PSALM 37:1–7

Trust in the LORD and do good; dwell in the land and enjoy safe pasture.
Delight yourself in the LORD and he will give you the desires of your heart.
Commit your way to the Lord; trust in him and he will do this.
– PSALM 37:3–5

If you are prepared to commit your life to the Lord and trust Him, He will take care of you and give you the desires of your heart, the psalmist writes. The prophet Isaiah also agrees that God is the One you can trust for life (cf Isa 33:6a). No-one who has ever committed their way to God and his promises has ever been put to shame.

Once you realise how great and omnipotent God is, and that this wonderful God loves you and promises to care for you, it becomes easy to surrender your whole life to Him, find your joy in Him and trust Him for everything in your life. If you find it hard to trust God unconditionally you can talk to other Christians who have already walked with God for quite a while, and use their practical experience to bolster your own faith in God.

You can also learn to strengthen your faith by discussing with God the things which undermine your trust. Spend more time with God, find 'trust' verses in your Bible and learn them by heart. Share with others how God has never put your trust to shame.

❧ Heavenly Father, thank you for the privilege of trusting You, of being able to commit my whole life into your hands because I know that You will care for me every day of my life. Amen.

November 21

God's will for your life

READ: COLOSSIANS 1:9–14

We have not stopped … asking God to fill you with the knowledge
of his will through all spiritual wisdom and understanding.
– COLOSSIANS 1:9

There are two groups of people: the one group is totally selfish, they focus only on themselves and do only what they want to do; the other group is prepared to discover God's will and live according to his will for them. Jesus' whole life was focused on doing the will of his Father. Before He did anything, He first consulted his Father to know his will. Even in the Garden of Gethsemane He was prepared to put God's will first although He pleaded fervently that God should remove the cup of suffering from Him: 'Yet not what I will, but what you will,' He prayed in Mark 14:36.

Only God Himself can reveal his will to people, and we can only know that will if the Holy Spirit gives us the wisdom and insight to do so. Although God's will and yours may be worlds apart, his will is always best for you. For this reason you usually experience inner peace and joy when you are prepared to obey God. And God's will is always that his children should live to the full, lovingly and honestly, that we should use our God-given gifts and fulfil our personal call. Finally it is God who works in you to will and to act according to his good purpose (Phil 2:13).

❧ Heavenly Father, please reveal your will to me by the wisdom and insight which your Spirit brings into my life. Make me willing to obey your will for my life, even if it differs from mine. Amen.

November 22

Seek God's will

READ: JEREMIAH 29:4–14

'I know the plans I have for you,' declares the Lord,
'plans to prosper you and not to harm you,
plans to give you hope and a future …
You will seek me and find me when
you seek me with all your heart.'
— JEREMIAH 29:11, 13

Just like parents who love their children and always want to give them the best, God's will for his children is also to profit them and not to harm them. He wants to give us a future, a hope, the prophet Jeremiah writes. And He makes it possible for us to know his will, provided we are willing to inquire about that will and obey it.

God has a specific task for each of his children. If we are willing to obey Him, we live within his will. Usually God's will for our lives is related to the special gifts or talents He has entrusted to us. If you would like to discover God's will for you, look at the gifts He has given you and then decide in what way you could use these things to the glory of God, to the extension of his Kingdom, and to the advantage of God's other children.

If you are willing to do this, if you want to seek God's kingdom and his will, He will give you all the other things as well, Jesus promises in his Sermon on the Mountain.

❧ Lord Jesus, thank you that your will includes my prosperity, that You are already preparing my heavenly future. Please show me in detail what your will for me involves and make me willing to obey You unconditionally. Amen.

November 23

Surrendering to God

READ: HEBREWS 10:32–39

You need to persevere so that when you have done
the will of God, you will receive what he has promised.
– HEBREWS 10:36

God has a universal will for his children: that we should live according to his will. Then He also has a specific will for each of us: that we
should develop and use the gifts He has entrusted to us.

Two things are required if you want to discover God's will in your
own life. You have to develop an intimate relationship with Him, because God will not reveal his will to you if you live far from Him and
refuse to obey his commands. Secondly, you have to be prepared to
persevere – because it is not always easy to do God's will – particularly not when it is contrary to your own desire and will. The second
last step of the twelve-step rehabilitation programme of Alcoholics
Anonymous reads: 'We strive to improve our conscious contact with
God through prayer and meditation, while we pray for knowledge of
his will for us and the strength to carry it out.'[7] Therefore, pray with
perseverance for knowledge of God's will and the strength to obey it.
Then you may rely on God to fulfil the promises for you which are
found in his Word. If you are willing to commit your whole life to this
will, you can take this beautiful promise in 1 John 2:17 for yourself
personally: 'The world and its desires pass away, but the man who
does the will of God lives for ever.'

❧ Heavenly Father, I pray that You Yourself will help me and give me the
necessary strength and perseverance to live the way You want me to, and to
do your will so that your promises can be fulfilled for me. Amen.

November 24

Happiness in this life

READ: PSALM 119:9–16, 54, 56

I rejoice in following your statutes as one rejoices in great riches …
Your decrees are the theme of my song wherever I lodge …
This has been my practice: I obey your precepts.
– PSALM 119:14, 54, 56

True happiness has very little to do with external circumstances. It is a feeling which comes from inside and which only God can give you. Your happiness depends on whether you obey God's commands. Those who do, experience God's peace and joy in their lives. The psalmist confessed that he rejoiced in obeying God's statutes as one would rejoice in great riches. But what exactly does this law of God involve? 'Let no debt remain outstanding, except the continuing debt to love one another, for he who loves his fellow-man has fulfilled the law,' Paul said in Romans 13:8.

God's two most important commandments are summarised by Jesus Himself in Matthew 22:37–38 in response to the Pharisee's question as to which is the greatest commandment in the Law: '"Love the Lord your God with all your heart and with all your soul and with all your mind." This is the first and greatest commandment. And the second is like it: "Love your neighbour as yourself."'

Happiness in this life therefore depends on your relationship with God and your relationship with your neighbour. Only when you love them sincerely (God above all and your neighbour as yourself) will you be able to claim true happiness.

❧ Heavenly Father, help me to love You above all, and others as myself so that I can experience consistent joy and peace in my life. Amen.

November 25

Rejoice despite suffering

READ: 1 PETER 1:3–9

In this you greatly rejoice, though now for a little
while you may have had to suffer grief in all kinds of trials.
These have come so that your faith ... may be proved genuine and
may result in praise, glory and honour when Jesus Christ is revealed.
– 1 PETER 1:6–7

It is humanly impossible to be happy at all times. For this reason
one of the lines of the prayer for serenity reads: 'so that I will be reasonably happy in this life'. When we look around us we do not see
many happy people left in the world. Violence, hatred, envy and
jealousy abound. Drug abuse, alcohol abuse, HIV/Aids and depres-
sion are increasing hand over fist. However, it is still possible to be
'reasonably happy' because God is present in the lives of his children
even during misfortune.

You can rejoice though you have to suffer misfortune and grief for
a while, Peter says, because these things prove your faith. God will be
able to see whether your faith is genuine or false by the way you respond. Ultimately misfortune produces positive results in your life,
because it teaches you to be able to 'write exams' so that your faith will
eventually prove genuine and will result in glory and honour when
Jesus Christ is revealed.

Ask God to give you his joy in your life – particularly in times of
trouble, so that others will be able to see that your faith is real.

❧ Heavenly Father, I now know that you want to use this trouble to prove
whether my faith is genuine. Please help me to pass the test. Amen.

November 26

God gives joy

READ: PSALM 16

Therefore my heart is glad and my tongue rejoices;
my body also will rest secure ... You have made known
to me the path of life; you will fill me with joy in your
presence, with eternal pleasures at your right hand.
– PSALM 16:9, 11

God Himself is our only Source of consistent joy – and best of all is that no-one and nothing can take this joy away from us. For this reason David rejoiced about his relationship with God in Psalm 16. He confessed that he belonged to God, that he had nothing to do with other gods, that God was his life and cared for him, that everything he had came from God (v 2–3, 5). Consequently his life was filled with joy – because God Whom he loved, was a source of abundant joy.

I have never met anyone who was 'radiant with joy' and not a Christian. True joy – the kind which does not have to depend on your circumstances at all – is impossible without God in your life. However, if you love and serve God you receive his joy freely and in such abundance that you will not be able to hide it from others. 'Splendour and majesty are before him; strength and joy in his dwelling-place,' reads the song of praise which David let Asaph and his men sing (1 Chron 16:27).

If God's consistent joy is still lacking in your own life, set your relationship with God right – then you will receive his joy as a bonus.

❧ Father, I pray that You will give me the abundant joy in my life which only You can give so that my life will overflow with your joy from now on. Amen.

November 27

A home in heaven

READ: 2 CORINTHIANS 5:1–10

Now we know that if the earthly tent we live in is destroyed,
we have a building from God, an eternal house
in heaven, not built by human hands.
– 2 CORINTHIANS 5:1

We have already discovered that God's children are actually strangers and aliens here on earth (see 19 November). For this reason it will be senseless to prepare grand homes on earth. We are merely tent-dwellers, Paul says in the core verse for today. However, one day when we no longer need this earthly tent, we have the promise of a permanent home in heaven – our real home. This heavenly home is not made by human hands – it is made by God Himself and is eternal.

You therefore no longer have to be so anxious about securities on earth and your future here in the world. If you belong to God, your life on earth is merely an in-between stage – a place where you are prepared for your life in heaven one day. As soon as you understand this fact well, your priorities should change and you will probably spend more time and attention on the things which really matter – those 'treasures in heaven' which Jesus spoke about in his Sermon on the Mountain. While you are on earth you should try to live the way God wants you to (cf 2 Cor 5:9).

✤ Father, thank you for the prospect that You Yourself are preparing my home in heaven - a home where I will live for ever. Please help me to live in accordance with your will while I am still on earth. Amen.

November 28

An immortal body

READ: 1 CORINTHIANS 15:42–55

The dead will be raised imperishable, and we will be changed.
For the perishable must clothe itself with the imperishable,
and the mortal with immortality.
– 1 CORINTHIANS 15:52B–53

When Jesus returns, incredible things will happen, Paul wrote to the church in Corinth. The dead will be raised and will live for ever, while the Christians who are still alive will be changed. When the last trumpet sounds at the second coming of Jesus, an imperishable, immortal body will replace our earthly, mortal bodies. When this happens death will have been destroyed completely, because God Himself will give us the 'clothes' in which we will meet Jesus and live for ever. *Die Bybellenium* calls it the 'robe of immortality'.

The older we are, the more aware we are of exactly how frail and perishable the mortal body is. As the years go by, we lose our strength, our senses become weaker and ailments increase. After sixty practically everyone suffers from some chronic ailment. Small wonder that some of the aged start longing for heaven! If you are battling with your earthly body at the moment, you may look forward to heaven with confidence. There you will always be healthy and without pain and your mortal body will be changed and clothed with honour and power, and you will be with God for ever.

❧ Heavenly Father, thank you that I will one day have an immortal, imperishable body when I will be with You for ever. Thank you that this fact makes it easier for me to live with my imperfect earthly body. Amen.

November 29

An end to all suffering

READ: REVELATION 21:1–8

And I heard a loud voice from the throne saying, 'Now the dwelling of God is with men, and he will live with them. They will be his people, and God himself will be with them and be their God. He will wipe every tear from their eyes. There will be no more death or mourning or crying or pain.
– REVELATION 21:3–4

On earth all of us have a hard time, but we have this promise that in the new heaven and the new earth which await all God's children we will experience a level of happiness such as we have never known before. There all pain, hurt and suffering will be over for ever. There we will always be with God and He will personally wipe away all tears. Christians therefore do not have to fear death at all. It is merely the way to get to God and heaven.

In the midst of the greatest suffering you can still hold on to this promise. 'Though outwardly we are wasting away, yet inwardly we are being renewed day by day. For our light and momentary troubles are achieving for us an eternal glory that far outweighs them all,' Paul promises in his letter to the Corinthians (2 Cor 4:16–17). One day in heaven our joy will be perfect because we will be with God. If you can build these three thoughts into your faith and allow them to change your life, you are on your way to a calm, joyful and wonderful life. Don't hesitate any longer.

Heavenly Father, it's wonderful to know that my suffering on earth will eventually lead to heaven where all suffering will be over and I will live with You for ever. Amen.

November 30

Heavenly Father,

please give me the ability
to pass on to You the things which
I cannot change – and to leave them with You.
Give me the courage to make positive changes
in my life, and the wisdom
to know the difference between
these two things.
Help me to be satisfied with the fact
that I cannot see far into the future,
and make me willing to live one day at a time,
and enjoy every moment.
Lord, I also pray for the grace to accept the difficult times
in my life as coming from You.
I realise that You want to use them to teach me valuable lessons
for life so that I will live even closer to You.
I know the world in which I live leaves
much to be desired – but I also know
that You will ultimately work
all things for my good.
In future I want to live in line with You so that
I will be able to be reasonably happy in this life.
Thank you for the promise that heaven awaits me –
that I will receive an immortal heavenly body
and a permanent heavenly home and
that all my suffering will then be over for ever.

Amen

Do you know about Jesus? _____

In December we celebrate the birth of Jesus. This month we will once again stand amazed at the magnitude of God's incomprehensible love for us; that He was willing to send his Son into the world and sacrifice Him to die the cruellest death imaginable so that we could be adopted as his children.

A remarkable sermon of Peter's is recorded for us in Acts 10 in which he confessed that he had not understood Jesus' ministry on earth before. In the light of this sermon we will now reflect on what each of us knows about Jesus and what his death on the cross meant to us personally.

It is my prayer that you will have a new understanding of Jesus' ministry on earth by the end of this Christmas season and also of the role that you should play in this ministry.

December

I now realise for the first time

READ: ACTS 10:9–35

Then Peter began to speak: 'I now realise how true it is that
God does not show favouritism but accepts men from
every nation who fear him and do what is right.'
– ACTS 10:34–35

By means of the vision of the sheet filled with all kinds of four-footed animals as well as reptiles and birds, which God commanded him to kill and eat, Peter got the very direct message from God that He is absolutely impartial. God told him that what He had made clean, people dare not regard as unclean. 'God has shown me that I should not call any man impure or unclean,' Peter told the men whom Cornelius had sent to him (Acts 10:28). He was immediately willing to accompany them to Cornelius' home.

Peter realised for the first time that God was no respecter of persons. In the past the Jews had regarded themselves as God's chosen people, and all other people as gentiles or heathen. Peter himself used to be intolerant; he wanted those who accepted Jesus to be circumcised – in other words they first had to become Jews. However, his attitude was changed and he realised that everyone has access to faith and mercy, provided they believed in Jesus.

Jesus had come into the world to convey this message: To everyone who believes in Him, God gives the right to be his child. Faith in Jesus is all we need to receive heaven. Do you realise that God has no favourites? It is to be hoped that you will be able to answer this question in the affirmative by the end of this Christmas season.

❧ Heavenly Father, thank you that You do not have favourites. Thank you that I may be your child because I believe in Jesus. Amen.

December 1

What Jesus came to do

READ: ACTS 10:37–48

*You know … how God anointed Jesus of Nazareth
with the Holy Spirit and power, and how he went around doing good and
healing all who were under the power of the devil, because God was with him.*
– ACTS 10:37–38

While He was on earth, Jesus did the work of his Father. Wherever He went He healed people, drove out demons and proclaimed the good news of the kingdom of God. He also gathered a small special group of people around Him who accompanied Him wherever He went and whom He equipped to carry on his work once He had returned to heaven.

Peter, one of that group of disciples, now told Cornelius and the people with him about the things which Jesus did and about his death on the cross and his resurrection. He also professed that everyone who believed in Jesus would receive forgiveness of sin. While Peter was still speaking, the Holy Spirit came on all who heard the message. The Jewish believers who had come with Peter were astonished that the gift of the Holy Spirit had been poured out even on the Gentiles. They were speaking in tongues and praising God. Thereupon Peter baptised all of them in the Name of Jesus Christ.

Every Christian should be a witness. God also expects you to proclaim his good news to others so that his kingdom can be extended throughout the world.

❧ Lord Jesus, please give me the confidence to convey your good news to everybody I meet like Peter. Amen.

December 2

Jesus died for us

READ: ACTS 10:39–43

They killed him by hanging him on a tree.
– ACTS 10:39

Sometimes we forget what our deliverance cost God and Jesus. When we look at the crucified Jesus we see God's love for sinners very clearly. God loved us so much that He gave his only Son to die for us. When Jesus was nailed to the cross and his blood was shed so that our sin could be forgiven it was actually God who was assuring mankind of his love for them.

The cross also shows us how much Jesus loves us: He gave up heaven for us to come into this sinful world. Here He did not even have a home of his own. He followed a simple lifestyle and during the last three years of his life, He and his group of disciples went from place to place to spread God's message of love. However, the fact that He was willing to suffer indescribable pain and humiliation on the cross, to lay down his life so that God could forgive our sin on the basis of his sacrificial death for us, is the absolute proof of Jesus' love.

The message of the cross 'seems like sheer silliness to those hell-bent on destruction, but for those on the way to salvation it makes perfect sense,' Paul wrote (1 Cor 1:18, The Message). Whenever you read about the cross, you should remember what it cost God to sacrifice his Son, and what it cost Jesus to pay the penalty for your sin.

❧ Heavenly Father, I praise You because the cross of Jesus not only demonstrates your love for mankind, but also Jesus' love for me personally. Amen.

December 3

The revelation of God's love

READ: 1 JOHN 4:7–13

This is how God showed his love among us:
He sent his one and only Son into the
world that we might live through him.
– 1 JOHN 4:9

Yesterday's reading reminded us that Jesus' death on the cross was a revelation of God's incredible love for mankind, for you and I. Jesus told Nicodemus about this love personally: 'God so loved the world that he gave his one and only Son, that whoever believes in him shall not perish but have eternal life' (John 3:16).

The French have a beautiful tradition at Easter of greeting one another on Good Friday with the words: *L'Amour de Dieu est folie* – 'God's love is folly'. When we think about the fact that the omnipotent Creator God gave his Son to die for sinful mankind we cannot comprehend it. It indeed sounds like folly. In terms of the standards of the world, God's love may indeed look like folly, but to us who believe in Him, it is a miracle which we should never take for granted. It should remain incredible to us every day, not only at Easter and Christmas, but for the rest of our lives.

Dozens of verses in the Bible assure us of this 'foolish' love of God for the world, yes, for you and me, too. Make a list of these verses and start every day by reading one of them and thanking God for loving you so much that He demonstrated his love by sacrificing his Son for you.

❦ Heavenly Father, your love for me amazes me! It is so undeserved that I cannot see how it can make any sense, but I accept it with gratitude. Thank you for loving me so much. Amen.

December 4

The love of Jesus

READ: EPHESIANS 3:14–19

And I pray that you … may have power, together with all the saints,
to grasp how wide and long and high and deep is the love of Christ,
and to know this love that surpasses knowledge …
– EPHESIANS 3:17–19

The cross of Jesus is not only the revelation of God's love for the world, but also of Jesus' love for you and me personally. He loves us so much that He was willing to leave heaven to come into the world as a man and die the cruellest death imaginable so that you and I can be God's children. While He was on earth, Jesus was a human being like we are. In Gethsemane his agony before the crucifixion was so severe that his perspiration became like drops of blood and He pleaded that his Father should take away the cup of suffering. He nevertheless remained obedient to his Father – even to death on the cross. Because He loves us so much He hung on the cross suffering the most indescribable pain and died so that your penalty for sin could be paid once and for all, so that you could become God's child and live for ever.

Jesus loved you so much that He was prepared to give his life for you – but He now expects you to live for Him. And when you think about the magnitude of his love for you, it should not be a difficult decision to follow Him.

❦ Lord Jesus, I cannot understand your love for me with my human mind, but I do understand how wide and high and deep and far that love reaches. In exchange I would like to offer You my love. Amen.

December 5

In Him was life

READ: JOHN 1:1–13

In the beginning was the Word, and the Word was with God,
and the Word was God ... Through him all things were made ...
In him was life, and that life was the light of men.
– JOHN 1:1, 3–4

Jesus was there from the beginning – He was involved in the creation with the Father. According to John's gospel everything was created through Him; nothing came into existence without Him, and what came into existence was Life, and this Life was Light to live by (*The Message*).

True life can only be created by God, and eternal life is only found with God. The most important purpose of Jesus' death on the cross was to make eternal life available to everyone who believes in Him. Only those who believe in Jesus can know that they have eternal life. 'Whoever believes in the Son has eternal life, but whoever rejects the Son will not see life, for God's wrath remains on him' (John 3:36).

Jesus gives new meaning to the word 'life' – before He came people did not know what 'eternal life' meant. However, by his resurrection He not only conquered death forever, but also assures everyone who believes in Him of eternal life. If you believe in Jesus, your whole life changes. You now know that you no longer have to fear death, because death does not have the last word about you – Jesus makes eternal life with God possible for you.

❧ Lord Jesus, thank you that your death means my life, that I know even now that I will one day live in heaven for ever because I believe in You. Amen.

December 6

God's Son and Himself God

READ: JOHN 1:14–18

The Word became flesh and made his dwelling among us.
We have seen his glory, the glory of the One and Only,
who came from the Father, full of grace and truth.
– JOHN 1:14

We are often so busy with this Jesus who was born as a human baby, who grew up in Nazareth, went throughout the land of Israel to proclaim God's message to the people and who eventually died on the cross, that we forget that not only was Jesus the Son of God, He was God Himself. The core verse for today underlines the incredible fact that God was prepared to become a human being for us – to live among us. In the original Greek the image used means that God actually 'pitched his tent' among us. Jesus became a man so that we could really hear and see and understand Him. However, we must never forget that He was also God. 'The Son is the radiance of God's glory and the exact representation of his being, sustaining all things by his powerful word … So he became as much superior to the angels as the name he has inherited is superior to theirs,' says the writer of the letter to the Hebrews (Heb 1:3–4).

When you celebrate Christmas this year, celebrate Jesus as God Himself, the Son who radiates God's glory, and Who 'mirrors God' perfectly (*The Message*), and through Whom God created the world.

❧ Lord Jesus, I worship You as the exact representation of God, the One who is the radiance of God's glory, yes, as God Himself. I praise You for having been willing to become man so that I could be accepted by God. Amen.

December 7

Jesus is risen!

READ: ACTS 10:40–41

But God raised him from the dead on the third day and
caused him to be seen. He was not seen by all the people,
but by witnesses whom God had already chosen …
– ACTS 10:40–41

Jesus conquered death and the evil powers forever by rising from the dead. At his resurrection He won the decisive victory over Satan, although the final victory will only be completed at his second coming. In the meantime his followers will still be involved in this battle against the evil one, but we know that we, like Jesus, can also be the victors in this battle because He who is in us is greater than the one who is in the world.

'I am the resurrection and the life. He who believes in me will live, even though he dies; and whoever lives and believes in me will never die,' Jesus promised Martha after her brother Lazarus had died (John 11:25–26). This promise still applies to everyone who believes in Him. Just as Jesus rose from the dead, his followers will also rise from the dead one day. 'Death has been swallowed up in victory,' Paul rejoiced in 1 Corinthians 15:54. God gives us that victory in Jesus Christ. Faith in Jesus also guarantees that you will one day be with Jesus in heaven forever. What's more, He is preparing your place for you in heaven right now.

❧ Lord Jesus, it is wonderful to know that you have already conquered death and the devil on my behalf and that You came to offer me the gift of eternal life. Amen.

December 8

Forgiveness of sin

READ: ACTS 10:34–43

They killed him by hanging him on a tree …
All the prophets testify about him that everyone who
believes in him receives forgiveness of sins through his name.
– ACTS 10:39, 43

Peter explained to Cornelius and the others gathered there that God forgives the sin of those who believe in Jesus. All of us sin from birth, and we are burdened with this sin, which God says deserves the death penalty because He is holy and cannot tolerate sin. But God is also merciful – He gives us a choice and a way in which we can be delivered from our sin: If we believe in Jesus and confess our sin, He forgives us our sin and adopts us as his children.

On the cross Jesus purchased you the right to be forgiven by God. You can therefore confess your personal sin with confidence because God will forgive that sin since his Son has paid the penalty for our sin. Jesus paid the penalty for your sin once and for all. No other sacrifice for your sin is now required because He died for you. In the Old Testament the blood of the sacrificial lamb promised forgiveness for the people of God for a little while, but this sacrifice had to be repeated regularly. However, the blood of Jesus guarantees God's forgiveness for ever – it is a once-only sacrifice which never has to be repeated: 'In him we have redemption through his blood, the forgiveness of sins, in accordance with the riches of God's grace that he lavished on us,' Paul said in Ephesians 1:7.

Lord Jesus, I praise You for having been prepared to sacrifice Yourself for my sin, so that God is now prepared to forgive all my sin. Amen.

December 9

We are witnesses!

READ: ACTS 10:39–43

*We are witnesses of everything he did in the country of the Jews and
in Jerusalem … He commanded us to preach to the people and
to testify that he is the one whom God appointed …*
– ACTS 10:39, 42

Peter concluded his eloquent sermon with the message that the disciples were witnesses of everything Jesus did on earth. Just as Jesus proclaimed the good news that God loved people and wanted to deliver them from sin, He also entrusted this message to his small group of followers to proclaim it throughout the known world after his ascension. The handful of disciples were given the huge task of proclaiming this message of Jesus' coming into the world and the deliverance which He brought to the world.

In his last message to them, Jesus also gave them this command personally: 'Go and make disciples of all nations, baptising them in the name of the Father and of the Son and of the Holy Spirit, and teaching them to obey everything I have commanded you' (Matt 28:19–20).

Jesus' command of reaching out to others still applies to his followers even in the 21st century. It is your task and mine to tell others about Jesus, and to confirm that God Himself had appointed Him. It is furthermore our responsibility to proclaim 'that everyone who believes in him, receives forgiveness of sins through his name' (Acts 10:43).

Are you fulfilling your task yet?

❧ Lord Jesus, please forgive me for being such an unenthusiastic witness; for having so many excuses as to why I cannot tell others about You. Thank you that You promised to assist your children when they witness for You until You return. Amen.

December 10

The message

READ: LUKE 1:76–80

The rising sun will come to us from heaven to shine on
those living in darkness and in the shadow of death,
to guide our feet into the path of peace.
– LUKE 1:78–79

Jesus is God's letter of peace to people. This is a message which the priest Zechariah, the father of John the Baptist, wants to stress in the verse for today. At that first Christmas this was also the message the angels delivered to the awe-stricken shepherds: 'Suddenly a great company of the heavenly host appeared with the angel, praising God and saying: "Glory to God in the highest, and on earth peace to men on whom his favour rests"' (Luke 2:13–14).

Peace on earth is a gift we should receive anew every Christmas. And in our country we have never needed peace as desperately as right now. Jesus' Christmas message says that He wants to guide your feet into the path of peace: He wants to give you his peace with the people around you, as well as peace with the God who sent his Son to die for you. And, as Jesus Himself said, the peace He gives is not like the peace of mankind at all because their peace is merely a truce. The peace which Jesus wants to give you this year, is a peace which will heal you; a peace which will guarantee you serenity and reconciliation for the rest of your life. It is probably one of the most wonderful Christmas gifts you will ever receive!

❧ Lord Jesus, thank you for your gift of peace at Christmas. Please help me to have the inner peace, which only You can give, in my heart for the rest of my life. Amen.

December 11

Peace between God and man

READ: EPHESIANS 2:11–18

For he himself is our peace, who has made the two one and has destroyed the barrier, the dividing wall of hostility, by abolishing in his flesh the law with its commandments and regulations. His purpose was to create in himself one new man … and in this one body to reconcile both of them to God through the cross, by which he put to death their hostility.
– EPHESIANS 2:14, 16

Before Jesus' birth Israel had looked forward to the birth of the promised Messiah for centuries. They thought that this Messiah would deliver them from the yoke of the Romans, but this did not happen. Jesus' kingdom differed totally from the kingdom which the Jews had expected, and instead of his people recognising Him as Redeemer, they had Him crucified because He did not fulfil their expectations.

At Christmas, which is literally round the corner, we celebrate the coming of the Holy Child into the world. He came to make peace between sinful mankind and a holy God. God is prepared to be reconciled to you, because Jesus has paid the penalty for your sin by dying on the cross. You should therefore take the matter of your relationship with God seriously, and make sure whether you are really pursuing the peace which Jesus gives. Everyone who confesses Jesus as Redeemer should be a living symbol of this peace, which only Jesus can give us. If you have made peace with God, his peace will rule in your life. Never make peace with the brokenness of the world around you. You should also always be willing to work towards peace, to set your relationship with others right, so that you can experience Jesus' lasting peace in your life.

❧ Lord Jesus, make me willing to work on my relationships so that the peace which You made possible between God and man will also be fulfilled in my relationships. Amen.

December 12

Peace among men

READ: COLOSSIANS 3:13–17

Bear with each other and forgive ... one another ...
Let the peace of Christ rule in your hearts, since
as members of one body you were called to peace.
– COLOSSIANS 3:13, 15

Peace affects your whole being because it stems from an unconditional relationship with God based on trust. Only when your relationship with Him is right will you be prepared to set your relationship
with others right.

The Greek word, which is translated as 'peace' means to be whole.
At Christmas everybody should try their best to mend the broken
relationships in their lives because there is always a close relationship
between peace with God and peace among men.

Once Christmas is past and we no longer hear Christmas carols,
when we look past the bright Christmas trees and presents and see
the darkness outside, it sometimes feels as if Jesus never really came
– because so little of the peace which He brought is visible among
people in our world.

The word peace concerns relationships. What do your relationships
with your husband, your children, your family, your acquaintances
and your church look like? Do you experience peace in your own life
because you serve the Prince of Peace?

The healing of relationships always assumes reconciliation between two parties. If you are aware of troubled relationships in your
own life, be reconciled to whoever is concerned.

❧ Father, there are still so many people with whom I often quarrel and with
whom I struggle to make peace. Forgive me, Lord. Help me to be reconciled
to You and others. Amen.

December 13

Peace or a sword?

READ: MATTHEW 10:34–39

Do not suppose that I have come to bring peace to the earth.
I did not come to bring peace, but a sword … anyone who loves his
father or mother more than me is not worthy of me; anyone who
loves his son or daughter more than me, is not worthy of me.
– MATTHEW 10:34, 38

You can have a wrong impression of peace. The peace which Jesus has in mind here involves a choice which will change your life dramatically. You must be willing to bear a cross for the sake of his peace, to follow Him on his way of the cross, to deny yourself, all for the sake of peace! If you really have a relationship with God, all other things, people and relationships should be subordinate to Him. You may not love anybody more than God – not even your husband or children or grandchildren who are so precious to you. Nothing and nobody may be more important to you than God. This is the message which Jesus wants to impress on your mind this Christmas. Only once you have really made peace with God all your other relationships will also fall into place.

However, peace is never a finalised agreement. As we are sinners, we can lose our peace time and again. Peace as a quality of the fruit of the Holy Spirit is possible in your life only if you are prepared to surrender the control of your whole life to God.

❧ Lord, forgive me for still regarding so many people and things as more important than You. Help me not to love anyone more than I love You. Amen.

December 14

God changes people

READ: LUKE 2:8–20

So they hurried off and found Mary and Joseph, and the baby,
who was lying in the manger. When they had seen him, they
spread the word concerning what had been told them about this child,
and all who heard it were amazed at what the shepherds said to them.
– LUKE 2:16–18

The dramatic events in the fields near Bethlehem that first Christmas night changed the lives of the group of shepherds forever. Initially they were panic-stricken when the angelic host appeared and the glory of God shone around them. Then they were reassured and amazed by the angel's message – that the long-expected Messiah had at last been born in Bethlehem. A great company of the heavenly host appeared and praised God and when they had gone back into heaven, the shepherds went to Bethlehem to see the newborn child with their own eyes. They were so moved by the events that they spread the word concerning what they had seen and what they had been told about the Child. Luke says that all who heard it were amazed at what the shepherds told them.

Meeting God always changes you. Those who surrender their lives to Him are made new by Him because He forgives their sins. When you meditate on everything that happened on that first Christmas, your life should also be changed. You should be amazed about the wonder of Christmas and share it with others. And you could also tell others at Christmas what God did for you – and how He made your life new when you acknowledged Jesus as your Saviour.

✣ Heavenly Father, thank you for still turning people who believe in the wonder of Christmas into new creatures. Please make me an enthusiastic witness for You this Christmas. Amen.

December 15

Reconciled to God

READ: 2 CORINTHIANS 5:16–21

All this is from God, who reconciled us to himself through Christ and gave us the ministry of reconciliation: that God was reconciling the world to himself in Christ, not counting men's sins against them.
– 2 CORINTHIANS 5:18–19

Today we celebrate the Day of Reconciliation. Israel also had such a festival, Yom Kippur, or the Day of Atonement. On this day they confessed their sins and asked God to forgive their sin. The high priest first brought a sacrifice for his own sin and the sin of the priests, and then a sacrifice for the sin of the people. This was the only day on which the high priest was permitted to enter the Holy of Holies of the temple.

Our core verse says very clearly that God reconciled mankind to Himself through Christ and our sins no longer count against us. Our sins are therefore forgiven and we are made new creatures only because Jesus paid the penalty for our sin and not because we do anything by which we can earn our forgiveness. Madeleine d'Engle says that the meaning of atonement is very clear when the word is divided into three words: *at-one-ment*.[1] Atonement therefore actually means becoming one with Christ so that his deed of atonement applies to us as well.

Think about your reconciliation to God this Christmas; remember that it can only be realised by the intervention of Christ. It cost Jesus his life to bring you to God. During this Christmas season you should reveal your gratitude about having been reconciled to God by being reconciliatory to others. God has, after all, 'committed to us the message of reconciliation' (2 Cor 5:19).

Heavenly Father, I praise You for your reconciliation; that You reconciled me to Yourself through Jesus. Make me willing to be reconciled to others too. Amen.

December 16

Power from on high

READ: LUKE 24:45–49

You are witnesses of these things. I am going to send you
what my Father has promised; but stay in the city until
you have been clothed with power from on high.
– LUKE 24:48–49

Jesus never commands us to do something without providing a way in which we will be able to obey Him. He knew very well that it would be impossible for his small group of followers to proclaim his gospel throughout the whole known world. He therefore promised them a gift, 'the promise of my Father', to help them to carry out their task. In John 15 He told his disciples that when He went back to his Father He would send his Counsellor to them to help them with their task: 'When the Counsellor comes, whom I will send to you from the Father, the Spirit of truth who goes out from the Father, he will testify about me. And you must also testify, for you have been with me from the beginning' (John 15:26–27).

'You will receive power when the Holy Spirit comes on you; and you will be my witnesses,' He promised them shortly before his ascension (Acts 1:8). God still gives his children instructions which seem rather impossible to us, but by the power of the Holy Spirit He enables us to do the impossible. Yesterday was the Day of Reconciliation. Make it your aim to be an instrument of God's reconciliation in the world this year. You will only be able to do this by the power of God's Spirit.

Holy Spirit, please equip me to be a witness in the world to carry out the message of Jesus' reconciliation. Amen.

Jesus, the true Light

READ: JOHN 1:1–9

The true light that gives light to every man was coming into the world …
In him was life, and that life was the light of men. The light shines
in the darkness, but the darkness has not understood it.
– JOHN 1:9, 4–5

At Christmas we celebrate the coming of Jesus, the Light of the world. In Isaiah 9:1 the prophet prophesied that the people who lived in darkness had seen a great light; that a great light would shine over those who lived in the dark land. This prophecy was fulfilled at the birth of Jesus although He had shone his light on mankind from the beginning. The light of Jesus drove away the darkness of sin in the world – because darkness cannot prevail against the light which He shines into our lives.

If you believe in Jesus, you are a person of light. 'The fruit of the light consists in all goodness, righteousness and truth,' Paul told the church in Ephesus. And he therefore commanded them, 'Live as children of light' (Eph 5:9, 8).

However, this is not all, Jesus' followers are not only people of the light, they are lights! 'You are the light of the world,' Jesus said in his Sermon on the Mountain, and added: 'Let your light shine before men, that they may see your good deeds and praise your Father in heaven' (Matt 5:14, 16).

Therefore live in such a way this Christmas season that everyone will be able to see that you are a child of the light, and so that they will glorify God because they know that the light in you comes from Him.

❧ Lord Jesus, I worship You as the Light of the world, and I not only want to live as a child of the light, but I want to be a light for You in the dark world this Christmas season. Amen.

December 18

What do you believe about Jesus?

READ: JOHN 1:1–13

He came to that which was his own,
but his own did not receive him.
– JOHN 1:11

The world responded in two ways to the Light: Some invited Him into their lives with joy and the rest turned their backs on Him. When Jesus started doing miracles, many people did not believe in Him. It is quite sad to think that the people in the village of Nazareth where He grew up refused to believe in Him. They never saw Him as more than 'Mary's son' whom they knew from childhood. In fact, the very people for whom Jesus came into the world actually rejected Him. His own people, the Jews, had Him crucified. And the irony of the whole matter was that they crucified Him because He called God his Father.

God spoke audibly to Jesus twice in the New Testament – once at his baptism and again at the transfiguration on the mountain, and both times He confirmed that Jesus was his Son. Millions of people still reject Him. Many religions recognise Him as a great prophet, but not as God. 'Jesus, the best expression of God's being, still evokes just as much rejection as in his day,' Philip Yancy writes.[2]

What do you believe about Jesus? What does He mean to you? Was He merely an exceptional human being, or the Son of God, God Himself, Who gave his life so that you could have eternal life?

✣ Lord Jesus, I worship You as the only Son of God and also God, and I praise You for having been prepared to come into the world and to die on a cross so that I can go to heaven one day. Amen.

December 19

When the Word became flesh

The Word became flesh and made his dwelling among us.
We have seen his glory, the glory of the One and Only,
who came from the Father, full of grace and truth.
— JOHN 1:14

Many Christmas sermons have been based on this verse. Yet we do not really understand what it means to us personally that God became a man for us, that He left heaven and came into the world to live and suffer here as an ordinary human being. Augustine's beautiful explanation gave me a new perspective of Jesus' becoming a man: 'The Maker of man became a man so that He, Ruler over the stars, would be nursed by his mother, so that the Bread would suffer hunger, the Fountain would become thirsty, the Light would sleep, and the Way would become tired of his journey; so that the Truth would be accused of giving false evidence, the Teacher would be whipped and the Foundation would be hung on a cross; so that the Power would become weak; the Healer be wounded; and so that the Life would die.'[3]

By this verse John wanted to tell us about the tremendous difference Jesus' becoming man made in our lives: He became a man so that we could know his glory and share in the glory ourselves by becoming more and more like Him. He became a man so that you and I could become God's children. Try this Christmas season to follow Jesus' example to make a positive difference in the world like He did.

❧ Lord Jesus, I stand amazed that You, the King of the Universe, were prepared to become an ordinary man and to live among us. Help me to make a positive difference where I live, like You did. Amen.

December 20

Christmas and the Holy Spirit

READ: ISAIAH 11:1–9

*A shoot will come up from the stump of Jesse; from his roots a Branch
will bear fruit. The Spirit of the LORD will rest on him – the Spirit of
wisdom and of understanding, the Spirit of counsel and of power,
the Spirit of knowledge and of the fear of the LORD.*
– ISAIAH 11:1–2

The Holy Spirit is inextricably part of Christmas. The prophet Isaiah
prophesied that a new shoot would come up out of the royal house of
David (the stump of Jesse). The person referred to here would find joy
in the service of the Lord. Verse 2 explains how it would be possible:
the Spirit of God would rest upon the 'sprout' which would come up
from the stump of Jesse. God would therefore bring a second 'David'
and He Himself would equip Him for his task. From God Himself He
would receive the various attributes which the King should have: wisdom and insight, counsel and power, knowledge and respect for the
Lord. He would also introduce a perfect rule of peace on earth.

The Holy Spirit would enable this 'new shoot', Jesus, to rule on
earth. The Holy Spirit quickened the life in Mary: 'The Holy Spirit
will come upon you, and the power of the Most High will overshadow you,' the angel told her (Luke 1:35). It was also the Holy Spirit
who let Elizabeth sing a song of praise to the glory of God and
Zechariah prophesied when he was filled with the Holy Spirit (cf
Luke 1:42–45, 67 –79).

During this Christmas season you can surrender your life to the
Holy Spirit anew.

❧ Spirit of God, thank you that You are part of Christmas, and that You
gave wisdom and insight; counsel and power and honour for God to Jesus
then, and to us now. Amen.

December 21

The glory of Jesus

READ: 2 CORINTHIANS 4:1–6

For we do not preach ourselves, but Jesus Christ as Lord,
and ourselves as your servants for Jesus' sake. For God, who said,
'Let light shine out of darkness,' made his light shine in our hearts to
give us the light of the knowledge of the glory of God in the face of Christ.
– 2 CORINTHIANS 4:5–6

In his letter to the church in Corinth, Paul said that they did not understand his preaching because their minds had been blinded by the devil. Consequently they could not see the glory of Christ. 'They're stone-blind to the dayspring brightness of the Message what shines with Christ who gives us the best picture of God we'll ever get' (2 Cor 4:4, The Message). However, Paul, who proclaimed Jesus as Lord, had knowledge of the glory of God which Jesus radiated.

In the previous chapter of his letter to the Corinthians he wrote that the veil which kept them blind would be taken away by Jesus because whenever anyone turns to the Lord, the veil is taken away – and they would reflect the glory of the Lord. And when this happens we would change more and more so that this glory will also be visible in our lives. The glory which Paul referred to here should increase steadily by the Holy Spirit working in our lives (cf 2 Cor 3:14–18).

During this month you should focus on the glory of Jesus; your life and your actions should radiate his glory so that others would see his glory in you. Let the glory of Jesus Christ increase in your life during this Christmas season.

❧ Lord Jesus, please let your light shine in my heart so that I will not only see your glory during this Christmas season but also reflect it in my life. Amen.

December 22

Peace on earth

READ: LUKE 2:13–15

Suddenly a great company of the heavenly host appeared with the angel,
praising God and saying, 'Glory to God in the highest, and
on earth peace to men on whom his favour rests.'
– LUKE 2:13–14

The angel's announcement of good news to a group of shepherds was followed by a host of angels who brought a message of peace to those who love God. Jesus is the King of peace who was born so that God's peace which was destroyed by the Fall could rule on the earth again. By the life and death of this Prince of Peace, reconciliation between the holy God and sinners would be brought about. This peace of which the angels were singing, is a peace which enables us to have God's peace in our hearts although we live in a world without peace; to be peacemakers because we love the Prince of Peace.

Isaiah prophesied the birth of the Child who would be the 'Prince of Peace' (Isa 9:6). Jesus brought about this peace by his death on the cross and this Christmas He once again offers you his peace. 'Peace is a way of life,' my husband once said in a Christmas message. 'Peace is the smile we give one another because we live day after day under the smile of God.' God wants to teach you to live in such a way from today that you will be able to live in peace with other people. May the God of peace become a reality to you this Christmas season.

❧ Lord Jesus, I worship you as the Prince of Peace. Please give me your lasting peace in my heart and life so that I can be a peacemaker on earth. Amen.

December 23

God's love for the world

READ: JOHN 3:13–21

For God so loved the world that he gave his one and only Son,
that whoever believes in him shall not perish but have eternal life.
– JOHN 3:16

When Jesus came into the world, God's love for us was demonstrated in a way which we cannot ignore. God gave his only Son so that you and I could have eternal life. This love reached a climax on Golgotha when Jesus died on the cross so that those who believe in Him will never be lost but have eternal life. I read somewhere that a writer posed the question: 'Does God really love us?' And then he answered his own question by saying: 'Look at the crucified Jesus. Look at the rough cross, at every thorn which penetrated his forehead, at every bruise where heavy fists struck Him. All these wounds expressed God's words: "I love you."'[4]

At Christmas we are once again reminded of the magnitude of that love. God's love for you should kindle love for Him and also for others in your heart. This year you and I can respond to this immeasurable love of God by making Christmas a day on which we will treat others with love and respect, pursue God's peace and radiate his joy so that the world can become a better place for everybody. May God's love, peace and joy be an inextricable part of your life every day so that the wishes for a 'Blessed Christmas' tomorrow will indeed be fulfilled in your life.

❧ Lord, thank you for your incredible love for me. Please fill me with your love, peace and joy this Christmas season so that it will be part of my life from today. Amen.

December 24

Three wishes for Christmas

READ: ROMANS 15:7–13

May the God of hope fill you with all joy and peace as you trust in him,
so that you may overflow with hope by the power of the Holy Spirit.
– ROMANS 15:13

In an article in the Christmas copy of the magazine, *Lééf* (2005), several people were asked about their dreams for Christmas. A police inspector said that during her 30 years as a policewoman she had rarely spent Christmas with her family. It nevertheless remains the most special time of the year to her because she believes in God. Her idea of a perfect Christmas, she said, was a Christmas without violence, a day when police would be unnecessary.

A tennis coach whose daughrter was involved in a nearly fatal car accident dreamt of sitting in the silence of a small thatched chapel close to the sea on Christmas morning and thanking God that his family was still intact. A former politician has a rainbow country wish – that everyone in our country should be able to celebrate Christmas with human dignity as members of one big family. And that we would be able to strengthen one another with the greatest gift ever: Christ in our lives.

What is your wish for Christmas? Perhaps you can have it fulfilled this year, because Christmas always remains a festival of hope, love and joy. Our core verse for today is therefore my three-fold Christmas wish for you: 'May the God of hope fill you with all joy and peace as you trust in Him this Christmas day, so that you may overflow with hope by the power of the Holy Spirit!'

Lord Jesus, thank you for having come to fulfil all our Christmas wishes. Strengthen our faith on this Christmas day so that our hope will become stronger by the power of your Spirit. Amen.

December 25

Jesus, the only door to God

READ: JOHN 14:1–6

Jesus anwered, 'I am the way and the truth and the life.
No-one comes to the Father except through me.'
– JOHN 14:6

In 2005 I talked to a well-known Afrikaans author. She made it very clear that the Bible was only of literary interest to her; that God is so big that He can save us without the intervention of his Son; that all the blood and suffering on the cross was unnecessary; that she would never believe that her Jewish and Muslim friends would not be able to reach God. After a few minutes I realised that it was as unlikely that I would be able to convince her, as she would be able to convince me. I nevertheless had several sleepless nights as a result of this conversation. Today many people believe that Jesus has become irrelevant, that we regard Him as far too important. Those who think like that are very wrong. As a well-known song says:

My God is so high you can't get over Him,
He's so low you can't get under Him,
He's so wide, you can't get around Him,
You must come in, by and through the Lamb.

If you do not know, follow and love Jesus you cannot know God. His blood shed on the cross is essential to wash away your sin. We can never overestimate Jesus, because without Him we cannot reach heaven.

❧ Lord Jesus, how can we thank You for having made it possible for us to reach God. I want to demonstrate my gratitude by committing my life to You. Amen.

December 26

Whoever has seen Him has seen the Father

READ: JOHN 14:8–14

Philip said, 'Lord, show us the Father and that will be enough for us.'
Jesus answered: 'Don't you know me, Philip, even after I have been among
you such a long time? Anyone who has seen me has seen the Father …
Don't you believe that I am in the Father and the Father is in me?'
– JOHN 14:8–10

God is too powerful to be seen by people. When Moses asked God whether he could see Him, God said, 'You cannot see my face, for no-one may see me and live' (Exod 33:20).

When Jesus came into the world, He told his disciples that they only had to look at Him if they wanted to get to know God better. 'Anyone who has seen me has seen the Father,' He told Philip.

Sometimes we wonder why God does not answer our prayers. Jesus knows how we feel because some of his prayers were not answered either. He prayed that the Father's will should be done on earth as in heaven; and when we look at the world as it is today, this prayer has not yet been fulfilled. In Gethsemane Jesus prayed that God should take away his suffering but God did not answer this prayer.

When God apparently does not answer our prayers it is not because He does not love us. From Jesus' deeds and words in the Bible we get to know his love for people. As we see the Father in Jesus we know that God, like Jesus, loves us and cares about us: 'Jesus gives God a face and tears are rolling down his cheeks,' writes Philip Yancy.[5] Should you ever wonder whether God is there, or whether He cares about you, look at Jesus. In Him you should be able to see God's love for you.

🪶 Lord Jesus, thank you for showing me how much God loves me. Amen.

Jesus came to show us the Father

READ: JOHN1:15–18

No-one has ever seen God, but God the One and Only [Son],
who is at the Father's side, has made him known.
– JOHN 1:18

Reinhold Niebuhr compares the revelation of God in Christ with the Rosetta stone. Before this stone was discovered, the Egyptologists had to guess the meaning of the hieroglyphics. Nobody really knew what the little picture symbols of the strange handwriting meant. However, then the Rosetta stone was discovered – a stone tablet on which the same text was written in Greek, in the ordinary Egyptian writing, and in the hieroglyphics, which had been indecipherable up to then. For the very first time the hieroglyphics could be deciphered by comparing these three translations. By means of this key all the other documents in which hieroglyphics were used could be interpreted and for the first time it was possible to form a clear picture of a lost civilisation.

Niebuhr says Jesus enables us to reconstruct our faith, to know God's love for us and to understand God's purpose for our lives. We can trust God because we trust Jesus. Should we doubt God, we merely have to look at Jesus, the Rosetta stone of our faith.[6]

If you look at Jesus you have to see God because He is the exact representation of the being of God, says the writer of the letter to the Hebrews (Heb 1:3). Now, although God is holy and you are merely a sinner, God is within reach because you know and love Jesus. Jesus' sacrifice furthermore enables God to forgive your sin and mine.

❧ Lord Jesus, when I look at You I realise the greatness and the glory of your Father for the first time, and I even understand a tiny part of his plan with my life. Amen.

December 28

Walk as Jesus did

READ: 1 JOHN 2:1–6

But if anyone obeys his word,
God's love is truly made complete in him.
This is how we know we are in him: Whoever
claims to live in him must walk as Jesus did.
– *1 JOHN 2:5–6*

Philip Yancy says he has always felt uneasy about participating in charismatic activities such as speaking in tongues or being slain in the Spirit. Instead of these 'manifestations of the Spirit' he prefers to look at the life of Jesus when he wants to visualise the Holy Spirit, because in Jesus the invisible God has a face. 'After all, Jesus' life on earth gave us a clear picture of what someone who belongs to God should look like. The qualities of the fruit of the Spirit which Paul discusses in Galatians 5:22–23 (the qualities by which Christians should be identified), are indeed the exact qualities which Jesus manifested on earth and He promised to make his home with us to encourage those very qualities,' Yancy writes.[7]

If you want to know how God wants you to live, look at Jesus. Look at the way He lived, what He said, what He did, how He treated others, and then 'do likewise'. Live in love like He did. Ask God to let the fruit of the Spirit grow in your life; then people who look at you will be able to see Jesus.

❧ Lord Jesus, please make the qualities which You manifested on earth visible in my life as well, so that those who look at me will be able to see You. Amen.

December 29

Jesus is King!

READ: HEBREWS 1:1–10

The Son is the radiance of God's glory and the exact representation of his being, sustaining all things by his powerful word. After he had provided purification for sins, he sat down at the right hand of the Majesty in heaven. So he became as much superior to the angels as the name he has inherited is superior to theirs.
– HEBREWS 1:3–4

Jesus was an ordinary human being like us – but without sin – therefore it is easy for us to acquire the habit of thinking of Him as an ordinary human being. However, Jesus is the exact representation of God; He sustains all things by his powerful word, the writer of the letter to the Hebrews says. He is superior to the angels. He is the Son of God. He was set far above the angels. He is the Son of God. His throne will last for ever and ever and righteousness will be the sceptre of his kingdom. Therefore God has anointed Him as King (cf Heb 1:5, 8–9).

Long before the birth of Jesus the prophet Isaiah prophesied that the Child who would be born would be a Prince of Peace; that his government and peace would have no end and that He would sit on the throne of David and reign forever. This king would establish the kingdom and uphold it with justice and righteousness, from that time on and forever (cf Isa 9:6–7).

Jesus is the greatest King ever. We must guard against becoming too familiar with Him, and always remember that He is God, that He is King for ever, that his kingdom will have no end and that He will bring justice and righteousness for ever.

❧ Lord Jesus, I worship You as the King of the heaven who will ensure justice and righteousness for your followers for ever. Amen.

December 30

God will go before you

READ: ISAIAH 52:7–12

The LORD will go before you, the God
of Israel will be your rear guard.
— ISAIAH 52:12

In Old Testament times God's people could have tremendous peace of mind: They were never without the presence of their God of the Covenant. In the desert his presence was visible to everyone: during the day as a pillar of cloud and at night as a pillar of fire. They nevertheless exchanged their God for heathen gods time and again, until He punished them by having them taken captive. Yet God was still merciful. Through the prophet Isaiah God sent a positive message to the exiles: He had not forgotten them – He was still going before them and He was still their rear guard.

Tomorrow is the first day of a new year. Every Christian may take the same promise as Israel with them into the unknown territory of the new year with confidence: God will go before you in the new year, and He will also come behind you to protect your back. May you experience the blessed presence of this God who loves you every day of your life in the year which lies ahead.

I would like to give you the prayer of Lancelot Andrews, which dates from the 14th century, for the year which lies ahead:

Lord, be in me to strenghten me, around me to envelop me, above me to protect me, under me to carry me, before me to guide me, behind me to prevent me from getting lost, around me to protect me. All glory be yours, O Lord, our Father, for ever and ever. Amen.[8]

December 31

Lord Jesus,

thank you that, during the past month, I could discover
anew Who You really are.
Like Peter I understand for the first time
why You came into the world:
that your birth and death demonstrate
God's infinite love for me;
that your death made life possible for me;
that You are not merely the Son of God, but God Yourself.
I praise You for your death on the cross
which makes God's forgiveness a reality for me;
and for your resurrection
which makes victory over death possible for me.
Make me a witness who will convey
your good news to others during this Christmas season –
and the new year which lies ahead.
Please place your lasting peace in my heart and life:
peace with You and with others;
change me and reconcile me to God and my neighbour.
I worship You as the light of the world
who brought light into the darkness of the sin in my life.
From now on I want to live in your light,
I want to be a light for You.
Holy Spirit, give me your wisdom and insight so that I will be able to see the
glory of Jesus and try to live like Him.
Lord Jesus, I want to invite You right now
to be the King of my life.
Please go before me and show me
the way which lies ahead in the new year.

Amen

Index of scriptures

Endnotes

JANUARY   *Live for God*

1. Smit, D. *Christen-wees in 'n weghol-wêreld* (Lux Verbi, Cape Town: 2002), 42
2. Nicol, W. *Godsdiens wat werk* (Lux Verbi, Cape Town: 2000), 174
3. Ibid, 179
4. Ibid, 178
5. Wright, N. *Together for Good* (Harvest House Publishers, Oregon: 2000), 17 February
6. Stanley, C. Quoted in Wright, N. *Together for Good* (Harvest House Publishers, Oregon: 2000), 19 January

FEBRUARY   *Bear fruit!*

1. Wilkinson, DM. *Die geheimenis van die wingerdstok vir vroue* (Christelike Uitgewersmaatskappy, Vereeniging: 2003), 84
2. Wilkinson, B. *Die geheimenis van die wingerdstok* (Christelike Uitgewersmaatskappy, Vereeniging: 2003), 40
3. Vosloo, W & Van Rensburg, F (Ed). *Die Bybellennium* (Christelike Uitgewersmaatskappy, Vereeniging: 2003), 1357
4. Wilkinson, B. *Die geheimenis van die wingerdstok* (Christelike Uitgewersmaatskappy, Vereeniging: 2003), 26
5. Ibid, 99
6. Maxwell, John C. *Beginsels om oor te besin* (Christelike Uitgewersmaatskappy, Vereeniging: 1999), 37

MARCH   *The Way of the Cross*

1. Vosloo, W & Van Rensburg, F (Ed). *Die Bybellennium* (Christelike Uitgewersmaatskappy, Vereeniging: 2003), 1181
2. Ibid, 1366
3. Ibid, 1237

APRIL   *Glorify God*

1. Warren, Rick. *The Purpose-Driven Life* (Zondervan, Grand Rapids, Michigan: 2002), 56
2. Wilkinson, DM. *Die geheimenis van die wingerdstok vir vroue* (Christelike Uitgewersmaatskappy, Vereeniging: 2003), 184
3. Vosloo, W & Van Rensburg, F (Ed). *Die Bybellennium* (Christelike Uitgewersmaatskappy, Vereeniging: 2003), 1523

MAY   *In the footsteps of Hosea*

1. *Devotions for May based on Smit, J. Die wonder van die Woord* (Carpe Diem Media: Vanderbijlpark: 2002)

JUNE   *Walking on water*

1. Ortberg, J. *If You Want to Walk on Water, You'll Have to Get out of the Boat* (Zondervan, Grand Rapids, Michigan: 2001)
2. Ibid, 9–10
3. Ibid, 35
4. Ibid, 36
5. Ibid, 56
6. Henry T Blackaby. Quoted in Ortberg, J. *If You Want to Walk on Water, You'll Have to Get out of the Boat* (Zondervan, Grand Rapids, Michigan: 2001), 70
7. Ortberg, J. *If You Want to Walk on Water, You'll Have to Get out of the Boat* (Zondervan, Grand Rapids, Michigan: 2001), 71–73
8. Ibid, 138
9. Ibid, 149
10. Ibid, 155
11. Ibid, 166
12. Warren, Rick. *The Purpose-Driven Life* (Zondervan, Grand Rapids, Michigan: 2002), 48

JULY   *Psalms of praise*

1. Cilliers, J. *Het God 'n handvatsel?* (Christelike Uitgewersmaatskappy, Vereeniging: 2003), 7
2. Yancey, P & Brand, P. *Na God se beeld* (Struik Christian Books, Cape Town: 2005), 283, 384
3. Vosloo, W & Van Rensburg, F (Ed). *Die Bybellennium* (Christelike Uitgewersmaatskappy, Vereeniging: 2003), 696
4. Simpson, N, Van Rensburg, E & Ludik, B. Die wonder van gebed (Lux Verbi.BM, Wellington: 2000), 40

AUGUSTUS   *The purpose of suffering*

1. Gibran, K. *Die Profeet* (JL van Schaik, Pretoria: 1995), 32
2. William Taylor. Quoted in Cowman, LB. *Streams in the Desert* (Zondervan, Grand Rapids, Michigan: 1997 [revised edition]), 221
3. *The Amplified New Testament* (Zondervan, Grand Rapids, Michigan: 1958), 751
4. Paul Brand. Quoted in Yancey, P. *Spirituele oorlewing* (Christelike Uitgewersmaatskappy, Vereeniging: 2005), 68
5. Charles H Spurgeon. Quoted in Cowman, LB. *Streams in the Desert* (Zondervan, Grand Rapids, Michigan: 1997 [revised edition]), 148
6. Yancey, P. *Reik na die onsigbare God* (Zondervan ZA, Johannesburg: 2000), 58
7. Madame Jean de Guyon. Quoted in Yancey, P. *Reik na die onsigbare God* (Zondervan ZA, Johannesburg: 2000), 54
8. Ibid, 55
9. Henry Jowett. Quoted in Cowman, LB. *Streams in the Desert* (Zondervan, Grand Rapids, Michigan: 1997 [revised edition]), 20

SEPTEMBER *Wealth*

1. Naudé, P. *Geesgedrewe gelowiges* (Lux Verbi.BM, Wellington: 2005), 149
2. Foster, R. *Money, Sex and Power* (Hodder & Stoughton, London: 1985), 73
3. Ibid, 55
4. Ibid, 29
5. Yancey, P. *Rumours from Another World* (Struik Christian Books, Cape Town: 2004), 211
6. Foster, R. *Money, Sex and Power* (Hodder & Stoughton, London: 1985), 44

OCTOBER *Surrender*

1. Warren, R. *Die doelgerigte lewe* (Jonathan Ball, Jeppestown: 2002), 67
2. Ibid, 63
3. L'Engle, M. *Glimpses of Grace* (Harper, San Francisco: 1996), 103
4. Redpath, A. Quoted in Maartens, M. *Gebed kan my lewe verander* (Lux Verbi, Cape Town: 1989), 19
5. Warren, R. *Die doelgerigte lewe* (Jonathan Ball, Jeppestown: 2002), 73

NOVEMBER *The peace God gives*

1. Hudson, T. *The Serenity Prayer* (Struik Christian Books, Cape Town: 2002), Introduction
2. Ibid, 22
3. Ibid, 44
4. Ibid, 73
5. Ibid, 75
6. Ibid, 101
7. Vosloo, W & Van Rensburg, F (Ed). *Die Bybellennium* (Christelike Uitgewersmaatskappy, Vereeniging: 2003), 1523

DECEMBER *Do you know about Jesus?*

1. L'Engle, M. *Glimpses of Grace* (Harper, San Francisco: 1996), 77
2. Yancey, P. *Reik na die onsigbare God* (Zondervan ZA, Johannesburg: 2000), 137
3. Ibid, 127
4. Ibid, 129
5. Ibid, 130
6. Ibid, 130–131
7. Ibid, 165
8. Smit, N. *Die groot boek van Christelike aanhalings* (Christelike Uitgewersmaatskappy, Vereeniging: 2005), 18

Bibliography

Amplified New Testament, The (Zondervan, Grand Rapids, Michigan: 1958)

Ban Breathnach, Sarah. *Simple Abundance* (Bantam Books, London: 1997)

Cowman, LB. *Streams in the Desert* (Zondervan, Grand Rapids, Michigan: 1997 [revised edition])

Eareckson-Tada, Joni. *When God Weeps* (Zondervan, Grand Rapids, Michigan: 1997)

Foster, R. *Money, Sex and Power* (Hodder & Stoughton, London: 1985)

Gibran, K. *Die profeet* (JL van Schaik, Pretoria: 1995)

L'Engle, M. *Glimpses of Grace* (Harper, San Francisco: 1996)

Maxwell, John C. *Beginsels om oor te besin* (Christelike Uitgewersmaatskappy, Vereeniging: 1999)

Naudé, P. *Geesgedrewe gelowiges* (Lux Verbi.BM, Wellington: 2005)

New English Bible (University Press, Oxford: 1970)

Nicol, W. *Godsdiens wat werk* (Lux Verbi.BM, Cape Town: 2000)

Ortberg, J. *If You want to Walk on Water, You've Got to Get out of the Boat* (Zondervan, Grand Rapids, Michigan: 2001)

Smit, D. *Christen-wees in 'n weghol-wêreld* (Lux Verbi.BM, Cape Town: 2002)

Smit J. *Die wonder van die Woord* (Carpe Diem Media, Vanderbijlpark: 2003)

Smit, N. *Die Groot Boek van Christelike Aanhalings* (Christelike Uitgewersmaatskappy, Vereeniging: 2005)

Warren, R. *Die doelgerigte lewe* (Zondervan ZA, Johannesburg: 2002)

Wilkinson, B. *Die geheimenis van die wingerdstok* (Christelike Uitgewersmaatskappy, Vereeniging: 2001)

Wilkinson, DM. *Die geheimenis van die wingerdstok vir vroue* (Christelike Uitgewersmaatskappy, Vereeniging: 2003)

Wright, N. *Together for Good* (Harvest House Publishers, Oregon: 2000)

Yancey, P & Brand, P. *Na God se Beeld* (Struik Christian Books, Cape Town: 2005)

Yancey, P. *Reik na die onsigbare God* (Zondervan ZA, Johannesburg: 2000)

Yancey, P. *Rumours from Another World* (Struik Christian Books, Cape Town: 2004)

Yancey, P. *Spirituele oorlewing* (Christelike Uitgewersmaatskappy, Vereeniging: 2005)

We would like to hear from you.
Please send your comments about this book to us at:
reviews@struikchristianmedia.co.za